Sub-Imperialism Revisited

Studies in Critical Social Sciences

Series Editor

David Fasenfest
(*Wayne State University*)

VOLUME 105

Critical Global Studies

Series Editor

Ricardo A. Dello Buono
(*Manhattan College, New York*)

VOLUME 7

The titles published in this series are listed at *brill.com/cgs*

Sub-Imperialism Revisited

Dependency Theory in the Thought of Ruy Mauro Marini

By

Adrián Sotelo Valencia

Translated by

Jacob Lagnado

BRILL

LEIDEN | BOSTON

Cover illustration: Created by María del Carmen Solanes Carraro.

Library of Congress Cataloging-in-Publication Data

Names: Sotelo Valencia, Adrián, author.
Title: Sub-imperialism revisited : dependency theory in the thought of Ruy Mauro Marini / by Adrián Sotelo Valencia ; translated by Jacob Lagnado.
Description: Leiden ; Boston : Brill, [2017] | Series: Studies in critical social sciences ; volume 105 | Series: Critical global studies ; volume 7 | Includes bibliographical references and index.
Identifiers: LCCN 2017008347 (print) | LCCN 2017022194 (ebook) | ISBN 9789004319417 (E-book) | ISBN 9789004319400 (hardback : alk. paper)
Subjects: LCSH: Economic development--Latin America. | Capitalism--Political aspects--Latin America. | Imperialism. | Marini, Ruy Mauro.
Classification: LCC HC125 (ebook) | LCC HC125 .S6854 2017 (print) | DDC 338.98--dc23
LC record available at https://lccn.loc.gov/2017008347

Typeface for the Latin, Greek, and Cyrillic scripts: "Brill". See and download: brill.com/brill-typeface.

ISSN 1573-4234
ISBN 978-90-04-31940-0 (hardback)
ISBN 978-90-04-31941-7 (e-book)

This book is printed on acid-free paper and produced in a sustainable manner.

In memory of Ruy Mauro Marini

Contents

Foreword

Adrián Sotelo Valencia's new book, *Sub-Imperialism Revisited: Dependency Theory in the Thought of Ruy Mauro Marini,* represents a serious attempt to bring Marini's work up to date theoretically and empirically in light of the major issues facing Latin America and the world today. A student of Marini with numerous works published in different languages, here Sotelo puts the central arguments of the Marxist theory of dependency as conceptualised by Marini to the test of time by throwing them open to debate within the social sciences.

In the first two of the book's eight chapters, the author compares the specific nature of the Marxist theory of dependency to other perspectives, including ECLA's developmentalism and modernization theories; endogenism; neo-Gramscianism; postcolonial theory; world-systems theory and the Weberian and developmentalist interpretations of dependency. He argues in favour of developing the Marxist version of dependency theory and rejects hybridisations which only mischaracterise it and make developing its concepts that much harder. Chapters 3, 4, 5 and 6 discuss the specificity of dependency theory in relation to the theory of imperialism; the chief features of imperialism and dependency in their current phase, and the particular place occupied by sub-imperialism within dependency theory. In doing so, Sotelo draws out sub-imperialism's economic roots in the capital accumulation process and its relationship with political forces and the State, as well as the characteristics it has assumed in contemporary Latin America and Brazil in particular.

The author goes on to situate the theory of sub-imperialism within the debate with those who claim Brazil is set to 'overcome' its peripheral and dependent condition and become an imperialist pole and world power, albeit one subservient to hegemonic capitalism. Ruy Mauro Marini passed away in 1997, and so Chapters 7 and 8 explore the relevance of his analysis today with a discussion of his concepts of the counter-insurgency state and the state of the fourth power which takes as its starting point the patterns of capital accumulation and contradictions between social classes and competing political forces present in Latin America since the 1980s.

As a leading exponent of the Marxist theory of dependency, Sotelo's theses are consistent with the view of contemporary capitalism he has presented throughout his body of work, namely that

1) Global capitalism has entered a new stage of dependency under a pattern of accumulation under the hegemony of fictitious financial capital.

Sotelo characterises this new stage as financial-neoliberal and one which has led to financialisation and two models of accumulation: a de-industrialising primary-exporter model, notwithstanding the mitigating effect of sub-imperialism in Brazil's case; and a secondary-exporter model, which in Mexico is based on the export of manufactures from the maquiladoras and cheap labour (mostly) to the United States.

2) The financialised model of accumulation, under the hegemony of fictitious capital, expresses but also exacerbates the crisis of surplus value production. This is because it is ultimately a result of the automation of productive processes and living labour being replaced by dead labour, which means extraordinary surplus value cannot depend solely on the circuit of commodity production being realised but also requires fictitious capital to be created via public debt and state monopoly capitalism. The ever increasing displacement of productive accumulation towards the fictitious sphere has made it harder to produce surplus value, thus triggering a fall in rates of profit, investment and economic growth. It has also led to labour super-exploitation being intensified throughout the global capitalist economy and spreading from the peripheries to the traditional imperialist centres such as the US and Western Europe, where it has fuelled the crisis of bourgeois democracy and capitalist civilisation.
3) Only the Marxist theory of dependency is able to theorise dependency as a historical process that has intensified over the last three decades and identify its different stages. In this sense it is possible to distinguish four principal models of dependent capital accumulation: (a) colonial dependency, (b) primary-exporter and financial dependency, (c) industrial dependency, and lastly (d) neoliberal dependency, dominated by fictitious capital and the scientific-technical revolution. Weberian dependency perspectives prioritise concrete analyses of dependency whilst rejecting its status as a theory, partly because they labour under the developmentalist illusion that 'interdependency' can be achieved via integration of a kind which is subservient to and dependent on imperialism. Similarly, perspectives which argue that a subordinate capital-imperialism exists in the most developed peripheral countries like Brazil fail to capture the contradictions and characteristics of the new stage of dependency because they ignore its structural differences with capital's dynamic in the core countries.
4) The cycle of rising commodity prices during the first decade of the 2000s and following the crisis of the Washington Consensus created an opening which allowed the left and centre-left in Latin America to come to

power and implement poverty reduction policies. These policies became a badge of honour for these so-called progressive governments and Lula's two administrations especially, but became unsustainable as prices began falling again in the following decade, thus reversing the earlier trend. As a result political struggle in the region became more acute, bourgeois democracy entered into crisis and attempts were made via 'soft coups' to bring down progressive governments in the region and destroy their accumulated power and the social forces behind them – as with the Brazilian parliament's impeachment and subsequent removal from office of constitutional president Dilma Rousseff. These developments have put the counter-insurgency state back on the agenda. Counter-insurgency states seek to destroy their enemies by imposing a corporative state controlled by big capital or the fourth power. When unable to reach the next stage of the neoliberal offensive in Latin America via minimally competitive and representative elections, such states attempt to force the issue by restricting democracy and bringing it under the external control of big private capital. But the deepening of the economic crisis and continued slowdown in Chinese growth over the coming years will only serve to aggravate the neoliberal dependent model's crisis of reproduction. This will lead to renewed social struggle and the peoples of Latin America will once again make socialism their strategic goal.

5) Sub-imperialism is a far-reaching historical process which is simultaneously articulated with the dependent economy's cycle of capital at its monopoly and finance capital stage; the development of the State, and the contradictions between the dependent country's expansionist logic and imperialism. The contradiction between the expansion of productive processes and the limits imposed on the internal market by super-exploitation mean the State needs to stimulate the export of manufactures and investments through a policy of regional industrial development which makes use of any global spaces freed up in the course of their antagonistic cooperation with imperialism. The conclusion is that not all peripheral countries can be sub-imperialist, with the exceptions proving the rule. Brazil, due to its regional influence, is perhaps the only example of a sub-imperialist country in Latin America, as the US's geopolitical and strategic domination of Central America prevents countries like Mexico from attaining such a condition.

6) Sub-imperialism is a structural process of dependent capitalism and therefore did not end along with the civic-military dictatorships but instead developed further during the democratic period and, somewhat

> paradoxically it would seem, under Lula and Dilma's centre-left governments, as both sought to strengthen Brazil in its condition as a regional power rather than break with the cycle of dependency.

Although Lula and Dilma tried to pursue a foreign policy based on cooperation with their Latin American neighbours through MERCOSUR, UNASUR and CELAC, Brazil's economic links abroad were mostly fostered by other institutions such as the BNDES state investment bank, which financed the expansion of big Brazilian corporations' cycle of capital into the rest of Latin America and Africa. Proof of this was provided by Brazil's positive trade balance in respect of these regions (dominated by manufactures), and by the increased share of remittance-based revenues on its balance of payments. The expansion of Brazil's so-called trans-Latin companies is a new and important feature of contemporary Latin American sub-imperialism compared to when it first emerged in the 1970s.

In the best tradition of learning, Sotelo encourages readers themselves to fashion the key theoretical concepts which will underpin the Marxist theory of dependency in the 21st Century. And whether or not we fully agree with his arguments, we are invited to think about today's world from a critical, emancipatory vantage point – one that can shine a light on the most crucial aspects of the patterns of capital accumulation represented by contemporary neo-imperialism and neo-dependency.

Carlos Eduardo Martins
Universidad Federal de Rio de Janeiro (PEPI/UFRJ)

List of Diagrams, Figures and Tables

Diagrams

Figures

Tables

Introduction

> The Leninist theory of imperialism (...) is an obligatory point of reference in the study of sub-imperialism. It should not be invoked to prevent such a study from being conducted, because, among other reasons, it is the Leninist theory of *imperialism*, not *sub-imperialism*.
>
> RUY MAURO MARINI
>
> *Subdesarrollo y revolución* [*Underdevelopment and Revolution*], 1969

∵

The present work re-assesses the concept of sub-imperialism as formulated by Ruy Mauro Marini in his key writings using the Marxist theory of dependency (MTD): a theory inspired by the best of classical Marxist thought (Marx-Engels, Lenin) and Latin American critical thought. Sub-imperialism has been the subject of renewed interest in recent times, provoking intense and productive debate in the light of Brazil's increasingly important role as one of the BRICS in the international relations system and specifically in its 'natural' area of influence of Latin America's Southern Cone. Its active role in Mercosur is another relevant factor, as is the portrayal of recent Brazilian governments as progressive and even left-wing, similar in that sense to others in the region such as Bolivia, Venezuela and Argentina. This image can be explained at least partly by the political history of two of the country's recent presidents – Luiz Inácio Lula da Silva (2003–2011), a former metalworker, and Dilma Rousseff (2011–2016), an ex-guerrilla.

These factors have been marshalled to dismiss a whole range of theses which had previously and especially during the military dictatorship (1964–1985) characterized Brazilian governments as counter-insurgent and sub-imperialist, with a marked tendency to extend capital accumulation and state influence beyond the country's borders. That perspective has been replaced by one which sees the arrival of 'democracy' and 'civil society' in the mid-1980s as having changed Brazil in structural and geo-strategic terms. In this new perspective, Brazil is now a modern country with a strong claim to being a new world power of the kind which historically emerged after WWII in the shadow of the dominant imperialist power in the form of the United States. And although the US still just about retains that status, it has increasingly had to give ground

 | DOI 10.1163/9789004319417_002

in recent decades to newly emerging powers such as China, Russia, India, South Africa and Iran.

In this work we question the thesis that Brazil has become a major developed power similar to the world's most consolidated Western imperialist powers such as the US, UK, Germany or France, whose influence in terms of international relations, the global division of labour and military power is essential to maintaining the capitalist system as a whole. We look at the most representative examples of this theory in order to then offer our own interpretation of Brazil's current position as both dependent and sub-imperialist—an *intermediate power*—in light of the theoretical, methodological and analytical propositions which make up Marini's MTD.

We certainly do not deny that the important and indeed transcendental historical and structural changes of recent decades have affected both the nature of dependency and the development of dependent capitalism in Brazil in particular. But neither do we believe that such changes negate the continued presence of dependency characteristics within the framework of a global capitalist order now experiencing widespread and severe upheaval. Rather we believe that a dialectical synthesis is needed which renews the 'old' on the basis of the new by openly acknowledging the chief transformations that have affected the Brazilian economy and society. Only then can we really grasp the global dynamics at work in the current historical and structural context.

As noted, the chief arguments developed by Marini between the 1970s and 1990s as part of his Marxist theory of dependency are once again under discussion. Many authors claim the theory is no longer relevant because of the changes to affect capitalism and society globally in recent years. Even initially, the MTD and its political and ideological implications clashed head-on with authors and tendencies, including the majority of endogenist ideologues and intellectuals in the different communist parties, who refused to allow it any epistemological space (or indeed any other space) as a perspective or theory for analysing Latin America's socio-historical, political and economic processes. For some on the left, Marx and Lenin's theories of capitalism and imperialism respectively were quite sufficient for the purpose of understanding the nature of the region's socio-economic processes. Dressed up in Third International and then Soviet theses, this position permeated the main theoretical and political currents of a left which was to virtually disappear in the 1980s and 1990s as its proponents adopted other approaches—structuralism, functionalism, neoclassical theories or theoretical eclecticism—in order, they claimed, to finally understand said regional processes as a basis for analysing and understanding capitalism itself.

In doing so, however, it would appear to us that they often confused their method of inquiry with their method of presentation, in the manner observed by Marx in his *Afterword* to the second German edition of *Capital*,[1] and so drew conclusions from what was merely raw material awaiting theorisation. But the new issues and problems thrown up in the last few decades by imperialism and dependency in the context of an expanding capitalist mode of production, which have earned them the 'neo' prefix, simply express the form, and not the essence, of that mode of production, which has actually intensified and expanded further across the planet, conquering and destroying individuals, communities, indigenous peoples, natural resources, territories, nations and states. In this bid to create value and produce and appropriate surplus value the capitalist mode of production in fact perpetuates that frantic intensive-expansive movement which guarantees for capital as a whole, and permanently, high rates of profit and plentiful returns for the system's ruling classes.

In keeping with this theoretical and methodological principle, we think that just as important changes of form in recent decades have not meant the essence of the capitalist State has changed, (it has in fact been strengthened), so it is with *sub-imperialism* and *dependency*. Despite the changes they have concurrently undergone both internally and in the context of the global capitalist economy, they have only intensified and manifested themselves in new ways and through new structural cycles, notably in Latin America and in Mexico and Brazil in particular. This process is the subject matter of this book and the chapters that follow.

Chapter 1 provides some theoretical and ideological context by summarising the main currents or paradigms prevalent in Latin American thought immediately prior to and during the emergence of dependency theory. In confronting these tendencies, dependency theory strengthened its own theoretical and analytical framework and the main theses and positions upon which it would build an understanding of the nature of dependency and underdevelopment in Latin America. We follow this in Chapter 2 with a short personal tribute to Marini's thought and work. This helps to locate the present subject matter of dependency theory and sub-imperialism within the theoretical contexts of both his time and the present day, which allows us to appreciate the continuing relevance of his thought. It also underlines the power of his ideas to not only describe but also to explain the essential nature of the current period.

Chapter 3 then summarises what we consider to be the new features of imperialism (neo-imperialism) and dependency (neo-dependency). We revisit the original theoretical assumptions of Lenin's theory of imperialism and Marini's theory of dependency and reassess their systematic unity within the contemporary capitalist order in order to present our own interpretation of the current phase of global imperialism/sub-imperialism (in contraposition

---

1 Karl Marx, *Capital Volume One* (London: Lawrence and Wishart, 1974).

to that of the authors discussed in Chapter 6). By locating the general question of the imperialist system in the current period, Chapter 4 examines how dependency theory was originally formulated and outlines the key features of sub-imperialism described by Marini in his writings, drawing out the specific nature of sub-imperialism in contrast to both the so-called classical theories of imperialism and its more recent interpretations. The chapter also looks at sub-imperialism in the context of contemporary capitalist crisis as a starting point to understanding how it relates to this contradictory and ever changing process. We would note at this point, however, that the theory of sub-imperialism does not in any way contradict or 'supersede' the theory of imperialism, but that the two instead complement one another in a dialectical and dynamic relationship which recreates both theories in the light of the basic contradictions afflicting contemporary capitalism in crisis.

In Chapter 5 we move on to discussing the relationship between the United States and Brazil using Marini's concept of 'antagonistic cooperation'. In our view this concept clearly designates one of the central features of Brazilian sub-imperialism.[2] Antagonistic cooperation is not the same as the relationship enjoyed by countries which may have certain sub-imperialist features but are not fully sub-imperialist, such as Mexico. Hence we argue that while all sub-imperialism is dependent, not all dependent countries are sub-imperialist. In the case of Mexico this holds true however high a level of capitalist development it achieves over its history, and however much it acts in a 'sub-imperialist' fashion towards other countries in its 'natural area' of expansion of Central America and the Caribbean.

Chapter 6 moves on to discuss a range of positions, among which we find two main schools of thought: one which from the outset dismisses dependency theory (and in some cases sub-imperialism) in both its Marxist and reformist versions as being 'unhelpful or ineffective'; and another which may have initially made a qualified defence of dependency theory, pointing out both its strengths and weaknesses, but which later ended up joining the first school of thought by also dismissing it. We discuss three authors who belong to this latter group.

In Chapter 7, we compare and contrast the counter-insurgency state and the state of the fourth power (*Estado del cuarto poder*). In so doing, we show that sub-imperialism as a socio-economic and political phenomenon is bound up with class structure and the specificity of capital reproduction. It does not

2 The term 'privileged satellite' has also been used with regard to this relationship, but as Marini notes in his Memoria it represents a rather different concept.

therefore correspond to just one particular phase of Brazilian capitalism – the period of military rule – as held by authors who disregard the close and indeed dialectical relationship between sub-imperialism and democracy in times of constitutional civilian rule. Then in Chapter 8 we bring our theoretical assumptions about Brazilian sub-imperialism to bear on our discussion of Brazil's current role regionally and globally, looking at what the recent expansion of Brazil's so-called trans-Latin companies can tell us about sub-imperialism in the context of the contemporary crisis of capitalism.

Lastly, the epilogue reviews the main conclusions of the present work and anticipates likely medium and long term processes and tendencies in the current crisis of global and Latin American capitalism. Aside from short periods of weak and relative recovery such as the one currently experienced by the United States, we would appear to be heading towards a systemic, structural and civilizational crisis of unfathomable proportions. The severe economic slowdown now faced by Brazil and Latin America signals the end of a historical cycle of economic growth which seemed to have set the region apart from countries experiencing either economic stagnation, such as in the European Union and Japan, or very low growth rates, such as the United States. Instead, the whole world seems to be hurtling towards a crisis which is deeper and more widespread than ever before, and whose future path and consequences are almost impossible to predict.

CHAPTER 1

Dependency Theory in the Post-1945 Development Literature of Latin America

Ruy Mauro Marini passed away in Rio de Janeiro in 1997 after a long illness, having previously spent over 20 years of his life in exile because of his political and ideological activity on the Latin American revolutionary left. In the present work we pay tribute to him by giving an overview of his thought and work, and then demonstrating its relevance to current developments across the world and in Latin America in particular. We shall begin by briefly surveying the main currents of thought which emerged in Latin America after the Second World War and were later challenged by dependency theory in general and by Marini in particular.

Development Theory in the Latin American Social Sciences

Development theory reflected the reorganisation of the capitalist world after the Second World War under the unshakeable economic, political and military domination of the United States. Its aim was to justify US control over peoples and nations who were appearing on the world-historical stage amidst intense processes of decolonization and struggles to create new nation states. These new countries emerging out of decolonization (some capitalist, others socialist) were characterized as 'underdeveloped', in contrast to the 'developed' industrialized nations of capitalism's historical centre. *Quantitative methods of measurement* were used to differentiate and separate the two sets of countries on the basis of neoclassical and functionalist theories of development.

Despite their differences, all theories of development share certain common traits, which can be synthesized in *two* theses which to this day continue to influence the social sciences, especially with regard to the method used to compare developed and underdeveloped industrial societies. The first thesis sees underdevelopment *itself* as a necessary *prior stage* along a *continuum*[1]

1 Ruy Mauro Marini, "La crisis del desarrollismo," in *La teoría social latinoamericana*, Ruy M. Marini and Márgara Millán, eds., vol. 2 of *Subdesarrollo y dependencia* (Ciudad de México: El Caballito, 1994), 137.

 | DOI 10.1163/9789004319417_003

which countries must progress along before acquiring the features of fully developed capitalism. This linear process is the key concept behind the developmentalist notion of *take-off*, according to which a country must fulfil the conditions of the first stage (underdevelopment) in order to then 'take off' and achieve 'fully' developed capitalism by travelling a path identical to that followed by Western societies.

The second thesis is quantitative and determinist, and is expressed by a set of formal benchmarks to 'measure' underdevelopment. Described by Gunder Frank as the "gap approach",[2] it uses 'indexes' of *literacy, nutrition, birth and death rates, per capita income, poverty levels, rates of fixed capital formation, and productivity*. Later converted into 'mathematical models', these benchmarks 'express' the *level* a society has reached along the trajectory of the evolutionary *continuum*. For advocates of this approach there can be *no* other way forward outside of these systemic limits and in the direction of a *non*-capitalist future.

One of the leading proponents of development theory, later to be passively adopted by Latin America's most liberal and conservative currents, was Walt Whitman Rostow.[3] He rather mechanically divided development into five successive, lineal stages: (*a*) the traditional society, (*b*) the pre-conditions for take-off (*c*) the take-off itself, (*d*) maturity, and (*e*) the mass consumption of goods and services.[4]

Translated into social equations and 'ideal models', these theories of development are reduced to quantitative measurements of the kind which became popular after the Second World War as part of an ideological and political attempt by the centres of capitalist power to justify a new postcolonial order controlled by a US-led imperialist system. Later, modernization would provide the basis for theories emanating from the United Nations Economic Commission for Latin America (ECLA)[5] which would prove highly influential (if not altogether successful) in their attempt to provide an explanation of development underpinned by an evolutionist understanding of modernization as the transition from a traditional society to a developed one, or from 'outward development' to 'inward development'.

---

2 André Gunder Frank, *Latin America: Underdevelopment or Revolution* (New York: Monthly Review Press, 1969), 39.

3 Walt Whitman Rostow, *The Stages of Economic Growth: A Non-Communist Manifesto* (Cambridge: Cambridge University Press, 1960). Rostow wrote this book at a CIA-funded US research centre.

4 Rostow, *The Stages of Economic Growth*, 16.

5 In 1984 the English name was changed to ECLAC (United Nations Economic Commission for Latin America and the Caribbean) in order to reflect the membership of the Caribbean countries. [Translator].

Structural Dualism

Structural dualism is a variant of the cultural anthropology of development, and although its origins date back to the beginning of the 20th Century and the 'indigenous question',[6] its real heyday was in the 1950s and 1960s. It was heavily influenced by North American structural-functionalism, which tried to explain the structures of change and characteristics of the Western 'model' of society. For Marini "...the issue of modernization and the notion of structural dualism inspired most of the sociological and anthropological work produced during this period."[7] One of the leading representatives of structural dualism was the French geographer Jacques Lambert,[8] who is associated with the idea of the *enclave*[9] as an extension of the dominant foreign metropolis during the historical period developmentalists call 'outward development'. Thus structural dualism refers above all to the concentration of highly productive units in restricted areas within a national territory. These areas constitute economically evolved enclaves where the fruits of technological progress are concentrated, and underdevelopment appears as the *antipode* of development. *Structural duality* exists in the sense that capitalist and non-capitalist structures are connected to one other by the metropolis.[10] The concept is present not only in different schools of functionalism but also in the orthodox Stalinist strand of

---

6 Aníbal Quijano, "La nueva heterogeneidad estructural de América Latina," in *¿Nuevos temas, nuevos contenidos*? Heinz R. Sonntag, (Caracas: UNESCO / Nueva Sociedad, 1989), 30; and Itagaki Yoichi, "A Review of the Concept of the 'Dual Economy'," *The Developing Economies* 6:2 (1968): 143–157.

7 Ruy Mauro Marini, *América Latina: dependência e integração* (Sao Paulo: Brasil Urgente, 1992). 72. This and subsequent citations from this source have been translated from Portuguese to Spanish by the author and into English by the translator [Translator]. Gunder Frank offers a critique of dualism in *Latin America: Underdevelopment or Revolution*. See Chapter 14 in particular: 'Dialectic, not Dual Society,' 221–230.

8 Jacques Lambert, *América Latina, estructuras sociales e instituciones políticas*, 2nd ed. (Barcelona: Ariel, 1970), and *Os dois Brasis* (São Paulo: Editora Nacional, 1976).

9 Fernando H. Cardoso and Enzo Faletto, *Dependencia y desarrollo en América Latina* (Ciudad de México: Siglo XXI, 1969); Vania Bambirra, *El capitalism dependiente latinoamericano* (Ciudad de México: Siglo XXI, 1974).

10 André Gunder Frank, *El subdesarrollo del desarrollo. Un ensayo autobiográfico* (Caracas: Nueva Sociedad, 1991).

historical materialism[11] as 'coexisting modes of production'. The only difference between the two is that historical materialism allows for the existence of relations internal to modes of production within a country and a degree of State intermediation.

For dualism, modernization is the key to 'overcoming' underdevelopment and lack of progress whilst building a *fully* capitalist country with its corresponding social and juridical relations: private property, development of the productive forces and advanced Western style (i.e. Eurocentric) political and electoral systems. As Gunder Frank notes:

> The political strategy usually associated with these factually and theoretically erroneous interpretations of development and underdevelopment is for the bourgeois the desirability of extending modernism to the archaic sector and incorporating it into the world and national market as well, and for the Marxists the desirability of completing the capitalist penetration of the feudal countryside and finishing the bourgeois democratic revolution.[12]

Modernizing Functionalism and Social Change

Modernization theory "corresponds to the high point of Parsonian influence on Latin American social research"[13] and has been internalised by the cognitive and academic structures of social and human sciences on the continent. One of the structural-functionalist school's greatest proponents of modernization theory (also known as *scientific sociology*), along with Aldo Solari, was the sociologist Gino Germani.[14] For his biographer Joseph Kahl,[15] this Italian-born but later Argentina-based intellectual's greatest contribution was to combine traditional classical European theory with the new empirical research methods being used in the United States at the time.

11 Quijano, "La nueva heterogeneidad," 31.

12 Frank, *Latin America: Underdevelopment or Revolution*, 223.

13 Quijano, "La nueva heterogeneidad," 30.

14 His most notable works include Gino Germani, *La Sociología en la América Latina* (Buenos Aires: Eudeba, 1964) and *Política y sociedad en una época de transición* (Buenos Aires: Paidós, 1968).

15 Joseph Kahl, *Tres sociólogos latinoamericanos* (Ciudad de México: ENEP / Acatlán, 1986), 117.

Another pioneer of this school was Medina Echavarría. Linked to ECLA, one of his most important works was *Economic Development in Latin America: Sociological Considerations* (1963), which looked at what was then a key issue in classical sociology: the social consequences of economic development and the relationship between economy and society in Latin America. Echavarría's analysis was strongly influenced by Max Weber's *interpretive sociology*, and in particular Weber's *Economy and Society*, which Echavarría himself translated for Fondo de Cultura Económica in 1944.

The main issue in the 1950s and 1960s was the dichotomy between 'traditional' and 'modern' society. It was thought this could be 'resolved' by modernizing socio-economic structures and political systems which would lead in turn to full industrialization. During the period of stagnation and crisis that followed in the 1970s and 1980s, governments and ruling classes turned to this ideological version of modernization as they embarked upon programmes of capitalist restructuring and modernization of the productive apparatus, thus foreshadowing the neoliberalism defined by one author as "a neo-Weberianism which reconciles formal democracy with finance capital".[16]

ECLA's Developmentalism

Another school of thought to strongly influence the Latin American social sciences and social thought was developmentalism. Also derived from neoclassical theories but with a strong dose of Keynesianism, it is associated with ECLA's work from the late 1940s and 1950s under the outstanding leadership of Raúl Prebisch.[17] Following Rostow, most developmentalist authors understood 'dependency' as one more stage in a 'linear succession' along the path to a fully developed stage of capitalism, and so placed their emphasis on industrialization, improved income distribution and the possibility of 'autonomous' capitalist development.

16 Gilberto Felisberto Vasconcellos, *Gunder Frank. O enguiço das ciências sociais* (Florianópolis, Brasil: Editora Insular, 2014), 177. Translated from Portuguese to Spanish by the author and into English by the translator [Translator].

17 For a relevant study see Octavio Rodríguez, *La teoría del subdesarrollo de la CEPAL*, 8th ed. (Ciudad de México: Siglo XXI, 1993). Other theoretical expressions also existed at the time and indeed had been developing for several decades, including functionalism, the non-academic Marxism of the various communist parties, and the philosophical positions taken up by 'essayists' and 'thinkers' in areas as varied as law, anthropology and psychology.

Structural Heterogeneity

This school represented an attempt to elucidate the specific nature of capitalism in backward and dependent countries. It was Prebisch who did most to formulate the concept, although it originated with the Chilean Aníbal Pinto. In general terms, it took the position that the transition from 'outward development' (1850–1930) to 'inward development' (1930–1982) reinforced the *structural heterogeneity* of modernized economies. In other words "their historical heterogeneity, in which economic units coexist that are representative of phases separated by centuries of evolution, from primitive agricultural and sometimes even pre-Columbian times to huge steel works or car plants built in the very image of those of an open economy."[18]

Quijano observes[19] that the concept of structural heterogeneity was developed in contraposition to the dualism of an anthropological functionalism immersed in modernization theory and the different versions of orthodox historical materialism present in Latin American thought in the context of a fierce debate over whether the region should be characterised as feudal or capitalist.[20] Unlike structural dualism, which separates the 'traditional' from what is 'modern', the essential idea of heterogeneity is that both dimensions can coexist in a single national or regional space, although the former gradually becomes marginalised to the point of becoming 'informal'. As Pinto argues,

> The so-called 'structural heterogeneity' of Latin American economies (and societies) entails the coexistence at the regional and national level of systems or modalities that correspond to very different phases of development. It is a more general and complex reality than that of the much-discussed 'dualism', which is typically associated with the structure of an 'enclave' economy consisting of a 'modernized' exporting 'centre' and a *hinterland* that is relatively or absolutely separated and removed from the dynamic core.[21]

18 Aníbal Pinto, "Concentración del progreso técnico y de sus frutos en el desarrollo latinoamericano," in *Inflación: raíces estructurales* (Ciudad de México: Serie Lecturas del FCE, 1985), 43.

19 Quijano, "La nueva heterogeneidad," 30.

20 See Carlos Sempat Assadourian *et al.*, "Modos de producción en América Latina," in *Cuadernos de Pasado y Presente* 40 (Buenos Aires) (1973).

21 Aníbal Pinto, "Factores estructurales y modalidades del desarrollo, su incidencia sobre la distribución del ingreso," in *Inflación: raíces estructurales* (Ciudad de México: Serie Lecturas del FCE, 1985), 164.

In the late 1950s and 1960s other authors such as Córdova and Michelena[22] in Venezuela developed the concept of structural heterogeneity "to mean the co-existence and inter-connectedness of different modes of production in a single social formation, offering a new interpretation of dependency."[23]

Endogenism

What we call 'endogenism' rode the Marxist and historical materialist currents that developed in Latin America between the late 19th and latter half of the 20th Century before they virtually disappeared in the 1980s, transforming themselves into social democratic political parties. Endogenism's influence goes back to the emergence of socialist (later communist) parties in the early 20th Century, starting with the Partido Socialista Obrero de Chile [Socialist Workers Party of Chile) in 1912, founded by Luis Emilio Recabarren, the Mexican Communist Party (1919), and then other Communist Parties in Brazil (1921), Cuba (1925), Guatemala (1925), El Salvador (1930) and Peru (1930), all of which were affiliated to the Third International (1919–1943).

Also known as 'orthodox Marxism'[24] in the history of Latin American thought, endogenism gives precedence to 'internal factors' such as class struggle, capital accumulation, the State and oligarchies in explaining historical-social phenomena. In doing so it relegates 'external factors' – imperialism, global accumulation and division of labour, world trade – to a 'secondary' level of importance. Sergio de la Peña, a leading proponent of endogenism, explains his method of understanding underdevelopment in these terms:

> In order to analyse [underdevelopment] one must firstly understand the internal relations which characterise how capitalism functions in a society, before then understanding how its external relations operate.[25]

---

22 Armando Córdova and Héctor Silva Michelena, *Aspectos teóricos del subdesarrollo*, 4th ed. (Caracas: Época, 1977).

23 Heinz Rudolf Sonntag, *Duda, certeza y crisis. La evolución de las ciencias sociales en América Latina*, 2nd ed. (Caracas: UNESCO / Nueva Sociedad, 1989), 47.

24 Sonntag, *Duda, certeza y crisis*, 36. See also Raúl Fornet-Betancourt, *Transformación del marxismo, historia del marxismo en América Latina* (Ciudad de México: Plaza y Valdés / Universidad Autónoma de Nuevo León, 2001).

25 Sergio de la Peña, *El antidesarrollo de América Latina*, 13th ed. (Ciudad de México: Siglo XXI, 1999), 85–86.

As a tendency it mostly found its expression in the communist parties and their ideologues. Their strategy was to build alliances with the dependent bourgeoisie, whom they saw as an 'alternative' they could turn to in order to 'isolate' the 'main enemy' in the shape of the feudal landowning classes, also called oligarchies, whilst also speeding up progress towards 'full' capitalist development and carrying out the 'bourgeois democratic' revolution against imperialism. In this way socialism would be gradually phased in as part of a peaceful revolution achieved mainly through the ballot box. But the September 1973 military coup against the Allende government in Chile showed that it in fact it was unrealistic to see the bourgeois democratic electoral process as the only path to socialism.

So it was that the communist parties followed what was then the Moscow line of advocating an 'alliance' of the proletariat and the peasantry with a supposedly progressive bourgeoisie, even though dependency theory had already characterised the latter as a backward-looking and dependent 'lumpenbourgeoisie' which was integrated into the dominant imperialist bloc whilst remaining very different from the bourgeoisie of the core countries.

Neo-Gramscianism

Neo-Gramscianism became a distinctive feature of the political and ideological trends in Latin America in the 1970s, especially as the region's industrialization and import substitution-based model of capital accumulation was hit by a structural crisis and developmentalist strategies and modernizing sociological functionalism finally ran out of steam, giving way to the neoliberalism which would become hegemonic over the next three decades.

Politically and ideologically, its rise[26] expressed both the cycle of military dictatorships in Latin America between 1964 and 1985 heralded by the 1964 coup in Brazil; and the emergence of Eurocommunism as an expression of the crisis of a European left which was somewhat disdainful during the 1970s of 'really existing socialism' and the events which brought Salvador Allende and his Popular Unity government to power in Chile. These events, along with the military coup which subsequently toppled Allende, would give rise to a 'new' and predominantly political theorisation of developments in Latin America, a task for which certain intellectuals found Gramsci to prove the perfect fit. Located in the limited terrain of ideological superstructure, neo-Gramscianism

26 For Gramsci's reception in Latin America and the background to it see José Aricó, *La cola del diablo, itinerario de Gramsci en América Latina* (Buenos Aires: Siglo XXI, 2005).

would apply concepts such as 'State', 'civil society', 'hegemony', 'east-west', 'war of positions', 'historic bloc' and 'subaltern classes' to Latin America in a supposedly far-reaching explanation of political phenomenology. For Marini, neo-Gramscianism emerged as a critique of the originally Leninist organizations and ideologies which had hegemonised the 'Chilean road to socialism', and whose main thesis was that the struggle for power should not mean conquering the State apparatus first of all, as Lenin and Trotsky had argued, but instead a process which would culminate in such a conquest. This thesis thus ended up legitimising a legal and strictly electoral route to socialism.[27]

In the 1980s neo-Gramscianism was to fall victim along with endogenism to the blows of the economic crisis and the political-ideological effects of the democratization of the capitalist State, together with the progressive decline of the dictatorships. These developments saw both paradigms fall into (formal) disuse, giving way to various ideological defences of neoliberalism.

Postcolonialism or Dependency?

The late 1950s saw a new approach emerge across art, literature, and culture in the United Kingdom. Known as Cultural Studies, its leading figures included the likes of Raymond Williams, William Hoggart, Edward P. Thompson and Stuart Hall.[28] Cultural Studies originally took a critical Marxist position, giving shape to a profound and "…systematic critique of reductive and mechanical

27 Ruy Mauro Marini, "La década de 1970 revisitada," in Ruy M. Marini and Márgara Millán, eds., vol. 3 of *La teoría social latinoamericana* (Ciudad de México: El Caballito, 1995), 39–40. Note that we distinguish Gramsci the theoretician who viewed Marxism as the *philosophy of praxis* from the different uses made of his categories and concepts by Latin American and European thinkers seeking to defend the peaceful road to socialism in Latin America and Eurocommunism in Europe. For a systematic treatment of this issue see Néstor Kohan, *Fetichismo y poder en el pensamiento de Karl Marx* (Buenos Aires: Editorial Biblos, 2013), especially 283 *et seq.*

28 Estela Fernández Nadal, "Los estudios poscoloniales y la agenda de la filosofía latinoamericana actual," *Herramienta* 24 (2003–2004): 94; Ramón Pajuelo Teves, "Del 'poscolonialismo' al 'posoccidentalismo': una lectura desde la historicidad latinoamericana y andina," *Comentario Internacional* 2 (Quito: Universidad Andina Simón Bolívar, 2001): 113–131, http://repositorio.uasb.edu.ec/handle/10644/2040; and Santiago Castro-Gómez, "Latinoamericanismo, modernidad, globalización. Prolegómenos a una crítica poscolonial de la razón," http://www.periodismo.uchile.cl/talleres/teoriacomunicacion/archivos/teoriassindisciplina.pdf. See also Raymond Williams, *Culture and Society 1750–1950* (Harmondsworth, UK: Penguin Books, 1961).

understandings of ideological processes, and the discovery of culture as a relatively autonomous sphere".[29] After the fall of the Soviet Union and the rise of the Washington Consensus (1989)[30] it was taken up in the United States where, unsurprisingly, its critical content and global vision were replaced in the universities by a fragmented, postmodern perspective under a neoliberal, capitalist logic. This perspective would give birth to 'multiculturalism' – the 'ideology of global capitalism'.[31] Cultural Studies subsequently spread to Latin America, drawing inspiration from thinkers such as Rawls,[32] a leading exponent, and Martín-Barbero.[33]

According to Coronil,[34] postcolonial studies failed from the very start to address two key issues. Firstly, by focussing on European colonialism in Asia and Africa it left out that of Spain, France, Portugal, Holland and England in America and especially Latin America, from where it would later project itself onto Africa and Asia. Its second serious omission was the absence of

---

29 Nadal, "Los estudios poscoloniales," 94.

30 The 'Ten Commandments' of the Washington Consensus (formally known as *Ten Areas of Policy Reform*) came out of an international conference organised by the Institute of International Economics in the United States on the 6th and 7th of November 1989. The conference was attended by economists from eight Latin American countries (Bolivia, Chile, Peru, Argentina, Brazil, Mexico, Colombia and Venezuela) and became the basis of John Williamson, ed., *Latin American Adjustment: How Much Has Happened?* (Washington D.C: Institute of International Economics, 1990). The Conference's conclusions became known as the Washington Consensus (7–38). Most governments in dependent and underdeveloped countries continue to follow its prescriptions to the letter.

31 Nadal, "Los estudios poscoloniales," 105.

32 John Rawls, *El espejo, el mosaico y el crisol. Modelos políticos para el multiculturalismo* (Barcelona: Anthropos, 2001).

33 Jesús Martín-Barbero, *Al sur de la modernidad. Comunicación, globalización y multiculturalidad* (Pittsburg, PA: University of Pittsburg, 2001). Other authors suggest that from a Latin American perspective, postcolonial theory took the form of *posoccidentalismo* [postoccidentalism] – a "continuation and deepening of the postcolonial critique" (Pajuelo, "Del 'poscolonialismo' al 'posoccidentalismo"), whose 'geopolitical coordinates' are 1) *Postmodernism* (both European and North American versions and best represented by authors such as Lyottard and Baudrillard); 2) *Postcolonialism,* both in its Indian version as represented by Guha, Baba, Spivak and *'subaltern studies'* and its *postorientalist* version, notably Edward W. Said; and 3) Postoccidentalism, best represented by authors such as Mignolo, Coronil, Dussel, Quijano, and Lander.

34 Fernando Coronil, "Naturaleza del poscolonialismo: del eurocentrismo al globocentrismo," in Edgardo Lander, comp., *La colonialidad del saber: eurocentrismo y ciencias sociales. Perspectiva Americana* (Buenos Aires: CLACSO / UNESCO, 2000), 246 *et seq.*

imperialism as an analytical category, despite its *continuing to play* a fundamental part in the analysis and reflections of Latin American thinkers.

When a group of North American university researchers of Latin American origin applied multiculturalism to 'Latin American studies' this gave rise to what became known as 'subaltern studies' or 'postcolonial theory.' Latin American and Caribbean authors such as Fernando Ortiz, Franz Fanon, Aimé Césaire, Edouard Glissant and Fernández Retamar are all cited as precursors of this theoretical trend. In Latin America itself it is associated with authors like Walter Mignolo, Ileana Rodríguez, Santiago Castro, Eduardo Mendieta, Fernando Coronil and Alberto Moreiras.[35] But it was undoubtedly Edward Said who, with *Orientalism* (1978), became the chief inspiration for the postcolonial theory of authors such as Spivak, Guha, and Aijhaz Ahmad from India, and the South African Benita Parry.[36] Postcolonial did not mean 'postcolonialist' however, and they were certainly not on the right.

World-Systems Analysis

The theory or analysis of the *capitalist world-system* is undoubtedly one of the most important schools of contemporary thought, and the closest to the MTD. For *world systems analysis,* rooted in a systemic perspective and the ideas of Fernand Braudel's Annales School,[37] the global factor overdetermines national factors, so only the world system is described as *capitalist,* while countries and regions are viewed in isolation despite being 'parts' of the world system. It fails to take into account the world economy as understood by Marxist authors such as Lenin, Bukharin, or Marx himself, who began by establishing the dialectical relationship between—as opposed to the sum of—national economies and the world capitalist economy. In, his monumental three volume work The Modern World-System, Wallerstein set himself the task of reconstructing the global history of capitalism and modernity from the 16th Century to the present, and coming up with a theory of this historical process. This would

35 Nadal, "Los estudios poscoloniales," 95–96. See also *A colonialidade do saber. Eurocentrismo e ciências sociais. Perspectivas Latino-americanas,* Edgar Lander, ed. (Buenos Aires: CLACSO, 2005).

36 See the discussion in Jonah Birch, "La teoría postcolonial en debate. Entrevista a Vivek Chibber," *Herramienta* 53 (2013): 157–169, http://www.herramienta.com.ar/revista-herramienta-n-53/la-teoria-postcolonial-en-debate-entrevista-vivek-chibber.

37 Carlos Antonio Aguirre Rojas, *Braudel a debate* (Ciudad de México: JGH Editores, 1997), and *La escuela de los anales* (Madrid: Montesinos, 1999).

culminate in world-systems analysis,[38] in which states belong to one of three clearly defined areas: the centre, the semi-periphery, or the periphery.[39]

Conclusion

The foregoing discussion shows that the different paradigmatic expressions of post-WWII social thought in Latin America represented progress but also displayed certain limitations. Today, the two main currents with the potential to overcome those limitations are world-systems theory and the MTD. For now, each of these currents continues to plough its own furrow, crossing paths but without joining forces. Ideally, if more time were devoted to such encounters then the two schools could pursue common subjects of study and common goals. For its part, dependency theory needs to perfect its methods and concepts to the point where it can venture empirically verifiable hypotheses in order to help us grasp the essence of the different phenomena which determine Latin American reality today. And that is where the MTD provides the theoretical-methodological and ideological tools needed in order to formulate the kind of lines of enquiry and analysis capable of producing concepts and categories which strengthen the study of dependency and underdevelopment in the tragic context of the crisis of contemporary capitalism.

38 Carlos Antonio Aguirre Rojas, *Immanuel Wallerstein, crítica del sistema-mundo capitalista* (Ciudad de México: ERA 2003), 37.

39 Immanuel Wallerstein, T*he Modern World-System: Capitalist Agriculture and the Origins of the European World-Economy in the Sixteenth Century* vol. 1 (New York: Academic Press, 1974). See also World-System Analysis. An Introduction (Durham: Duke University Press, 2004) by the same author.

CHAPTER 2

Marini's Marxism and Dependency Theory Today

This chapter outlines the main features of Marini's theoretical and political approach within the framework of general Marxist theory and the theory of imperialism, with a particular focus on the background to his Marxist theory of dependency and its most salient aspects. Our purpose is to locate the subject of the present work – sub-imperialism – and understand it in terms of its chief categories and concepts as well as its contemporary dynamics. Later we shall see how these very dynamics can be explained by both dependency theory itself and sub-imperialism's own economic and strategic geopolitical cycles.

A Personal Tribute

I first met Ruy Mauro Marini in 1975 as a sociology undergraduate at the Faculty of Political and Social Sciences of the Universidad Nacional Autónoma de Mexico (UNAM). By then he had already spent several years (with some interruptions) in exile from his native Brazil as a result of the 1964 military coup against constitutional president Joao Goulart – a coup which at the same time heralded the historical-political cycle of military dictatorships in Latin America which lasted into the mid-1980s.

As a lecturer in *World Economic and Social History* his academic qualities and subject knowledge always shone through, in particular his grasp of Latin American and Brazilian history. What really set him apart however was his ability to describe this history in both abstract and concrete terms and then explain it within a dynamic global context. Indeed this was true for all the courses he taught, not just in the Faculty of Political and Social Sciences but also in other higher education and postgraduate institutions such as the Postgraduate Studies department in UNAM's Economics Faculty, which he co-founded and where his teaching and research earned him his position as a tenured lecturer of the highest rank.

Respected by friends and enemies alike, Marini was always honest and rigorous in his theoretical analysis of social phenomena. He left an indelible mark on Mexico in the 20-odd years he spent there, where his role in nurturing leading Mexican intellectuals and guiding and inspiring new generations brought him recognition as one of that unique breed of Marxists and humanists who light up the path towards radical social change and human progress. Most importantly, he did so in a way that highlighted the need to overcome

 | DOI 10.1163/9789004319417_004

capitalism as an entire economic system and social formation, and not just one of its facets such as neoliberalism or neo-developmentalism.

Marini was always alert to contemporary developments, and invariably had the right concept, category or hypothesis to hand with which to try and get to the bottom of them. This he did in a creative and rigorous fashion, excelling in his description of the processes and tendencies at work. He never imposed his opinions, and showed respect for and interest in those of others, always listening to them before setting out and defending his own ideas with clear, solid, and constructive arguments which rarely failed to convince. Whether lecturing to students, presenting and debating his ideas in academic forums, or writing, Marini never avoided addressing opposite viewpoints, and would do so with utmost calm. Unlike those who turned their back on their old convictions, at no point in his life did he ever hold back from freely and openly displaying his belief in Marxism and the struggle for a better world beyond capitalism, as represented in his eyes by democratic socialism.

Marini is most widely known in Mexican and Latin American academia as the author of *Dialéctica de la dependencia* [The Dialectic of Dependency]. Nowadays this work is seen as a classic 'must-read' of Latin American contemporary thought and the social sciences in general in which, as elsewhere, he used solid arguments to put paid to claims of a 'paradigmatic crisis' and crisis of Latin American thought during the 1970s and 1980s. Indeed, the *International Sociological Association* classified *Dialéctica de la dependencia* as one of the most important works of the 20th Century, alongside universal classics such as *One Dimensional Man* by Herbert Marcuse; *Phenomenology of Perception* by Maurice Merlau-Ponty, *Marx's Theory of Alienation* by István Mészáros, *Political Power and Social Theory* by Barrington Moore; *Value in Social Theory* by Gunnar Myrdal, *Essai sur la qualification du travail* by Pierre Naville; *Structure and Process in Modern Societies* by Talcott Parsons and *The Principles of Genetic Epistemology by* Jean Piaget.

Anyone who has not read *Dialéctica de la dependencia* knows neither the author nor his work. But to understand either one also needs to look at the full breadth of his writings, which appeared in a range of different newspapers, magazines, reports, books and other formats. His other major works include *Subdesarrollo y revolución* [Underdevelopment and Revolution], *El reformismo y la contrarrevolución: estudios sobre Chile* (Reformism and Counter-revolution: Studies of Revolution) and his last book in Portuguese, *América Latina: depêndencia and integração* [Latin America: Dependency and Integration]; published in Spanish in Venezuela by Nueva Sociedad but unfortunately unavailable in English. He also coordinated the publication of *La Teoría social latinoamericana* [Latin American Social Theory], a joint 4-volume work published by Ediciones El Caballito (1994–1996), and the accompanying textbook

Textos escogidos [Selected Works], both of which have contributed enormously to the education of new generations of social scientists in Mexico and Latin America.

Marini's thought and work have penetrated the classrooms and lecture theatres of Mexico's leading universities, ranging from those based in the capital (the UNAM, the Universidad Autónoma Metropolitana, the Instituto Politécnico Nacional, El Colegio de Mexico, etc.) to regional universities of national standing such as Autónomas de Puebla, Zacatecas, Guerrero, Colima, Baja California and Universidad Veracruzana. His ideas have also reached the academic and research institutions of Europe and the United States, enriching the discussions of teachers, students and specialists seeking a critical understanding of the world we live in. Moreover they have helped forge whole generations of university students, not just in Mexico but also in other parts of Latin America, including Chile, Argentina and Central America. Wherever he worked, Marini guided his students patiently and was always responsive to their concerns. He would supervise their undergraduate and postgraduate theses in a relaxed and friendly style, showing them different theoretical and methodological approaches and relevant sources. Rigorous critical analysis was always at the heart of his thinking.

In Brazil, dependency theory broke out of academic confines to take its place in the ideological, scientific and political debate surrounding the two then dominant paradigms in Brazil and Latin America represented by the Brazilian Communist Party (PCB) and ECLA. Amidst the discussion, a new workers' party was set up in Brazil: *Politica Operaria* (POLOP). It was independent of the traditional workers' parties and the PCB-controlled peasant leagues, and Marini joined it:

> That led me, even though I was still in France, to contact the group publishing the Socialist Party youth magazine Movimiento Socialista in Brazil, (who printed my article taking national-developmentalism to task), and in particular with Eric Sachs. Upon my return I struck up a wonderful friendship with Eric, whose experience and political culture would influence me enormously. The group's main sections were based in Rio de Janeiro, Sao Paulo and Belo Horizonte. It later became the Organización Revolutionaria Marxista-Política Obrera (POLOP in Portuguese) – the first Brazilian expression of the revolutionary left which was to emerge throughout Latin America.[1]

1 Ruy Mauro Marini, *Memoria*, Ruy M. Marini Archive, http://www.marini-escritos.unam.mx/002_memoria_marini_esp.html.

This new *revolutionary left*, as it was called in order to distinguish it from the reformist left, would become well-known in the following decades and nowhere more so than in Chile, home to many of the debates between advocates of the theses associated with endogenism, ECLA and the 'dependency perspective'. In the mid-sixties after the coup in Brazil (1964–1967), the notion of dependency finally succeeded in discrediting the idea of 'autonomous national development' of Latin American capitalism as supported by the old theories of development and ECLA's structuralism. As Cardoso noted,

> ...the critique of 'development sociology' and the 'critique of functionalism' burst onto the scene at the same time as the critique of national populism and the political positions associated with it. Taken together, these critiques constitute the political and intellectual forerunners of dependency-based analysis.[2]

As a result, many Latin American scholars began using dependency as a unique theoretical, conceptual and methodological tool for understanding and analysing the socio-economic and political problems of the periphery, and Latin America and the Caribbean in particular, as a bloc of underdeveloped countries subordinated to the development and expansion of global capitalism and imperialism. In his investigation of the origin, nature and meaning of dependency, Cardoso noted that

> ...we have tried to analyse...the types of relationships between dependent countries (classes, states and economies) and imperialist countries. Therein lies the potential basis of a dependency theory. As I have stated elsewhere, this is not an alternative to the theory of imperialism, but complements it. As such, it is vital for dependency theory that the periodisation of the global capitalist economy and understanding of the current stage of imperialism are continually updated.[3]

At the time Cardoso still believed in constructing a *theory* of dependency, but at no point during his journey along the well-trodden path from reformist Weberianism to orthodox neoliberalism did he actually use dependency to 'update' the theory of imperialism. Instead, he simply retained it as a

2 Fernando Henrique Cardoso, "Notas sobre el estado actual de los estudios de la dependencia," in Sergio Bagú *et al.*, *Problemas del subdesarrollo latinoamericano*, 3rd ed. (Ciudad de México: Editorial Nuestro Tiempo, 1976), 98.

3 Cardoso, "Notas Sobre el Estado Actual...," 103.

Weberian device within the conservative version of 'interdependency', which understands dependency as at most a 'category in transition'. But he was certainly right in stating that (abstract) concepts should relate to the concrete historical circumstances of dependency and should therefore be continuously redefined depending on how the development of capitalism as a historical mode of production is periodised. Any such periodisation must take into account all the social, political and economic changes to affect capitalism worldwide in its cooperative and imperialist phases, through the age of big industry and manufacturing, and right up to the current information age in which a financialised economy is ruled by fictitious capital and fictitious profits.[4]

It is important to highlight two ideas regarding the origin and nature of dependency theory respectively. Firstly, as Raúl Fornet-Betancourt notes, the influence of the Cuban revolution and the failure of the Alliance for Progress helped make the social sciences the key site of development of Marxist theory and analysis in Latin America from the mid-1960s onwards. Within this process, he adds, we can see

> ...the formulation of dependency theory (or theories) as the real centrepiece of the development of this new Latin American social science, because it offers a new paradigm for understanding the situation on the subcontinent and also, logically, provides a basis for political action.[5]

But as Marini argued, dependency theory did not *originate* within Marxist thought, but rather *incorporated* Marxist tools. As the theory developed it "found itself in ever greater need of Marxism, until finally planting its flag firmly in the Marxist camp". And as only Marxist theory could properly analyse and understand dependency, so dependency theory needed to free itself completely of the structuralist and functionalist influences of its early days.[6]

Only by following Marini in *Marxist-izing* dependency theory in this way is it possible to arrive at a systematic critique grounded in a long term historical perspective, one which might against all the odds offer an alternative that goes

4 On this topic see Reinaldo Carcanholo, *Capital, essência e aparência*, vol.2 (Sao Paulo: Expressão Popular, 2013). As far as the present author knows, he is the first to link Marx's idea of *fictitious capital* (explained in Volume III of *Capital*) to that of *fictitious profits*.

5 Raúl Fornet-Betancourt, *Transformaciones del marxismo. Historia del marxismo en América Latina* (Ciudad de México: Plaza y Valdés, 2001), 276.

6 Sotelo, Adrian, "Entrevista con Ruy Mauro Marini: Las perspectivas de la teoría de la dependencia en la década de los noventa," *Estudios Latinoamericanos* 9 (1990): 53.

beyond not just the currently dominant ideological universe of neoliberalism but also dependent capitalism in its neoliberal phase. In contrast, the two dominant positions of neodevelopmentalism on the one hand and postmodernism and its sub-products (postcolonialism, occidentalism) on the other are both concerned, explicitly or implicitly, with the continued reproduction of dependent neoliberal capitalism through structural reforms and alliances with the ruling classes and the State.

The second idea of note concerns the characteristics of dependency and the level at which we classify dependency theory as a theory and as a method. Vania Bambirra defines it thus:

> Obviously not in the sense of a general theory of a mode of capitalist production, because that was done by Marx; and not as a 'dependent mode of capitalist production' either, as that does not exist, but rather as the study of dependent capitalist socio-economic formations, i.e. a lower level of abstraction capable of capturing the specific combination of modes of production to have co-existed in Latin America under capitalist hegemony.[7]

However, Bambirra's notion of a 'combination of modes of production' is questionable: although pre-capitalist productive structures certainly existed in the past, capitalism only really developed in Latin America once the advanced capitalist centres had somehow managed to subordinate these pre-capitalist productive formations and systems, thus providing the structural basis for the region's backwardness and underdevelopment. As Chilean Marxist historian and *dependentista* Luis Vitale puts it:

> ...the mode of production of the Hispano-American colonies was not feudal. Neither did it share the distinctive features of a modern, industrial, capitalist nation. The origins of capitalism there were different to those of Europe. History does not advance in a straight line, and Latin America did not follow the process typically followed by European capitalism,

7 Vania Bambirra, *Teoría de la dependencia: una anticrítica* (Ciudad de México: ERA, 1978), 26. Bambirra stresses the internal, adhered nature of imperialism within the structures of dependency. The level of social formation captures the specificity of the concept of country even, and how it differs from the concept of mode of production as described by Marx. For a discussion of this issue see V.I. Lenin, *What the "Friends of the People" are and How They Fight the Social-Democrats* (Moscow: Progress Publishers 1970).

> because it went straight from primitive communities to an incipient capitalism mainly producing precious metals and raw materials.[8]

Rather than discussing this issue in any more detail, our point here is to highlight the level at which dependency theory is constructed, which might be described as intermediate. The theoretical and methodological tools used to do this are drawn not only from Marxism and the theory of imperialism, but also from the specific features of Latin American formations apparent in the way societies and social classes, patterns of life, work and production, and territories and nation-states are all constituted. These particularities make for diverse and complex structural aspects and configurations.

With these two caveats, Marini's approach can be said to dialectically articulate the notion of dependency with that of imperialism without undermining their unity:

> For dependency theory, imperialism is not something external to dependency insofar as both are the product of the development of world capitalism. In fact, imperialism permeates dependent economies and societies completely, representing a factor that constitutes their socioeconomic structures, their State, their culture. Such an analysis offers new perspectives to historical and sociological studies in Latin America.[9]

Thus, in confronting the theses of both ECLA and the so-called orthodox Marxism commonly associated with the Latin American communist parties, Marini makes it clear that imperialism is a world system. As such it is therefore an integral part of the cycle of capital and patterns of capitalist reproduction in Latin America, as opposed to something external that needs to be 'isolated' as part of the 'autonomous national development' proposed by the aforementioned theses. In making this point Marini goes to the very heart of his disagreement and rupture with ECLA and also with other schools of dependency theory – including the self-styled and reformist (even conservative) dependency *perspective* – as well as with other approaches not really based on dependency, such as 'styles of development' and 'structural dualism'.[10]

---

8 Luis Vitale, *Interpretación marxista de la historia de Chile* (Santiago de Chile: LOM Ediciones, 2013), 172–173.

9 Marini, *América Latina: dependência e integração*, 90.

10 On the currents in Latin American thought see my book *América Latina, de crisis y paradigmas: la teoría de la dependencia en el siglo XXI* (Ciudad de México: Plaza y Valdés / FCPyS / UOM, 2005). Our essay "Teoría y neodependencia: una revalorización del

Dependency Perspective or Dependency Theory?

It was long thought that the only theory of dependency in existence was the one represented by the Cardoso School. This was partly because Marxists like Marini who had been developing dependency theory were forced into exile after the coup in Brazil. It then took more than two decades for their arguments to be rediscovered and for thought to be applied to developing a true MTD capable of engaging not only with the historical past of Latin American countries but also with their present and future in the context of their dependent and subordinate insertion in the global capitalist market.

The 1960s was an important and productive period for the development of theoretical approaches which mirrored the conditions and changes occurring in Latin America and the world. At the time a new cycle of military dictatorships was underway which would give rise to what Marini described as *counter-insurgency states.* At the same time and articulated to this, the pattern of capitalist accumulation and reproduction which had flourished in Latin America after WWII was clearly entering a period of decline and crisis. This was especially true for Brazil, Argentina and Mexico, the region's biggest players in terms of organic composition of capital, urban/industrial development, size and population, and the central role of the State in accumulation and reproduction.[11] A series of economic problems led to the decline and later crisis of the import substitution model of industrialization which ECLA and others, including *dependentistas*, had advocated as the main 'development strategy' to pursue. Globally, these problems only served to exacerbate the structural crisis of capitalist accumulation which would reach its zenith in the 1970s, paving the way for neoliberalism.[12]

The decisive decades of the 1960s and 1970s would be marked then by these twin processes of counter-revolution and the crisis of the post-war model of accumulation. The period drew to a close with the onset of democratization in the mid-1980s, to be followed soon after by the fall of the Soviet Union, the consolidation of the *Washington Consensus*[13] and what became known as

---

pensamiento de Marini para el siglo XXI" (unpublished manuscript) looks at this issue in greater depth.

11 On capital reproduction as a concept see Ruy Mauro Marini, "Sobre el patrón de reproducción de capital en Chile," *Cuadernos de CIDAMO* 7, http://www.marini-escritos.unam.mx/061_reproduccion_capital_chile.html.

12 I discuss crisis in more depth in *Crisis capitalista y desmedida del valor: un enfoque desde los Grundrisse* (Ciudad de México: Itaca / UNAM / FCPyS, 2010), situating it in relation to the crisis of value and surplus value production.

13 See footnote 29.

globalization. In terms of epistemological developments, we find that the crisis coincided with both a regional crisis of the hegemonic thought represented by ECLA and a rise in the influence of dependency theories. I say theories rather than theory because, as we shall see, dependency theory would eventually branch off into the (reformist) *dependency perspective* and the *Marxist theory of dependency,* each with very different epistemological and methodological frameworks, diagnoses and conclusions.

As we have seen, it was the whole set of concepts adopted by ECLA and its leading theorists that entered into crisis. But in my view these concepts were never actually put to the test. The capitalist crisis of the 1970s would ensure they remained merely a well-intentioned hypothesis – namely that dependent, underdeveloped and backward countries such as ours *might,* given certain social, economic, political and administrative conditions, develop an *autonomous capitalism* driven by large-scale intervention and social and economic planning by the State.

This position was evident among leading ECLA theorists such as Celso Furtado, María da Conceição Tavares, Aníbal Pinto, Juan Noyola, Aldo Ferrer and Raúl Prebisch. It was Prebisch who first gave development theory a theoretical, methodological and analytical framework based on a heterodox structuralist perspective. He would use this framework to develop his *core-periphery theory,*[14] upon which he later built his own concept of *peripheral capitalism.*[15] Under Prebisch, ECLA was able to add new elements to the then widely-held theory of international trade based on comparative advantage by conceptualizing and setting out the division of the world economy as a whole whilst highlighting the existence of a hegemonic *centre.* Crucially, in this view, whilst the dominant relationships and cycles of reproduction at the heart of the hegemonic centre do create growth and development, they are the same relations that create a subordinate, dependent and backward *periphery.*

This perspective represented the biggest contribution made by ECLA's structuralist version of development theory to Latin American thought, and one which Marini would confront. It incorporated the ideas of the influential

14 The foundational document was originally published in 1950: Raúl Prebisch, *The Economic Development of Latin America and Its Principal Problems* (New York: United Nations, 1950). Available online at http://prebisch.cepal.org/en/works/economic-development-latin-america-and-its-principal-problems.

15 Raúl Prebisch, *Capitalismo periferal: crisis y transformación,* (Ciudad de México: Fondo de Cultura Económica, 1987).

radical Brazilian thinker Celso Furtado, also associated with the organisation,[16] and whilst certainly drawing on Marx, it also drew on Keynes and the Keynesian school generally. ECLA sought to reduce social injustice and wealth concentration through State intervention in the economy in defence of society's collective interests.[17] It saw such intervention along with industrialization as the two keys to (capitalist) development in general and reducing 'external dependency' in particular. That said, the organisation unsurprisingly never saw socialism as a social formation and mode of production capable of providing an alternative path of socio-economic development.

At the heart of these ideas lay the belief that dependent countries 'might' be able to rely on the same characteristics, mechanisms and public policies as the likes of Mexico, Brazil, Argentina or Chile in order to 'adopt' US-style integrated development, with its model of a society based on the mass consumption of manufactured goods (Weber and Rostow's "ideal type")[18] and the patterns of capital accumulation and reproduction such a model entails. However, the *organic composition* of capital is *lower* in dependent countries than in advanced capitalist countries, and the former do not share the same class structure as British, North American or German society.[19] Furthermore, during the 1950s and 1960s at least 70–80% of the population in dependent countries lived in rural areas. Urbanization rates were very low, and development processes were based on agriculture, livestock production and extraction. 'Traditional society', whose income came from agriculture or mining, prevailed over the 'fully developed', 'educated' and industrialised section of society.[20]

Just as the ECLA model entered into crisis, new approaches such as the 'dependency perspective' and Marxist-Marinist *dependency theory* emerged in mid-1960s Brazil. In their theoretical and political understanding of global and

16 A useful discussion of this topic can be found in Osvaldo Sunkel and Pedro Paz, *El subdesarrollo latinoamericano y la teoría del desarrollo*, 9th ed. (Ciudad de México: Siglo XXI, 1976).

17 See for example Celso Furtado, *O capitalismo global* (Rio de Janeiro: Paz e Terra, 1998).

18 Max Weber, *Ensayos sobre metodología sociológica* (Buenos Aires: Amorrortu, 1982) and "The Five Stages of Growth – a Summary," in Rostow, *The Stages of Economic Growth.*

19 For Marx, the organic composition of capital is the synthesis of the relation between the value composition and the technical composition of capital. See Chapter 25 of Marx, *Capital Volume One*, 574. On the concept of the pattern of capital reproduction see Marini, "Sobre el patrón de reproducción de capital en Chile."

20 Gino Germani, *Política e massa*. Estudos Sociais e Políticos 13 (Minas Gerais, Brazil: Revista Brasileira de Estudos Políticos, 1960); Germani, *La sociología en América Latina* (Buenos Aires: Eudeba, 1964); Germani, *Política y sociedad en una época de transición* (Buenos Aires: Paidós, 1968).

Latin American capitalism, these new approaches offered a radical alternative to the theories of social change represented by ECLA, endogenism, modernization, and functionalism, once popular but all now facing an epistemological crisis. So let us momentarily clarify what the 'dependency perspective' is and why it differs from a theory of dependency as advocated by Marini and others.

For a long time, academics, social scientists and even the media identified dependency (as a school, perspective or theory) solely with the dominant version represented by Cardoso and a series of other theorists. But although this group had originally shared some common ground with Marini they eventually took a different path. Thus two distinct schools of thought emerged around dependency: the dominant tendency of the Cardoso School; and that represented by Marini and others, which sought to deepen understanding of dependency in order to explain events in Latin America and the world through *ad hoc*, purpose-built categories and concepts. It thus became apparent that there were two approaches: one a *perspective* and the other a *theory.* The first was a means or method of approaching the study of social reality. The second chose *dependency* itself as the *subject of study*.[21] Through debate and a process of differentiation these two tendencies were identified in political and ideological terms as bourgeois nationalist and reformist on the one hand; and revolutionary and Marxist on the other.[22]

For Heinz Sonntag, closely aligned to the Cardoso School, the two approaches reflect very different understandings of dependency. In his view the 'dependency perspective' method involves a "concrete analysis of concrete situations of dependency", giving priority to the study of class and the system of domination. In contrast, Marini's dependency theory supposedly undervalues these aspects of social reality, and instead sees dependency as a structural category with its own *theoretical status*, thus making it a *subject of study.* This leads Sonntag to the false and absurd conclusion that dependency theory therefore "denies" the possibility of capitalist development in our countries.[23]

Such a conclusion is completely inconsistent with the main theses and positions developed by dependency theorists. For Marini in particular, dependency as a category has its own historical and structural character, and its cycles of capital accumulation and reproduction are dialectically linked to the dynamics of class, class struggle, and State power. Furthermore, he places emphasis not on the 'impossibility' of capitalist development in the so-called periphery, but on the systematic transfer of value and surplus value from the periphery

21 These two perspectives are explained in Sonntag, *Duda, certeza y crisis*, 98 *et seq*.

22 Sonntag, *Duda, certeza y crisis*, 98.

23 Ibid., 101.

to the imperialist centres of hegemonic capitalism. At the same time, the super-exploitation of labour power serves to compensate for the loss of value and surplus value which the ruling classes in dependent countries suffer as a consequence.

It was in fact other authors, closer to ECLA, who proposed a theory of economic stagnation for Latin America. So for Furtado, growth was 'strangled' because technical progress largely benefitted only the most efficient and profitable productive units, and also as a result of 'high income concentration'. This, he argued, led to a *tendency* to stagnate, concluding that "the decline in economic efficiency is usually caused directly by economic stagnation",[24] and that "the problem of economic stagnation can therefore be understood as a structural issue".[25] For Marini it was rather the Cardoso School which dismissed dependency as a category only to end up embracing the conservative and neoliberal notion of 'interdependency'. And in this he was not mistaken, given that for Cardoso the dependent economy was an 'accidental occurrence' in the historical development of capitalism rather than an 'immanent condition'[26] of it.

From an MTD viewpoint, dependent capitalism does not develop historically and structurally 'outside' of the imperialist system as it does in 'dependency perspective', endogenist and ECLA theories, but is rather a (subordinated) constituent part of it. This is the essential notion underlying the MTD, expressed in theoretical and methodological terms as dependency's five historical forms:

(a) *Traditional or original dependency* of a colonial kind (1521–1850). The Argentine historian Sergio Bagú's notion of *colonial capitalism* is important here as a response to arguments for the existence of feudalism in Latin American societies[27] and theories of articulation of modes of production. There is also the monumental work of Chilean historian Luis Vitale, who countered 'feudalist' theses which "medievalised" Spanish colonial

24 Celso Furtado, *Subdesarrollo y estancamiento en América Latina* (Buenos Aires: Eudeba, 1966), 97.

25 Furtado, *Subdesarrollo y estancamiento en América Latina*, 100.

26 Ruy Mauro Marini, *Dialéctica de la dependencia* (Ciudad de México: ERA, 1973), 91. The Cardoso article Marini refers to is "Notas sobre el estado actual…".

27 Sergio Bagú, *Economía de la sociedad colonial. Ensayo de historia comparada de América Latina* (Ciudad de México: Grijalbo / Consejo Nacional para la Cultura y las Artes, 1992). For a compilation of articles by different authors on the feudalism/capitalism debate in Latin America see Carlos Sempat Assadourian *et al.* "Modos de producción."

society with his theory of early capitalist development in our Latin American countries.[28]

(b) *Commercial export-based dependency* in the context of the oligarchic / big landowner system (1850–1930).

(c) *Financial-industrial dependency* (1930–1950).

(d) The end of import substitution and the new wave of direct foreign investment gave a new and largely technological and industrial character to dependency (1950–1975).

(e) The current period as characterized by neoliberal dependency, which is primarily financial and technological in nature. Its dominant features include fictitious-speculative capital aimed at financial services and information technology; the world market as the main hub of accumulation and profiteering; new peripheries created by the global division of labour, specialising in the production of natural resources, foodstuffs and minerals; and the export of cheap labour from dependent countries to developed ones (Spain, United States, France, United Kingdom).

This modern structure of dependency does not mean that the cycles of capital, especially productive and mercantile capital, now lack their own dynamic. But it does mean that their dynamic is now dictated by subordination to fictitious capital and technological disadvantage.

The current phase of global capitalist restructuring and deindustrialization enables us to locate the social and political structural transformations currently affecting society in different ways – in particular the impact of quantitative and qualitative changes on the world of work in both developed and dependent/underdeveloped countries. We should likewise acknowledge that every structural and material change to society and its sum of social and political relationships will eventually shape social thought and the theoretical trends that historically constitute its methods, concepts and categories of analysis.

The Neoliberal Offensive and Marini's Response

Latin America did not escape neoliberalism's ideological offensive in the 1980s and 1990s, and in fact the region served as both a laboratory for putting it into

28 See Luis Vitale, *Interpretación marxista de la historia de Chile*, 4 vols. (Santiago de Chile: LOM Ediciones, 2013). André Gunder Frank makes similar arguments in *Capitalism and Underdevelopment in Latin America: Historical Studies of Chile and Brazil* (New York: Monthly Review, 1967).

practice and as the 'empirical proof' of its effectiveness. Various theoretical currents were marginalised and displaced from social science discourse and academic and research institutions, including the critical Marxist dependency-based approach associated with Marini and other noteworthy intellectuals. Neoconservative, neoliberal thinking even displaced non-Marxist currents which were nevertheless critical of the system, such as neodevelopmentalism and the endogenism traditionally espoused by Latin America's communist parties. In doing so, it managed to *rearticulate* functionalism within neo-structuralism and the different schools of neoclassical economic theory, resulting in an eclectic theoretical cocktail whose key feature, both then and now, is that it subjects capitalist economies and societies to the will of the markets and private companies with minimal state intervention in the economy or public ownership.

Marini and other authors such as André Gunder Frank, Vania Bambirra, and Orlando Caputo used the Marxist theory of dependency to confront neoliberalism's ideological onslaught. They did so by rearticulating Marx's theory and dialectical approach within a global perspective that unmasked the deep contradictions in the way the capitalist mode of production operates in dependent and underdeveloped countries – contradictions which the 'neoclassical models' and functionalists had tried to hide behind complex mathematical models of the region's social and economic conditions.

The forceful criticisms of dependency theory in the 1980s and 1990s actually had the opposite effect to that intended, as they led to it reasserting its critical role and thus emerging even stronger from the deep crisis of Latin American capitalism during the 'lost decade'. Those who, from the shaky ground of eclecticism and revisionism, predicted the death of the Marxist theory of dependency were profoundly mistaken, because today it is more alive than ever. As Marini wrote "...returning to dependency theory as the starting point means reacquainting ourselves with the best thinking on the left..."[29] However, as he himself warned, that does not mean it has a definitive answer to the problems faced by Latin America and the world.

The search for such an answer is a task incumbent upon critical Marxist Latin American thought as a whole, and not as some might think, the individual efforts of certain 'enlightened intellectuals'. That is why Marini always argued that dependency theory is not a finished theoretical product, as many critics claimed, but an outline – a project awaiting further development. What he did was to lay the foundations of the first critical theory and school of thought to recognise the nature of contemporary dependent capitalism without the

29 Marini, *América Latina: dependência e integração*, 101.

interference of dominant theories of European and North American origin. Thus at the end of *Memoria*, he concludes that

> (...) however one is to judge dependency theory, one cannot deny its unique and decisive contribution in encouraging the study of Latin America by Latin Americans themselves, and its ability to invert the relationship between the region and the major capitalist centres for the first time, so that Latin American thought went from being influenced by to itself influencing progressive thought in Europe and the United States.[30]

There has never been a more urgent need for this contribution than in the university of the 21st Century and pre- and postgraduate higher education generally, where the *pensée unique* of neoliberal ideology has strived to make itself the sole guiding light of all human thought.

In *Memoria* we are fortunate enough to have a guide to the genesis of Marini's thought and his personal and political journey up until 1990, along with a detailed list of his work, both published and unpublished.[31] It is therefore a valuable tool for reconstructing what was a key period for the revolutionary left in Latin America and especially in Mexico and Chile, where he was exiled. It shows us how he used his training as a Marxist and constructive, dialectical criticism to expose the conservative and bourgeois essence of the largely North American theories of development and the developmentalist and neo-developmentalist currents so widespread on the continent, as well as to critique endogenism and the neoliberalism driving our economies and societies today.[32]

Unlike many authors, Marini broke with and challenged ECLA's developmentalist ideology and communist party thinking of his time. In doing so he cast light on the true origins of dependency theory:

---

30 Marini, *Memoria*.

31 Including "Estado y crisis en Brasil," *Cuadernos Políticos* (Ciudad de Mexico) *13* (July–September 1977); "Las razones del neodesarrollismo (Respuesta a F.H. Cardoso y J. Serra)," *Revista Mexicana de Sociología* (Ciudad de México) xl (1978); "El ciclo del capital en la economía dependiente," in Úrsula Oswald, ed., *Mercado y dependencia* (Ciudad de México: Nueva Imagen, 1979); "Plusvalía extraordinaria y acumulación de capital," *Cuadernos Políticos* 20 (April–June, 1979); "Sobre el patrón de reproducción de capital en Chile,"*Cuadernos de CIDAMO* 7 (1981); "Crisis, cambio técnico y perspectivas de empleo," *Cuadernos de CIDAMO* 9 (1982).

32 For a critical examination of development theories which came to the fore after WWII see Frank, *Latin America: Underdevelopment or Revolution*). For a critique of Latin American currents see Marini, *América Latina: dependencia e integração.*

> ...current interpretations see it as an academic sub-product of (and alternative to) ECLA's developmentalist theory, but really dependency theory is rooted in ideas developed by the new left, particularly in Brazil, although its political development in opposition to communist party ideology was greater in Cuba, Venezuela and Peru.[33]

Thereafter dependency theory would make its own efforts to develop categories and concepts out of a complex regional panorama. This began with original and innovative concepts such as *labour super-exploitation* (the cornerstone of Marini's thought); *unequal exchange;*[34] *the counter-insurgency state* and *sub-imperialism; the integrated bourgeoisie, the state of the fourth power,* and *antagonistic cooperation,* as well as Marini's important contributions at different points of his life to the developing theories of democracy and socialism.

---

33 Marini, *Memoria.*

34 It is useful to recall the original discussion around unequal exchange between Emmanuel, Bettelheim and Amin, which appeared to have no impact (at least not directly) on the debate in Latin America or, notably, on the development of dependency theory. Emmanuel was one of the main authors to go beyond a theory of comparative costs of international trade based on price analysis by studying unequal exchange between nations on the basis of an exchange of unequal quantities of labour – to the detriment of underdeveloped countries. He asked whether there were "for certain reasons that the dogma of immobility of factors [i.e. capital, labour] prevents us from Seeing, a certain category of countries that, whatever they undertake and whatever they produce, always exchange a larger amount of their national labour for a smaller amount of foreign labour?". By answering in the affirmative he was able to then develop his theory of unequal exchange. Arghiri Emmanuel, *Unequal Exchange: A Study of the Imperialism of Trade* (New York: Monthly Review, 1972), xxxi. Originally published in French as *L'Échange inégal. Enssai sur les antagonismes dans les rapports économiques internationaux* (Paris: Maspero, 1969). The unequal exchange debate appears in Arghiri Emmanuel *et al.*, "Imperialismo y comercio internacional," *Cuadernos de Pasado y Presente* 24 (Buenos Aires) (1971). It should be noted that Marini's work contains no reference to this debate and that ECLA (represented by Raúl Prebisch, for example) only developed a theory of the 'deterioration of the terms of exchange'. This theory failed to mention the important problem of value transfers and production prices at the level of the open market. Blomström and Hettne therefore argued that "The development of a theory of unequal exchange was therefore not directly linked to the Latin American dependency school, although a number of Latin Americans also worked on it", Magnus Blomström and Björn Hettne, *Development Theory in Transition* (London: Zed Books, 1984), 81. One exception was Gunder Frank, who not only partook in the discussion but made some strong criticisms of much help in incorporating the issue in recent Latin American studies. See André Gunder Frank, *Dependent Accumulation and Underdevelopment* (London: Macmillan, 1978), 103 *et seq.*

These theoretical concepts make up the backbone of dependency theory in Marini's thought, and are used as the methodological and theoretical tools of a living, anti-dogmatic Marxism. Applied to the study of Latin American economies and historical-social formations, and indeed other dependent and underdeveloped areas of the world economy, they provide an understanding of the hidden and contradictory dynamics which ultimately explain why in the 21st Century such countries remain structurally incapable of overcoming dependency, underdevelopment and backwardness. The current crises in Brazil, Argentina and elsewhere in Latin America are the living proof of such a failure. Indeed, since the 1980s, these conditions, far from being eradicated, have in fact become more entrenched than at any time in recent history, thus reconfirming how the general laws of capitalism operate in Latin American social formations which form part of a world market and international division of labour dominated by the advanced capitalist countries.

In "Underdevelopment and revolution in Latin America" (1967), Marini put forward one of his key theses and one which still applies today:

> This essay reflects the essential aspects of my research since late 1965. Its content is summed up by the opening statement that '*the history of Latin American underdevelopment is the history of the development of the world capitalist system.*

In it he goes on to show that underdevelopment is simply the particular means by which the region became integrated into global capitalism.[35] This thesis is still eminently applicable today. In arguing that the contemporary problems of underdevelopment in Latin America, Asia and Africa are essentially a product of the extraordinary development of 20th Century industrial capitalism, he unmasks the everyday contradictions which we face in the social, economic, political and cultural spheres, in our wage packets and in our living and working conditions. But on a more general macroeconomic level it is the monstrous size of the foreign debt held by underdeveloped economies which today exemplifies an effective, modern and 'financial' means of 'underdeveloping' our countries whilst contributing towards an unprecedented level of concentration and centralization of capital in the developed centres.

Despite being opposed by all and sundry when it appeared, this thesis actually explains the restructuring of the world economy during the 1980s and the way new powers such as Japan, Germany and the US have achieved global

35 Marini, *Memoria*.

hegemony by keeping the most profitable parts of the productive process and state-of-the-art technology for themselves, as Marini showed. At the same time, dependent countries have been forced to build up foreign debt, with the transfers of value that implies, and to increasingly de-industrialise – a process which in recent years has affected the whole of Latin America, but above all Mexico, Brazil, Argentina and Chile.

In this sense, *Dialéctica de la dependencia* is an undeniably original text which offers a new roadmap to Marxist studies in the region and a new framework for studying Latin America:

> Instead of following this line of reasoning, I held true to my belief that underdevelopment and development are two sides of the same coin, and studied the conditions under which Latin America had become integrated into the world market and how such a process had a) functioned for the global capitalist economy and b) affected the Latin American economy. From this perspective, the export economy which emerged in Chile and Brazil in the mid-19th century before spreading everywhere else represented both the process and end product of a transition to capitalism, as well as the form that capitalism took in the context of a particular global division of labour. This being so, the value transferred as a result could not be seen as an exception or a hindrance to the laws of the global market, but rather as their consequence. This transfer of value assisted the development of capitalist production in Latin America, which took place on the basis of two conditions: an abundance of natural resources, and labour super-exploitation (which itself assumed an abundance of labour). The first condition led to monoculture and the second led to the indicators of underdeveloped economies themselves. Subsequent industrialization would be shaped by the internal and external relations of production which flowed from these two conditions. Thus to my mind, having resolved the fundamental question, i.e. how capitalism had affected the essence of the Latin American economy and how surplus value was created, I went on to investigate how this surplus value was transformed into profit, and the specific features of this transformation. The text [*Dialéctica de la dependencia*] and other writings from the same period give some indication of how far this research took me, but I would only resolve the issue some years later in Mexico.[36]

---

36 Ibid. Influenced by Paul Baran, Gunder Frank makes a similar argument in his main writings.

And Marini did indeed take on the issue in later writings in which he would cast light on the causes of Latin America's recurrent economic crises:

> As for the theoretical issues raised by *Dialéctica de la dependencia*, I addressed them on three levels during my third exile: the *cycle of capital in the dependent economy, the transformation of surplus value into profit*, and *sub-imperialism*. Regarding the *cycle of capital*, my research took the circulation-production-circulation relation as its starting point, applying it firstly to changes in the Brazilian economy since the first oil shock. This was the subject of my talk at the second National Congress of Economists in Mexico in 1977, as appears in the *Memoria* of the event. Out of this talk came my essay "Estado y crisis en Brasil" ('State and Crisis in Brazil', published by *Cuadernos Politicos*. Then, in the context of said relation but at the level of general theory, I analysed the movement of the dependent economy in the context of the capital-money cycle. This was the theme of my talk at a seminar on the agrarian question and the market, the text of which is included in *Mercado y dependencia* ["The Market and Dependency"], a *reading* published in 1979.[37]

In 1980, the Mexican journal *Cuadernos Politicos* published "Plusvalía extraordinaria y acumulación de capital" [Extraordinary Surplus Value and Capital Accumulation], which was the dissertation Marini had presented in public examination to become a tenured lecturer at the UNAM Faculty of Economics. He described it as

> ...divided into three sections. In the first section I look at schemes of reproduction, an issue which has provoked much debate at different points in the history of Marxism. I seek to show their specific purpose in Marx's theory: to illustrate that the amount of value produced in different sectors of the economy is necessarily equal. I analyse the three premises that have caused so much controversy: a) exclusion from the world market, b) the existence of just two classes, and c) a constant level of exploitation of labour. In the second section, I use variation in this last factor to examine the effects of changes in the working day and the intensity of work and productivity on the relation between value and use value and on distribution. Then in the third section I look at how three different authors have addressed schemes of reproduction: Maria da Conceição Tavares (undated), Francisco de Oliveira and Fred Mazzuchelli (1977), and Gilberto Mathias (1977). I show that the first author not only fails to break with the

---

37 Ibid. (Italics added).

> traditional ECLA schema (agriculture-industry-State), but confuses use value with value. De Oliveira and Fred Mazzuchelli on the other hand sharply capture the national money-world money contradiction, but end up only focussing on circulation. Finally, Mathias offers an excellent analysis of the role of the State in determining the rate of profit, but fails to consider the profit-surplus value relation. (That year we resumed the discussion in Mexico, and Mathias admitted that his criticism of me on the issue of labour super-exploitation in his work had been mistaken). This essay, probably the least known of my writings, is a necessary complement to *Dialéctica de la dependencia*, because it shows the results of the research I had begun in Chile on the effect of labour super-exploitation on the level of extraordinary surplus value.[38]

I include this long quote in order to show that Marini's writings were always logically and dialectically articulated with each another by the original and fundamental concepts he developed in *Dialéctica de la dependencia.* These concepts had nothing at all to do with structural dualism or the functionalist theory of modernization centred on the transition of traditional societies to supposedly modern and industrial ones,[39] as opponents of Marxist thinking on dependency have wrongly claimed. *In my view, this articulation should be at the heart of any attempt to continue developing Marini's thought as part of the more general effort to develop Marxism in the 21st Century as the only perspective and methodology which is critical of capitalism in all its forms.*

Secondly, Marini's method of taking the global economy as his starting point before looking at the internal problems of the mode of production specific to dependent countries, which he always used in opposing endogenist theories, should be revived in the light of recent changes to the capitalist economy. Just as he anticipated, this is now a truly global economy increasingly capable of subjecting national economies to trade blocs, with the latter overdetermining the former. For dependent economies, globalization has not brought with it an 'autonomous development' whose continuity is assured by reaching ever more mature and advanced stages of industrialization (as suggested by ECLA's 'centre/periphery' theory). On the contrary, it could be said that we are actually witnessing the return of the 'old' 19th Century export economy but with 'modern' foundations (e.g. in financial speculation and the import of IT and microelectronics) at the expense of the 'endogenous development' of industry and internal markets, particularly where the latter rely on mass consumption. This is the scenario presented by Marini in *America Latina: dependência e*

38 Ibid.

39 For a radical critique of dualism see Frank, *Latin America: Underdevelopment or Revolution.*

integração. It is one which leads to various conclusions concerning economic growth and development and more specifically the effect on the jobs, wages and training of a workforce who face increasingly precarious conditions as a sub-product of this process of global capitalist restructuring. This precarity has fed into the widespread expansion of labour super-exploitation, in a process which has demanded radical political and institutional changes in employment relations and the world of work generally.[40] One only needs to observe the impact of the Troika's extreme austerity measures on Greece and of similar policies as they are applied once again in Latin America in the context of its current economic crisis to find proof of what we are describing here.

In my view we need to follow the path laid by these theoretical-methodological and research premises in order to get a full picture of dependent capitalism as a social formation in contemporary Latin America, which is the level at which Marini began developing the MTD. Referring to these origins, he once stated in an interview that:

> ... dependency theory was not *originally* Marxist, but rather *incorporated* Marxist tools... and as it developed its positions it found itself in ever greater need of Marxism, until it finally planted its flag firmly in the Marxist camp.[41]

This is why Marini insisted that only by using Marxist theory could dependency be properly studied and understood, and that therefore dependency theory needed to free itself completely of the structuralist and functionalist aspects acquired in its early days.

Criticisms of the MTD were often poorly formulated, tending to ignore (deliberately or otherwise) the epistemological level of mid-1960s political debate in Latin America, which it entered seeking to explain backwardness, dependency and underdevelopment and the paths to transformation and liberation. This was partly due to the silence imposed by the military dictatorship and the institutionalized nature of intellectual and media censorship. Indeed in Marini's case his 20 year exile has meant that only recently is his work being read again in Brazilian universities, and even then in the face of opposition from the dominant tendencies and even from the left in those such as Sao Paulo and UNICAMP. Not only the institutions themselves but also the majority of

40 I expand on this in *The Future of Work. Super-exploitation and Social Precariousness in the 21st Century*, Amanda Latimer, trans. (Leiden-Boston: Brill, 2016).

41 Sotelo, "Interview with Ruy Mauro Marini", 53.

teaching staff are still very resistant to the idea of engaging with Marini's work, and it is often the same story throughout the rest of Latin America.

Marini himself suggested that revitalizing *dependentista* thinking of the Marxist kind would involve

> ...picking up the thread where we lost it in the 1970s, picking up Marxism again as the only effective weapon the left has to analyse and comprehend the (capitalist) world it lives in, and develop a radical critique of capitalism as part of a mass democratic project of the future which would rescue Latin America from crisis and forge a new kind of economy in the interests of the majorities and not just national and foreign capital.[42]

This of course implies a collective task of theoretical, methodological and political reconstruction which takes into account the many and ongoing changes to have affected global capitalism in recent years.

As Gilberto Vasconcellos has noted,[43] despite attempts to discredit him and obscure his legacy, on an epistemological level Marini is experiencing something of a revival, together with the likes of Gunder Frank and the hitherto almost unknown Brazilian philosopher Álvaro Vieira Pinto. This is evident not so much among the generation which gave in and took up new and fashionable pro-market theories, but more among their successors, including workers and social movements. For example, the Brazilian MST has identified with Marini, and other popular movements along with academics and students have all been increasingly turning to and discussing the MTD. It has also become a focus of discussion for various groups on social media.[44]

In sharp contrast to the intellectuals and social democratic governments identified with the Third Way, the Marxist theory of dependency in its most radical version does not allow for the possibility of 'reforming' capitalism. Instead it sees a transition to an original and profoundly democratic socialism as the only way of overcoming private ownership of the means of production, the exploitation of labour power by capital and a system of imperialist domination which, as James Petras has argued, acts in partnership with the State.

Certainly the MTD does need to take up new issues and lines of research. Conceptually speaking, the prefix *neo* needs to be given meaning within the

---

42 Ibid., 56.

43 Gilberto Felisberto Vasconcellos, *Gunder Frank. O enguiço das ciências sociais* (Florianópolis, Brasil: Editora Insular, 2014), 101 *et seq.*

44 For example, *Rebelión*, http://www.rebelion.org/; *La Haine*, http://www.lahaine.org/ and *Periodismo Internacional Alternativo* (PIA), http://www.noticiaspia.org/.

core structure of dependency as outlined by Marini. The foundation of this structure is the super-exploitation of labour power i.e. capital's partial expropriation of the worker's reproduction fund and the value of labour power, in order to convert them into a source of capital accumulation. Marini applied this concept to structurally dependent countries, especially in Latin America. But today, scientific and technological developments, together with the secular crisis of historical capitalism exemplified by the fall in its combined growth rates and productivity, make it applicable to the whole capitalist system.

Events such as the fall of the Soviet Union and the consolidation of the Washington Consensus were ideologically exploited by neoliberalism to proclaim the 'end of history' and the 'dawn of democracy' as an 'antidote' to socialism. But notwithstanding their negative effects on social thought, these events, along with the structural, systemic and civilisational crisis that hit capitalism in 2008–2009, signalled a turning of the tide. Despite slow and uneven progress, critical thought and Marxism have once again become popular theoretical and analytical tools for a significant number of intellectuals in Europe and indeed the United States. In contrast to the one-dimensional fragmentation of knowledge imposed by neoliberalism, holistic thinking is back on the agenda, and having cast off the straightjacket of neoliberal thought we can now revisit themes such as the law of value, unequal exchange, the transfer of surplus value to the advanced centres, the role of the State and labour super-exploitation in order to get to the heart of contemporary social, economic, political and cultural problems.

These then are some of the ideas which justify paying tribute to a man who deserves to be recognised by the social sciences, critical intellectuals and the revolutionary left as a true organic intellectual of the social and economic struggles of the workers and the oppressed and exploited peoples of dependent Latin American countries on the periphery of the capitalist-imperialist world system. The structural transformations which their struggles have generated as part of a broader socio-historical process are a powerful expression of the mounting difficulties and contradictions faced by global capitalism in the 21st Century.

Conclusion

Neoliberalism, social democracy and neodevelopmentalism are in crisis. They once offered a promising future to what the likes of the World Bank, IMF, OECD and BID call 'developing' (i.e. dependent) countries – a future of 'independence' and 'sovereignty' for them and their workforces alike. Dependency theories on the other hand see a tendency for labour super-exploitation and class struggle to intensify as the 'structural reforms' promoted by the dependent bourgeoisie and international financial institutions impose ever greater labour flexibility. Moreover, the structural crisis of global capitalism has seen sub-imperialism revitalized by new forms of expansion on the part of countries and capitals such as Brazil, Israel, Iran, South Africa and Nigeria. This is in addition of course to imperialism's own tendency towards militarism and military intervention (Syria, Iraq, Libya, the Ukraine), which can be seen as an attempt to retain hegemony as it loses ground to the emerging powers of China and Russia and to progressive governments demanding sovereignty in the face of the Balkanization process promoted by leading imperialist powers such as the US, UK, Germany, France, and Japan.

These then are the chief new issues that need to be addressed from a critical and contemporary perspective capable of fully explaining the driving forces behind them. Such an understanding should contribute to the development and organisation of struggles by workers and popular movements aiming not only to overcome neoliberalism—a strategically important goal—but also to overcome dependent capitalism and capitalism itself as the ultimate cause of *all* the calamitous problems suffered by workers and society generally worldwide: exploitation, inequality, poverty, hunger, despair, injustice, inflation, unemployment, environmental destruction and fratricidal wars which threaten humanity's very existence.

Rather than serving as a pretext to reject Marini's thought, these issues should be used to critically renew it in the context of a capitalism which is coming up against its historical limits. We are not talking about its final downfall, as desirable as that may be, but unsustainable structural limits which need to be fully comprehended before new concepts and categories can be created. Then, and only then, can we build a better future and help speed up the imminent historical decadence of the horrendous system of wage slavery and poverty sustained by the capitalist mode of production.

Achieving this strategic goal of Marini's thought whilst self-critically reviving the best of 20th Century Latin American social thought requires a *new theoretical model* fit for the 21st Century which is able to capture historical reality, its underlying tendencies and the secular cycles experienced by the people of Our America. Out of the current renaissance of critical thought we need a scientific theory to emerge which offers the peoples of the world a clear path towards the creation of a new social and economic order: one that is free of exploitation, domination and poverty and is, instead, for the first time in human history, based on freedom, democracy, and relationships of equality and fraternity between individuals and societies. But we have to act now if we are to avoid mass destruction!

CHAPTER 3

Neo-Imperialism and Neo-Dependency: Two Sides of the Same Historical-Political Process

The theory of imperialism allows us to understand the theoretical, material, political and geostrategic basis of imperialism in the 21st Century, its historical antecedents and its modern-day characteristics. In this chapter we briefly review the theory's main features in order to locate it within a contemporary analysis of globalised capitalism, thus providing the necessary context for understanding the sub-imperialist system associated with some countries, including Brazil in recent years.

Revisiting the Theory of Imperialism

Some authors have observed that the title originally given to Lenin's *Imperialism: the highest stage of capitalism* contained the word 'latest' and not 'highest', which appeared when it was officially published in the USSR. For Beinstein,

> Apart from disputes over the terminology, the Marxist school tried to conceptualize a real process located in a specific period (the late 19th and early 20th Century). Their aim was to describe a *contemporary imperialism* which was subject to the hegemony of finance capital...[1]

This hegemony, we would add, corresponds to the cycle of domination of industrial and banking capital by finance capital and monopolies.

Similarly, Gerard de Bernis notes that in the essay's 1917 edition, Lenin was analysing *contemporary imperialism*:

> The title Lenin gave to the first (1917) edition of his work was *Imperialism: the latest stage of capitalism*. In 1920 the title literally became 'the highest', which is perfectly compatible with the idea of latest. The most recent

1 Jorge Beinstein, *Capitalismo senil, a grande crise da economia global* (Rio de Janeiro: Record, 2001), 255 (italics added).

 | DOI 10.1163/9789004319417_005

> period is the latest but is not necessarily the last, with nothing to come afterwards.[2]

Hence there are absolutely no grounds for arguing that Lenin had a teleological view of imperialism, or for defending a Fukuyama-style 'end of history' perspective. The Soviet version of the work (Progress Publishers: Moscow, 1978) notes that

> *Imperialism, the highest stage of capitalism*, was written between January and June 1916 (…) In the middle of 1917 it was published under the title of *Imperialism, the Latest Stage of Capitalism. Popular Outline* with a preface by Lenin dated 26 April 1917 (Publisher's Note, no page number).

These observations take away from criticism that Lenin's theory represented a 'quasi-eschatological' version of imperialism later shown to be false by the fall of the USSR and the socialist bloc in the late 1980s/early 1990s, when the US became the sole imperialism and apparently the hegemonic power among capitalist nations. If instead we understand imperialism as the *latest* phase (corresponding to Lenin's time, which stretched from the end of the 19th Century into the first two decades of the 20th), then the theory and historicity of the concept open up whole new avenues of analysis when it comes to understanding the new core features it has acquired in the 21st Century. As Severo Salles argues,

> In the last five decades, capitalism has been characterised by the internationalisation of the social relation of capital, more commonly known as globalization. This has been a result of ever increasing centralization and concentration of capital and socialization of production during capitalism's highest stage—imperialism. In the last 30 years, financial globalization and neoliberalism have emerged as its dominant forms. Social breakdown is everywhere. Both these forms have been in crisis now for more than a decade.[3]

2 Gerard de Bernis, *El capitalismo contemporáneo* (Ciudad de México: Nuestro Tiempo, 1988), 19.

3 Severo Salles, *Lucha de clases en Brasil (1960–2010)* (Buenos Aires: Peña Lillo / Ediciones Continente, 2013), 22. This book is useful for understanding the historical, social, political and cultural background to the cycle of popular and class struggles in Brazil from the period of military dictatorship until the first decade of the 21st Century, including the systematic violation of human rights and forced disappearances. Starting from solid theoretical and methodological foundations and a critical intellectual outlook rooted in the best tradition

Rather than heralding a new 'post-imperialist' or 'post-capitalist' paradigm, what actually happened during the 'thirty glorious years' was that the world capitalist system became more heterogeneous and imperialism expanded[4] in a way that was consistent with the general interests of capital. As Atilio Boron puts it,

> It is evident that a phenomenon such as today's imperialism – its structure, its logic, its consequences and its contradictions – cannot be adequately understood from a close reading of classic texts by Hilferding, Lenin, Bukharin and Rosa Luxemburg. This is not because they were wrong, as the right loves to claim, but because capitalism is a changing and dynamic system that, as Marx and Engels wrote in the *Communist Manifesto*, 'constantly revolutionizes itself'. Therefore, we cannot understand early twenty-first-century imperialism by reading *only* those authors, but neither can we understand it *without* them. The goal is to move forwards in a reformulation that, departing from the Copernican revolution produced by Marx's work, which provides us with an interpretative clue that is essential for explaining capitalist society, will reinterpret with audacity and creativity the classical heritage of imperialism in the light of the transformations of the present. Today's imperialism is not the same as the one that existed thirty years ago; it has changed, and in some ways the change has been very important, but it has not changed into its opposite, as neoliberal mystification suggests, giving rise to a 'global' economy in which we are all 'interdependent'.[5]

Lenin formulated his theory of imperialism as a synthesis of the best work on the topic by his contemporaries, and the way forward does not in our view lie in dismissing it. Instead we should make it our starting point for investigating and analysing the world today, just as we should also use other theoretical and analytical tools such as Marx's schemes of reproduction of capital. Only thus

of scientific Marxism, the author reflects on the root causes of the establishment of the 21-year dictatorship, which lasted virtually until democratization led to the first 'free' elections being held, in which the first post-dictatorship civilian government was appointed following an 'indirect election'. The new government chose Tancredo Neves as President of the Federative Republic of Brazil, who was succeeded upon his death by vice-president José Sarney (1985–1990).

4 Salles, *Lucha de clases en Brasil*, 23.

5 Atilio Borón, *Empire and Imperialism: A Critical Reading of Michael Hardt and Antonio Negri* (London: Zed Books, 2005), 2–3.

might we comprehend the emerging problems and tendencies of the current historical period.

The New Features of Imperialism

The perspective described above frames our understanding of the *new* features of imperialism. From embryonic beginnings, these features have emerged to the point where now they visibly describe (neo) imperialism as a modern-day socio-economic, political, technological, cultural and military formation. Moreover, neo-imperialism is by no means limited to just one country (the United States) but is present across the globalised capitalist system and corresponds to a particular historical period. Paraphrasing what Lenin said in relation to imperialism, Boron calls it:

> ... an essential – and inherent – feature of contemporary capitalism. What happened with neoliberal globalization was that imperialism expanded its presence far and wide across the planet, and its actions became more oppressive and predatory than ever.[6]

Let us consider then what the features of neo-imperialism are:

a) *The rule of fictitious capital:* this is capital that does not create wealth, productive jobs, or an income for workers; only profits for its wealthy owners. It is the most common cause of the low growth rates typical of capitalism's current, semi-stagnant neoliberal phase.
b) North American imperialism remains a greater military power than the European imperialisms (Germany, Italy, UK, France, Spain) and Japan,[7] and directs its attacks against nations and peoples in underdeveloped and dependent parts of the world. A current example of this is Venezuela, which the Obama administration has accused of being a 'danger' to US national security.
c) Under classic imperialism capital exports were more important than commodity exports, but today the picture is far more complex. Within

6 Atilio Borón, *América Latina en la geopolítica del imperialismo* (Ciudad de México: UNAM, 2014), 39.

7 According to the Pentagon, in 2008 the US had "...865 installations in more than 40 countries...with over 190,000 soldiers in more than 46 countries and territories". As well as these bases the US has 7 more in Colombia, giving a total of 872. See Alfredo Jalife-Rahme, *El híbrido mundo multipolar. Un enfoque multidimensional* (Ciudad de México: Orfilia, 2010), 38.

the contradictory centre-periphery-dependency relationship, dependent countries not only continue to export the products of mining and along with labour power (i.e. remittances), but also export manufactured goods (mostly produced by foreign companies) and huge quantities of both material wealth (oil, iron, gas, livestock, water, and forest, marine and agricultural resources), and monetary and financial resources to the global centres of economic and political imperialist power, feeding the latter's ongoing expansion.

d) The IT revolution: the widespread use of computers, the Internet and social networks have speeded up the circulation and valorisation of global capital, leading to wave upon wave of mergers and acquisitions of companies, assets, workforces, means of production and consumption. This has the effect of concentrating and centralizing capital even further into the hands of a few multibillionaire capitalists.

e) After WWII the world was formally divided up between the leading imperialist powers. But now, and since 11 September 2001 especially, the US bourgeoisie and imperialism have pursued their geostrategic interests by imposing dependent neo-colonialism through military action and the annexation of countries and territories (Afghanistan, Iraq). Along with the US invasion of Iraq (1990) and Hurricane Katrina (2005), the 11 September attack turned out to be another example of what Naomi Klein termed *disaster capitalism:* a huge opportunity for capital to generate business and expand into new markets on the back of all manner of natural calamities and human tragedies.[8]

For Erick Pernett, 11 September 2001 marked a watershed in what Marini understood as global geopolitics – the geographically-based decision-making behind global policy:

> The attack on the US on Tuesday 11 September 2001, directed at the World Trade Center in New York (destroying the Twin Towers) and the Pentagon in Washington had unimaginable worldwide repercussions. Globally, it seemed to usher in a period of structural transformations and changes in the logic and discourse of geopolitics.[9]

---

8 Naomi Klein, *The Shock Doctrine* (New York: Metropolitan Books, 2007). Klein defines "disaster capitalism" as "... orchestrated attacks on the public sphere in the wake of catastrophic events, combined with the treatment of disasters as attractive market opportunities...," 26.

9 Erick Pernett, *La geopolítica tras el 11 de septiembre*: *¿absolutismo global o crisis de hegemonía mundial*? (Medellín: Lealón, 2005), 40.

The Twin Towers attack and other calamities were to feed into a whole geopolitical ideology based on the idea of 'failed states'. The concept was originally defined by Gerald Helman and Steven Ratner, who were 'concerned' that 'ungovernable' states, in other words states increasingly incapable of maintaining their place in the 'international community' (itself a misapplied and ambiguous term), were presenting a risk to both their own citizens and neighbouring countries.[10] The fall of the Soviet Union brought with it the need to find a new pretext for imperialist domination. 'Failed states' fitted the bill perfectly, and they became the face of the (new) 'axis of evil', which took over the role played by 'communism' during the Cold War and Latin America's military dictatorships.

Another definition of the geostrategic concept of 'failed state' comes from the CIA's 1995 State Failure Task Force Report.[11] The Report's aim was to identify which countries could be considered 'failed', thereby representing a potential 'risk' to both 'international security' and US domestic security. But the key catalyst in the development of the concept of failed states was provided by the Twin Towers attack, which "... clearly united academic and government thinkers alike in seeing weak and failed states as a fundamental threat to global security"[12] (as was clearly the main objective!).

We can understand better what the attacks signified and the reasons for President Bush's 'preventive war' in the name of his national security doctrine by turning to neoliberal author Francis Fukuyama:

---

10 Gerald B. Helman and Steven R. Ratner, "Saving Failed States," *Foreign Policy* 89 (1993).

11 Daniel Esty *et al.*, *Working Papers: State Failure Task Force Report* (McLean, Virginia: Science Applications International Corporation, 1995), http://www.researchgate.net/publication/248471752_Working_Papers_State_Failure_Task_Force_Report. In 1998 the same authors published a second report: Daniel C. Esty *et al.*, *State Failure Task Force Report: Phase II Findings*, http://wilsoncenter.org/sites/default/files/Phase2.pdf. It is worth noting that Samuel Huntington's *The Clash of Civilizations and the Remaking of World Order* (New York: Simon & Schuster, 1996) came out in between the publication of the two reports. Huntingdon's thesis argues for the superiority of Western capitalism over non-Western societies and systems, which will end up being influenced by the former, either by strengthening their relationships with countries such as Russia, China or Japan, or simply through military superiority and intervention.

12 Patricia Moncada Roa, "El fenómeno de la debilidad y el fracaso del estado: un debate inconcluso y sospechoso," in Moncada, ed., *Los estados fallidos o fracasados: un debate inconcluso y sospechoso* (Bogotá: Siglo del Hombre Editores / Universidad de los Andes, 2007), 32.

> …The logic of American foreign policy since September 11 is driving it toward a situation in which it either takes on responsibility for the governance of weak states or else it throws the in the lap of the international community. While denying that it has imperial ambition, the Bush administration has nonetheless articulated, in the president's June 2002 West Point speech and in the *National Security Strategy of the United States* (2002), a doctrine of pre-emption or, more properly, preventive war that in effect will put the United States in position of governing potentially hostile populations in countries that threaten it with terrorism.[13]

In 2002, following the 11 September attacks, President Bush's National Security Council set out an integrated strategy for intervention and cooperation in failed states, describing them as a risk to US national security.

f) In the past imperialism expanded across different countries and regions by invasion and by grabbing human and natural resources. Today, however, many experts agree that this expansion has hit real limits. The US armed forces' capacity to continue guaranteeing effective control has been brought into question by, for example, its partial retreats in Iraq and Afghanistan (although without ever abandoning the aim of domination). These retreats reflect the US's diminishing ability to sustain a successful military occupation, which in turn reflects a certain loss of global hegemony on its part.

g) It is especially worth mentioning the heightened threat of a nuclear attack on North Korea or Iran, which would affect most of the Middle East. As Chossudovsky notes,

> The distinction between tactical nuclear weapons and the conventional battlefield arsenal has been blurred. America's new nuclear doctrine is based on "a mix of strike capabilities". The latter, which specifically

13 Francis Fukuyama, *State-Building: Governance and World Order in the 21st Century* (New York: Cornell University Press. 2004), 94–95. As well as outlining the doctrine of 'preventive war', President Bush's speech at the West Point Military Academy on 1 June 2002 also referred to an "axis of evil" which threatened national and international security and had to be destroyed as part of a global conflict between "good and evil." See "President Bush Delivers Graduation Speech at West Point," http://georgewbush-whitehouse.archives.gov/news/releases/2002/06/20020601-3.html.

> applies to the Pentagon's planned aerial bombing of Iran, envisages the use of nukes in combination with conventional weapons.[14]

Indeed, perhaps the most notable feature of the new imperialist period – *our* 'highest stage' – is that in military terms it represents imperialism's most dangerous and destructive phase so far, and one that could have unthinkable consequences for humanity. As István Mészáros rightly warns us:

> For what is at stake today is not control of a particular part of the planet – no matter how large – putting at disadvantage but still tolerating the independent actions of some rivals, but the control of its totality by one hegemonic economic and military superpower, with all means – even the most authoritarian and, if needed, violent military ones – at its disposal. This is what the ultimate rationality of globally developed capital requires, in its vain attempt to bring under control its irreconcilable antagonisms.[15]

There is no contradiction between the aforementioned features of neo-imperialism, which articulate economic, cultural, ideological, strategic-military and psychological dimensions, and the features of imperialism identified by Lenin and other Marxists such as Bukharin, who defined the world economy as "… *a system of production relations and, correspondingly, of exchange relations on a world scale*".[16] In fact the former complement and enrich the latter whilst expressing the new global character of the imperialist system under neoliberalism. Furthermore, as Harvey notes, imperialism cannot exist independently of capitalism or vice-versa, but rather the two complement one other to give us 'capitalist imperialism', which is "a contradictory fusion of 'the politics of state and empire'…with 'the molecular processes of capital accumulation in space and time' ".[17] Severo Salles concludes that this whole process

> …has created a 'new imperialism', in which emergency rule is increasingly the norm, violence has proliferated, the molecular-digital technological

14 Michel Chossudovsky, "The Dangers of a Middle East Nuclear War," *Global Research* (17 February, 2006), http://www.globalresearch.ca/the-dangers-of-a-middle-east-nuclear-war/1988.

15 István Mészáros, *Socialism or Barbarism?* (New York: Monthly Review, 2001), 37–38.

16 Nikolai Bukharin, *Imperialism and World Economy* (London: Merlin Press, 1972), 26.

17 David Harvey, *The New Imperialism* (Oxford: OUP, 2003), 26.

> revolution has given imperial intervention added potency, and territorial control along with the supposedly anachronistic practice known as primitive accumulation are brought in line with financial globalisation. Primitive accumulation is unleashed by the generalisation of the superior commodity form as it replaces common wealth and public wealth as a result of neoliberal *privataria*;[18] by the spoils of war, and by the creation of something akin to colonies in the conquered countries with the fruits of the somewhat misnamed 'real socialism'.[19]

The original theory of imperialism described the *contemporary world* from the end of the 19th Century until the Soviet Union broke up in the early 1990s. But it failed to provide a specific theory of peripheral and colonial capitalism. That task would fall to the Marxist theory of dependency. Faced with a new post-Cold War global imperialist system, critical thinking needs to go beyond the classic features identified by Lenin and rework its theoretical and economic-political assumptions. Only then will it be in a position to understand what kind of world has developed on the dependent periphery of the dominant capitalist system. The concept of *dependency*[20] represents then a *necessary complement* to the theory of imperialism, because, uniquely, it recognises the nature of dependent and underdeveloped socio-economic formations – such as Latin America and the Caribbean – which are subordinated to the hegemonic capitalist imperialist system. As Fornet-Betancourt notes:

> It is important to point out that dependency theory has not been formulated as an alternative to the Marxist-Leninist theory of imperialism in the new Latin American social sciences. Instead it is seen as complementing and enriching Marxism, and its lines of argument relate to Latin America's particular historical situation. To highlight just one aspect that follows from that, the development of dependency theory means at the same time the development of Marxism as an essential component of a Latin American theory of liberation.[21]

---

18 A combination of *privatização* (privatization) and *pirataria* (piracy) in the original Portuguese.

19 Salles, *Lucha de clases en Brasil*, 23.

20 According to Marini, dependency is "…a subordinate relationship between formally independent nations, within which the subordinated nations' relations of production are modified or recreated in order to ensure the enhanced reproduction of dependency. Thus dependency can only produce yet more dependency, and getting rid of it necessarily means first putting an end to the relations of production which it involves," *Dialéctica de la dependencia*, 18.

21 Fornet-Betancourt, *Transformación del marxismo*, 277.

Today, Lenin's theory of imperialism and the Marxist theory of dependency are more relevant than ever to understanding national dynamics and neo-imperialism. It is by articulating the two with the 'new' features of imperialism listed here that we arrive at *neo-imperialism* as a means of describing the fusion of the features of classic imperialism (1860–1989) with the new aspects inherent in contemporary imperialism (1990–2016). And crucial among these new aspects are changes triggered by the breakup of the socialist camp (1989–1991) and the strengthening of "North American unilateralism", which "...in its militarist form, looks to strategies based on war, military logistics and the creation of vast armies and security apparatuses, with a huge increase in defence sector spending,"[22] as the US invasions of Afghanistan, Iraq, Somalia and other countries in the 1990s and early 2000s made irrefutably clear.[23]

It is in this context that neoliberalism acts in the interests of neo-imperialism by serving as a ruling class ideology in the imperialist countries which has been taken up by the bourgeoisies, oligarchies, trade union bureaucracies and organic intellectuals of dependent countries. These neoliberal interests are expressed by the imposition of structural and socio-political reforms driven by the irrational logic of the capitalist market, by the privatization of productive companies and public services, and by the commodification of the environment and almost every space of human and social life. One particularly relevant example of this is the neoliberal policy of labour market deregulation, which aims to 'free' labour power from the 'chains' of the old welfare state, from Fordist and Keynesian protectionism and from corporatist trade unionism, all of which prevent the creation of a flexible, precarious workforce fully adapted to the workings of 'liberalised markets'.[24]

It is the 'market' which 'regulates' the economy and social life, in other words business owners, landowners, oligarchs, media barons, and all those who own private property and control the banks and financial systems. Therefore worker participation in the latter through class-based organizations and the State itself is surplus to neoliberal ruling class requirements. No longer active subjects, workers then become passive and marginalised. In the tradition of Kayekian austerity,[25] the dominant ideology being imposed on the world in the form of the neoliberal ideal involves totally marginalizing humanity as an active historical subject and subordinating it to the despotic and totalitarian rule of capital.

---

22 James Petras, "El neoimperialismo," *Rebelión*, May 24 2004, https://www.rebelion.org/hemeroteca/petras/040524petras.htm.

23 See also the interesting articles published by British journalist Robert Fisk on this topic.

24 I look at this issue in *The Future of Work*. Leiden-Boston: Brill, 2016.

25 See Friedrich A. Hayek, *The Road to Serfdom* (UK: Routledge, 1944).

Neoliberalism expresses the interests of neo-imperialism and dependency at a time when huge transnational corporations hold sway and can rely on the political and military power of the imperialist State to ride roughshod over peoples, communities, social classes and nations which oppose its interests and designs. This is the destructive logic of imperial rule, which has become a threat to Iraq, Afghanistan, Iran, Syria, North Korea, Somalia, Colombia, Venezuela, Cuba, Mexico, and in fact any society which seeks to challenge and destroy neoliberalism and capitalism.

Conclusion

As a concept, neo-imperialism contributes to our understanding of the new historical and structural configuration of dependency and underdevelopment in the context of the global capitalist and imperialist system. But it needs to be articulated with Latin American thought rooted in the Marxist theory of dependency and the invaluable theoretical, methodological and political contributions made by Ruy Mauro Marini and others to this important current of critical and revolutionary 20th Century thought. One such contribution is of course the theory of sub-imperialism, which constitutes one of the theoretical and methodological foundations of Marini's thought, and without which his version of dependency theory would remain incomplete. As Matthew Flynn writes,

> Two theoretical frameworks are proposed for critically evaluating Brazil's contemporary foreign policy. The first is the thesis of sub-imperialism, which grew out of dependency theory, and the second is globalization, expressed in the theory of global capitalism.[26]

---

26 Matthew Flynn, "Between Subimperialism and Globalization. A Case Study in the Internationalization of Brazilian Capital," *Latin American Perspectives* 157, 34, No. 6 (2007): 11. In effect Marini develops the concept of *sub-imperialism* from *within* the theory of dependency and not outside of it, stressing that "the concept of sub-imperialism emerges from this. Formulated in the context of dependency theory and related to the vision the latter has of imperialist world integration, it was used by me and other authors…" Ruy Mauro Marini, "Geopolítica latino-americana", Arquivo pessoal de Marini depositado no Programa de Estudos de América Latina e Caribe-Universidade do Estado do Rio de Janeiro, ca. 1985, http://www.marini-escritos.unam.mx/066_geopolitica_latinoamericana.html#_top.

By re-evaluating the theories of imperialism and dependency as complementary paradigms, we can capture the fundamental changes to have occurred across the system as a whole in the final decades of the last century and the first decade of the current one. Latin America stands out because of its subordinate and dependent role as a producer of natural resources and commodities within a new pattern of accumulation and reproduction of dependent neoliberal capital specialising in production for export. Furthermore, since the fall of the Soviet Union and the socialist bloc new regional peripheries connected to the central countries have emerged, which in the long term will only serve to reinforce the structural aspects of dependency and underdevelopment in our region.

CHAPTER 4

Sub-Imperialism and Dependency

Of all the schools of left wing thought to come out of Latin America, dependency theory is undoubtedly the one to have most influenced the social sciences and higher education in the advanced capitalist countries. Developed over the course of the 1960s, it divided as we have seen into two opposing tendencies with differing research methodologies and theoretical frameworks. One tendency was reformist and social democratic, and described as an *enfoque* [perspective] by its advocates (see Chapter 2). The other was Marxist-Leninist in origin, and was committed from the outset to forging a *theory* of dependency as a *specific research goal*. It explicitly sought to understand Latin America reality in the context of the development of world capitalism.

In this chapter we show that sub-imperialism as a theory and practice of international relations is closely related to dependency theory. We also examine the relationship between dependency theory and Marini's theory of sub-imperialism in order to shed light on the specific nature of sub-imperialism in countries like Brazil within a regional and global context; in their processes of capital accumulation and reproduction, and in their global and socio-political relationships.

Capitalism: A Closed Circuit System

In the past there was much discussion about the nature of capitalism and its relationship with other modes of production, and in the 1970s the dichotomy between feudalism and capitalism in particular was vigorously debated, with a whole range of useful interpretations put forward.[1] But beyond those different positions, there can be no doubt that as a mode of production and reproduction of capital and of social and human relations, capitalism is now the same one system almost everywhere, and therefore eminently global.

In earlier times, advanced and colonial capitalism expanded at the expense of underdeveloped and dependent regions, which constituted pre-capitalist

1 See Luis Vitale, *Interpretación marxista*, Chapter 1. Vitale merits Sergio Bagú with being the first to formulate a theory of the non-feudal, *capitalist* nature of Latin America using the concept of "colonial capitalism." See Sergio Bagú, *Economía de la sociedad colonial. Ensayo de historia comparada de América Latina* (Ciudad de México: Grijalbo, 1992).

© KONINKLIJKE BRILL NV, LEIDEN, 2017 | DOI 10.1163/9789004319417_006

spaces and enclaves existing at the margins of the productive system for the hegemonic powers to realise capital and surplus value. This was explained in Rosa Luxemburg's great work[2] on capital *accumulation* and the *realisation* of surplus value in *non-capitalist* spaces, and her critique of Marx's *schemes of reproduction*, which she dubbed "theoretical fiction".[3] But in today's capitalist economy, organically integrated and operating within its own global mode of production, such *expansion* can only take place *within that economy's own sectors and limits* as they apply to production, circulation, exchange and consumption.[4] This restricts sub-imperialism's opportunities for expanding in peripheral countries to the extent that at most it can only act locally in regional geopolitical spaces and in some African countries such as Mozambique, Angola, Kenya, Cape Verde, Equatorial Guinea, Tanzania, Zambia and South Africa. Other authors such as Fritz Sternberg have also based their arguments concerning capitalism and imperialism on the assumption that Marx had been wrong on this point. Writing in 1926, Sternberg joined Luxembourg in considering that his work corrects and compensates for this 'deficiency' in Marx:

> She shares Marx's fundamental ideas: the stunning discovery that capital is not a technical concept, but a social one, and that only under very specific conditions can the means of production create capital. The consequence of this – that capitalism is not an eternal category but a unique historical formation, will always be regarded as one of Marx's great discoveries. Likewise, we think it is right not to build socialism in our minds but to show how the forces destined to give birth to it are present in capitalism itself. The great world-historical significance of Marx is that he placed superseding capitalism and realizing socialism in the hands of the class whose chief historical mission is to abolish class structures: the working class ... But he did not show the exact path towards that, towards the socialization of the means of production and a classless society

2 Rosa Luxemburg, *The Accumulation of Capital* (London: Routledge, 2003).

3 "It is quite different with the realisation of the surplus value. Here outside consumers *qua* other-than-capitalist are really essential. Thus the immediate and vital conditions for capital and its accumulation is the existence of non-capitalist buyers of the surplus value, which is decisive to this extent for the problem of capitalist accumulation." Luxemburg, *Accumulation of Capital*, 346. For an analysis of this, see Severo Salles, *Karl Marx y Rosa Luxemburg, La acumulación de capital en debate* (Buenos Aires: Peña Lillo / Ediciones Continente, 2009). For a critique of the ideas held by Luxemburg and other authors see Henry Grossman, *La ley de la acumulación y del derrumbe del sistema capitalista* 3rd ed. (Ciudad de México: Siglo XXI, 2004), especially 269 *et seq.*

4 See Volume 2 (Part 1) of Karl Marx, *Capital. Volumes one and two* (Ware: Wordsworth, 2013).

> where surplus value no longer exists. This was essentially because his analysis of the industrial reserve army, wages, the capital accumulation process and crisis was underpinned by the assumption that the world would only be made up of national economies engaged in capitalist production ... Only when an analysis of capitalism is produced that unfailingly acknowledges the decisive role played by non-capitalist spaces ever since capitalist production began, will it be understood that this book is not only a continuation of Marx's *Capital*, but that the very problems he examined are affected considerably by the existence of non-capitalist spaces... This is so true that the most important empirical arguments against Marx are easy to construct when the analysis of capitalism and the conditions of its reproduction takes into account the ever-present non-capitalist spaces.[5]

Sternberg sought to 'prove' in his outstanding work that Marx's methodological hypothesis, which sees capitalism as a closed system created 'in all its purity', prevented him from learning about 'essential relations' and is fundamentally untrue, because both capitalist and non-capitalist economic relations of production are united at the very core of the world system.[6] But what would he, Luxemburg and other students of imperialism have made of capitalism's condition today as a universal system which along with imperialism's influence is present in virtually every corner of the planet? This condition is what really sets current-day capitalism apart from previous periods. It was hinted at by Marx as a theoretical possibility in *Capital* Volume 2 (Part 1) under the first of three methodological premises he used to formulate his famous *schemes of reproduction*:

> But it is the tendency of the capitalist mode of production to transform all production as much as possible into commodity production. The mainspring by which this is accomplished is precisely the involvement of all production into the capitalist circulation process. And developed commodity production itself is capitalist commodity production. The intervention of industrial capital promotes this transformation everywhere, but with it also the transformation of all direct producers into wage-labourers.[7]

---

5 Fritz Sternberg, *El imperialismo* (Ciudad de México: Siglo XXI, 1979), 3–4.

6 Sternberg, *El imperialismo*, 15 *et seq*.

7 Marx, *Capital: Volumes one and two*, 636–699.

This tendency was to express itself in the creation of a truly global capitalist system, in which

> ...once those spaces on the periphery were incorporated into capitalist relations of production, imperialism continued to advance beyond the limits imposed by geography. It did this by commoditizing sectors of social and economic life once off-limits to the predatory markets, such as public services, pension funds, health education, security and jails. That is to a large extent the history of the last quarter of a century.[8]

The second methodological premise underpinning Marx's schemes of reproduction in Volume 2 of Capital assumes that there are only two social classes – the capitalist class and the working class.[9] Finally, his third premise allows for the reproduction of capital in circumstances where there is no change in the length, intensity and productivity of the working day.[10] As Marini rightly observes, in order to progress to a concrete analysis of capitalist reality we must revise these assumptions. This is especially true for constant productivity and its articulation with relative surplus value. Marini argues that Marx himself would have rethought this assumption because his quest to build a dynamic theory of the world market would have eventually led him to formulate a theory of imperialism.[11]

Thus for Marini, schemes of reproduction are neither isolated from nor clash with the other active components in this process of formulating a theory of imperialism. He also restates that only by using the labour theory of value in conjunction with the theory of surplus value as our starting point can we dialectically establish the organic relationship between the schemes of reproduction and the chief law of capitalism discovered by Marx: the permanent *tendency* for the rate of profit to fall discussed in *Capital* Volume III (Part 3), with the additional spur of the extraordinary rate of profit.[12] He goes on to conclude that schemes of reproduction are not valid by themselves alone when considered in relation to the production and realisation of surplus value. Instead they serve only as an analytical tool useful to the extent that they incorporate the other aspects of Marxist analysis: the law of value, the law of surplus value, and the tendency for capital's general rate of profit to decline.

8 Borón, *América Latina en la geopolítica*, 42.

9 Marx, *Capital: Volumes one and two*, 835.

10 Ibid., 822.

11 Marini "Plusvalía extraordinaria y acumulación de capital," 26–27.

12 Ibid., 38.

James Petras offers a more contemporary version of this based on a mature capitalism (arrived at via globalization), greater circulation of commodities, the use of state-of-the-art technology in productive processes, and increased capital accumulation. He argues that

> … There are clearly differences between what we are experiencing in this period and what happened in the past… Firstly, circulation has expanded enormously. Capitals are entering everywhere. There are no non-capitalist or pre-capitalist areas. In terms of extension, the space available is much greater than in any other period. We don't have feudalism now, we don't have economies separated from capitalism, we don't have collectivist systems which keep capitals out. Capital can penetrate, invest, profit etc., more extensively, and that is the difference. Secondly there is the question of degree. There is now a much larger volume than ever before of capitals circulating. And thirdly, there is the way capitals now move using new technologies. It's a fact that finance capital particularly is circulating incredibly fast and people talk about thousands and thousands of millions of dollars circulating every day. Also the division of labour is much more widespread and there is a greater autonomy of capital movement compared to the past…The final conclusion in this regard is that globalization is not inevitable.[13]

The Features of Sub-Imperialism

Many authors, both Marxist and non-Marxist, dismiss Lenin's theory of imperialism. At the same time they claim that despite Marini's undoubted 'merits' they cannot understand what is 'specific' about sub-imperialism. So in this section we shall summarise the specific elements which for Marini and others make up sub-imperialism. It is worth clarifying at this point that sub-imperialism as a concept does not just apply to the military dictatorship which ruled Brazil between the mid-1960s and mid-1980s, but also characterizes Brazil's current pattern of dependent capitalist reproduction based on the production and export of raw materials (soya, iron, steel) and the extent of its dependency on China. That notwithstanding and as Marini notes, the concept was originally used to describe how Brazil's military dictatorships managed to

13 James Petras, *Globaloney. El lenguaje imperial, los intelectuales y la izquierda* (Buenos Aires: Antídoto, 2000), 28–29.

weld the bourgeoisie's interests and the national interest into one common cause which it promoted across the world. Thus

> ...influenced by this critical position, more than one Brazilian author chose to view the country's recent development simply in terms of expansionism. The strength of the phenomenon known as sub-imperialism led the United Nations and its technical bodies to come up with the concept of newly industrialized countries, thus privileging sub-imperialism's economic dimension, and this term became widely used in the latter half of the 1970s. Some Marxist authors, such as Enrique Semo and Jorge Castañeda in Mexico, took a similar approach to this issue, and tended to suppress/obscure the qualitative differences between imperialism and sub-imperialism. In international politics theory, the phenomenon of sub-imperialism has led to importance being given to the concept of intermediate powers, which some authors differentiate from sub-imperialism. This term has even been incorporated into the official vocabulary of states such as Mexico and Brazil. Finally we should note that in the 1960s Vivian Trias, along with Paul Schilling, Rodolfo Puiggrós, Gregorio Selser and others, used the concept of privileged satellites to address the issue from a strictly geopolitical perspective. The 1973 coup in Chile reignited interest in this approach and led to the left producing more detailed analyses of geopolitical doctrine and its application in Latin America.[14]

Marini discussed the concept of sub-imperialism within the context of dependency theory at various points in his theoretical writings. He did so most comprehensively in *Subdesarrollo y revolución* [Underdevelopment and Revolution], the first edition of which was published in Mexico by Siglo XXI in 1969.[15] He returned to it in the *Preface* to the fifth edition because of a series of confusions created by authors such as Cardoso who had either not understood his formulation or had clearly disagreed with it. This was perfectly understandable in Cardoso's case given that his approach reflected more the theory of interdependency.

Many Marxist authors deny that there can be problems realising commodities under capitalism, or to be more precise, problems in the circuit of commodity capital: C...M {L/Pm}...P...C', although this is an issue which Marini did

---

14 Marini, "Geopolítica latino-americana," (italics in the original).

15 Also published in Italy as *Il subimperialismo brasiliano* (Turin: Giulio Einaudi, 1974).

fully address.[16] Instead they prefer to talk of a 'crisis of overproduction', obscuring the underlying mismatch between supply and demand – *effective* demand that is. This mismatch prevents the realisation of commodities and with it that of the surplus value stolen from the worker which is required to ensure the amplified reproduction of capital. Furthermore, as Reinaldo Carcanholo notes, "Categorising the current crisis as one of overproduction or over-accumulation says virtually nothing".[17] The same can be said for 'underconsumption', which is just a superficial way of describing the inner workings of capitalism, whereby the popular and working classes are partly or fully prevented from consuming commodities by falls in their income. Marini described this as the *divorce* of production from the consumer needs of the masses[18] that occurs when dependent capitalism is primarily focussed on satisfying the needs and demands of the middle and upper classes.

In this regard there are three key aspects of realisation which are dialectically articulated with one another in sub-imperialism and particularly in Brazil: (a) luxury consumption mainly by the middle and upper strata of the bourgeoisie, (b) exports as a factor in the realisation of internal production, and (c) the State's role as an investor and stimulator of demand, especially through public spending.[19] But as Carlos Eduardo Martins argues, the very fact that in the dynamic of sub-imperialism relationships are dialectical rather than mechanical means that, mediated by an increase in the organic composition of capital, the twin processes of industrialization and technological development give rise to a contradiction. This contradiction finds its expression in an increased number of stages of production and a limited domestic market in dependent countries. Hence

> ...State-led demand and luxury consumption partly compensate for the limits placed on mass consumption, but they are not enough to deal with the rise in productivity. This contradiction leads to a formation which the author [Marini] calls sub-imperialism. For Marini, the tendency in question is relative rather than absolute. So the internal market continues

---

16 See "Estado y crisis en Brasil," 76–84, and "El ciclo del capital en la economía dependiente," 37–55. See Marx, *Capital: Volumes one and two*, 635 and 639 in Volume 2, Part 1, Chapter 4.

17 Carcanholo, *Capital, essência e aparência*, 138.

18 Marini, *Dialéctica de la dependencia*, 74.

19 Ruy Mauro Marini, *Subdesarrollo y revolución*, 12th ed. (Ciudad de México: Siglo XXI, 1974).

> growing in a concentrated form, but commodities are increasingly realised on the international market.[20]

Separately or together, the three aspects of realisation noted above play a central role in times of both crisis and expansion. In both cases new productive sectors emerge, and during the military dictatorship in Brazil these were the nuclear industry and the 'military-industrial complex'. As Marini demonstrates, the sub-imperialist State is the main protagonist in this process, weathering crises and stimulating recovery and expansion by exploiting inter-imperialist contradictions and rivalries whilst basking in its relative autonomy vis-a-vis imperialism. This does not mean however that it overcomes structural dependency – the main category overdetermining and conditioning the sub-imperialist State. Brazil's development of its own nuclear programme and arms industry both during and after the dictatorship did nothing to change that fact:

> The problem here is essentially one of knowing to what extent a nuclear programme could reduce Brazil's technological dependency on the most advanced industrial centres (…) It must be pointed out however that this dependency is contradictory in nature because it grows in direct proportion to the raising of the dependent country's technological level. In other words, access to a superior level of technology brings with it a greater need for highly advanced techniques and components, the production of which is a privilege enjoyed by the developed countries.[21]

Breaking with or overcoming dependency first requires breaking the monopoly held by advanced countries' "in research and development, which facilitates technical innovation (…) making the other countries even more dependent."[22] It also means breaking their control of the processes whereby industries are transferred to underdeveloped countries. This control is exercised in two ways:

---

20 Carlos Eduardo Martins, *Globalização, dependência e neoliberalismo na América Latina* (São Paulo: Boitempo, 2013), 243.

21 Ruy Mauro Marini and Olga Pellicer de Brody, "Militarismo y desnuclearización en América Latina; el caso de Brasil," *Foro Internacional* 29 (1967): 21–22.

22 Ruy Mauro Marini, "Proceso y tendencias de la globalización capitalista," in *La teoría social latinoamericana vol. IV, Cuestiones contemporáneas*, Ruy M. Marini and Margara Millán eds. (Ciudad de México: El Caballito, 1995), 59, http://lahaine.org/amauta/b2-img/Mariniglobalizacion.pdf.

> …firstly, by giving priority to transferring less knowledge-intensive industries to the more backward countries; and secondly, by dispersing the different stages of commodity production across different countries, thus preventing the growth of nationally integrated economies.[23]

Nationally integrated economies are of course one of the defining features of capitalist development in the advanced countries. Furthermore, the extent to which this division of the world economy has concentrated technical and scientific progress in a select few developed countries is unprecedented, especially when it comes to basic and applied science. But however much technology these countries are willing to transfer to dependent countries, they will not include 'source code', the knowledge at the core of technological development, despite unproven assertions to the contrary by authors like Zibechi. Otherwise the conditions for overcoming dependency really would exist. To deal with the Brazilian Air Force's 'current vulnerability', Zibechi offers two alternatives: to either join forces with French manufacturers

> …to design and manufacture, in Brazil, a fifth generation jet fighter like those that already exist on the global market [or to] …purchase fifth generation fighters in a deal that includes a comprehensive and complete transfer of technology, including all source code. The purchase would be the first step towards national production of the jet fighters by Brazilian company with State involvement, which would eventually be capable of the whole production process.[24]

Evidently the second scenario would prove Marini and Pellicer's point that

> (…) access to a higher level of technology brings with it a greater need for highly advanced techniques and components, the production of which is a privilege enjoyed by the developed countries.[25]

This is a privilege that, we might add, the developed countries are unwilling to give up. Oliveira identifies two consequences of the molecular-digital revolution relevant to this discussion: firstly, that peripheral countries at most can only copy the disposable parts, and not the original design of technical-scientific

---

23 Marini, "Proceso y tendencias," 59.

24 Raúl Zibechi, *The New Brazil: Regional Imperialism and the New Democracy*, trans. Ramor Ryan (Edinburgh: AK Press, 2014), 106.

25 Marini and de Brody, "Militarismo y desnuclearización en América Latina," 21–22.

units from their advanced counterparts; and secondly, that capital accumulation deriving from the copy of something disposable very quickly becomes obsolete.[26] Hence technological, scientific and financial dependency is reproduced on a wider scale. It also deepens insofar as obsolescence requires new investment. This usually comes from foreign capital and international bodies such as the IMF and World Bank, with copyright always of course carefully protected.

In refuting the sub-imperialist thesis, Zibechi draws attention to the role of Brazil's military-industrial complex in helping it become an imperial power. But this is nothing new. Marini himself noted that despite the development of its armaments industry from the 1970s onwards Brazil still failed to overcome dependency:

> This path currently being taken by Brazilian economic policy, in its attempt to unblock capitalist accumulation by creating dynamic new sectors, has many implications. We will highlight three of these for now. Firstly, the message that the global capitalist crisis, caused primarily by the conflict between the leading capitalist powers, has not just precipitated the economic crisis in Brazil but has also provided the country with an opportunity to overcome that crisis. In relation to both nuclear energy and the arms industry, the Brazilian state today makes the most of the fierce competition between the United States and Western Europe, especially Germany and Japan, to ensure it captures the resources made available by the global circulation of capital, means of production and technology. *Brazil will not overcome this mode of dependency*, but by diversifying the ways it articulates itself with the global capitalist economy it can carve out an opportunity to put its plans for industrial development into practice and so assert its role as an intermediate power in the global division of power. In other words, the Brazilian state takes advantage of inter-imperialist contradictions to carry out its sub-imperialist project.[27]

Will Brazil continue furthering its sub-imperialist project by exploiting inter-imperialist contradictions? Of course it will! Today sub-imperialism makes the most of these contradictions to make relative progress with its own expansionist development projects based on the nuclear and arms industries, but without coming anywhere near overcoming dependency as understood by dependency

26 Francisco de Oliveira, *Crítica à razão dualista /O ornitorrinco* (São Paulo: Boitempo, 2003), 139.

27 Marini, "Estado y crisis en Brasil," 82 (italics in the original).

theory. Today these inter-imperialist contradictions can be seen to a certain degree in the competitive relationship between, for example, the US and France. This has allowed Brazil to implement its own geopolitical policies as a way of asserting its position regionally and internationally without disturbing the structures of domination. The same can be said of Argentina which, as Gambina notes, has experienced unprecedented primary export-based growth since its 2001 crisis, but without in any sense overcoming dependency:

> Argentina continues to be a dependent country within global capitalism – one that is subordinated to the power of the transnational corporations. That is why foreign capital dominates the strategic sectors of the local economy, be it in agriculture, industry or services. The presence of 'trans-Latin' Argentine companies among the region's transnationals does not alter its dependent condition, but rather shows that capital can only function effectively if it reaches the scale of global competition.[28]

One pre-condition of sub-imperialism is that it cannot operate without a strong State that enjoys a relative degree of autonomy from imperialism. Marini was quick to draw attention to this:

> As noted earlier, the Brazilian economy's pattern of realisation in its sub-imperialist phase is sustained by luxury consumption, the world market and the State. When I analysed this pattern for the first time some years ago, I pointed out that as the main means of sustaining it, luxury consumption also appeared to be the most precarious, with the most solid and in fact the only viable means in the long term being the world market. However the escape route for the Brazilian economy's problems of realisation—which of course are exacerbated during times of recession—is the State, which can promote demand to an almost unlimited degree as long as the conditions in which capital reproduces itself are not significantly altered. In other words, as long as labour super-exploitation is not threatened.[29]

Clearly then the State plays a strategic and functional role in sub-imperialist expansion in the region within a framework of super-exploitation and

---

28 Julio C. Gambina, "Economía a fines del 2011," *Rebelión*, 20 December 2011, accessed 21 January 2015, http://www.rebelion.org/noticia.php?id=141613.

29 Marini, "Estado y crisis en Brasil," 83.

dependency. Moreover, these latter two categories aid our analysis of dependent countries today. For example they help us understand the role of the Brazilian state in the structural and financial crisis of 2008–2009 and how the government tried to mitigate the crisis through measures which included wage rises; credit stimuli for hitherto excluded popular sectors to acquire consumer durables such as refrigerators, electrodomestic appliances and even cars, and programmes targeting extreme poverty such as the Lula government's 2003 Bolsa Familia programme, which according to the official Brazilian Institute of Geography and Statistics (IBGE) has lifted 30–36 million people out of poverty. Nevertheless, despite these figures, so often cited by the PT and the government in their electoral campaigns, the IBGE also reported that in 2013 about 7.2 million Brazilians went hungry or lacked a balanced diet, and another 52 million suffered food insecurity.[30] Neoliberalism and capitalism in general only mitigate poverty, whether 'normal' or extreme, for political reasons. They do not eradicate it because they need it to exist at a certain level in order to control unemployment and capital accumulation, as Marx showed in Chapter XXIII of *Capital* Volume I.

In discussing sub-imperialism as a particular feature of the dependent economy in the era of monopolies and finance capital Marini confined his description to Brazil in Latin America. But during this period dependent economies in general failed to become stronger or gain greater autonomy in the world market, whilst as countries they failed to achieve any real decision-making power over domestic affairs based on national sovereignty within an international framework of 'symmetrical relationships' with developed nations. Instead they ended up as dependent neoliberal economies which, however developed, remained at the mercy of the economic cycles of the hegemonic, advanced capitalist countries, as measured by the latter's organic composition of capital, level and development of productive forces, and share of average global rates of profit.

A dependent country like Brazil, whose level of capitalist development and political autonomy has earned it a place among the so-called BRICS (including South Africa), nevertheless remains peripheral and subordinate to the advanced countries of hegemonic capitalism. This is the condition described by Marini's concept of *sub-imperialism*. And although he also looked at other countries (Egypt, Iran, Israel…), he focussed on Brazil because that is where sub-imperialism manifests itself in its purest form, as well as being the country

30 IBGE, *Pesquisa nacional por amostra de domicílios. Segurança alimentar 2013* (2014), http://biblioteca.ibge.gov.br/visualizacao/livros/liv91984.pdf.

he was most familiar with. Mexico on the other hand is far from being typically sub-imperialist. As an exporter of manufactures assembled by US transnational-owned maquiladoras, Marini instead saw Mexico as an example of *economic annexation*, whereby local labour power is super-exploited and incorporated into North American capital accumulation:

> One way of manufacturing for export found in Mexico and which predominates in the Philippines, South Korea and Hong Kong is the maquiladora, whereby local plants finish or assemble parts and components received from foreign plants and then return them for the final process. But it is important to note that as long as the country hosting the *maquila* industry does not have to fight to conquer markets then this model is a long way from generating sub-imperialist tendencies. The essential characteristic of the maquila is that it is a stage of the production process relating to the reproduction cycle of an individual capital which is performed in a country other than that where the cycle takes place. This means that, as with the old enclave economy, a particular factor of production (in this case the workforce) is taken from the dependent economy and incorporated into the capitalist accumulation process of the imperialist economy, thus representing a case of *economic annexation*.[31]

As well as this *economic annexation* and its accompanying absorption of the labour power of millions of undocumented workers, another factor explaining why Mexico cannot be seen as sub-imperialist is its heavy dependency on the United States and specifically US cycles of capital reproduction. As Mathias Luce puts it:

> In Mexico, economic and political subservience to the ambitions of great US imperialism blocks national capital from having its own ventures. The degree of US imperialist penetration in Mexico hampers the state from putting into practice a relatively autonomous expansionist policy. In this manner, a subordinate formation in both Argentina and Mexico has matured but not as a relatively autonomous sub-imperialism.[32]

---

31 Ruy Mauro Marini, "La acumulación capitalista mundial y el subimperialismo," *Cuadernos Políticos* 12 (1977): 33. Mathias Luce examines sub-imperialism and especially Brazilian sub-imperialism in "La expansión del subimperialismo brasileño," *Rebelión*, 12 December 2008, http://www.rebelion.org/noticia.php?id=76977 and more recently in Mathias Luce, "Subimperialism, the Highest Stage of Dependent Capitalism," in *Brics: An Anti-Capitalist Critique*, Ana García and Patrick Bond, eds. (London: Pluto, 2015).

32 Luce, "Subimperialism," 34.

This subordination is exacerbated by the fact that Mexico and the US are neighbours who are separated by a 3185 km frontier. And it is the US which by far benefits the most from this proximity thanks to migratory flows and the remittances sent home by around 11 million Mexican workers.[33]

By distinguishing the main features of sub-imperialism we can see its similarities and differences with both non-sub-imperialist dependent countries and (neo) imperialist advanced capitalist countries. This may in turn help us to understand its specificities, with a view to identifying anti-capitalist (and not just anti-imperialist) advances by the workers and the popular masses. In challenging those who deny the existence of sub-imperialism as described by Marini, Luce highlights five specific features of dependent industrialization which together make up a *sub-imperialist system* that has lasted *beyond* the dictatorship:

a) The dependent country becomes a 'regional sub-centre' whose influence is felt in the countries and systems around it (for example Argentina in Paraguay, Uruguay, Bolivia and the Mercosur zone).
b) The unification of different bourgeois factions by displacing internal contradictions. In Mexico, for example, this unity was achieved after the last (failed) coup attempt, concocted by General Victoriano Huerta and German officials. The unity of the Mexican bourgeoisie and oligarchy remains in place today, held together by an authoritarian, presidentialist and partisan system run by the PRI and the government. But this unity has not led to sub-imperialism, partly because unlike in Brazil the state did not take on the form of an *estado de compromiso*.[34]

   The Mexican case is certainly different from that of Argentina, where in practice there really was no unity between the bourgeois factions. Nevertheless, Mexico still ended up as a dependent capitalist country and not a sub-imperialist power like Brazil. Even if we accept the authoritative opinion of Francisco de Oliveira in the sense that a new bourgeois faction emerged under the Lula/PT governments, all this new faction

33 On this topic see Ana Alicia Peña López, *Migración internacional y superexplotación del trabajo* (Ciudad de México: Itaca, 2012).

34 According to Oliver, the Brazilian state assumed the form of an *estado nacional de compromiso* or national state based on a compromise. This kind of state accurately reflected the unity between different classes and the dominant forces as represented fundamentally by big capital and the export oligarchy, a unity which was redefined when the military came to power "… under the hegemony of big transnational capital" (42). In contrast, he sees the Mexican state as a "national Jacobin unitary state" (40). See Lucio Oliver Costilla, *El estado ampliado en Brasil y México* (Ciudad de México: UNAM, 2009).

actually did was to take a share of power and get its cut of the surplus value and wealth handed out to leading government and party figures:

"...it is what explains the recent pragmatic convergences between the PT and PSDB, the apparent paradox that Lula's government is carrying out FHC's [Cardoso's] programme and taking it even further. It is not a question of a mistake, or of borrowing aspects of FHC's programme, but really of a new social class made up, on the one hand, of the technocrats and economists disguised as bankers at the core of the PSDB; and on the other, the workers-cum-pension fund managers at the core of the PT. The identity of both groups is bound up with controlling access to public funds and knowing how to get their hands on them".[35]

c) The development of a specific national and sub-imperialist political-ideological project. In Brazil this project was built on import substitution-led industrialisation. It reached its zenith across Latin America with the neoliberal policies of the early 1990s,[36] which led to deindustrialisation. Brazil then became an exporter of primary products upon adopting a dependent extractivist model.[37]
d) The formation of national capitalist monopolies or trusts (the so-called *trans-Latin companies*) that follow the trail of those from the advanced countries.
e) The simultaneous transfer of value from the sub-imperialist to the central countries, and appropriation of value and surplus value of the weakest countries by the sub-imperialist bourgeoisie for its own benefit. This feature is very specific to the sub-imperialist countries in contrast to both the dependent countries located below them and the imperialist countries.

On this last point, Brazil's DIEESE (Inter-Trade Union Department of Statistics and Socio-economic Studies) found that US$171,300,000 worth of profits were repatriated between 2006 and 2013. This was counted as part of the deficit in the balance of payments current account, and represented the value that transnational companies transferred on to their parent companies.[38] In 2013

35 de Oliveira, *Crítica à razão dualista*, 147. Translated from Portuguese to Spanish by the author and into English by the translator [Translator].

36 See María da Conceição Tavares, "Auge e declínio do processo de substituição de importações no Brasil," in *Da substituição de importações ao capitalismo financeiro* (Rio de Janeiro: Zahar, 1972).

37 Salles, *Lucha de clases en Brasil*, 25.

38 DIEESE, "Remessas de lucros e dividendos: setores e a dinámica econômica brasileira," *Nota Técnica* 137 (2014): 2.

the Netherlands captured 23.07% of this value transfer, the United States 20.14% and Spain 12.41%.[39] Transnational companies were concentrated during this period in the automobile industry, consumer goods (including drinks), telecommunications, retail and chemicals.[40]

Some, like Pedreira Campos, mistakenly think that sub-imperialism is simply about circulation and 'market constriction' which 'forces' companies to invest abroad:

> Without ignoring such accounts of the phenomenon as the thesis of Brazilian sub-imperialism, we think that the explanation given by Ruy Mauro Marini and his followers is not sufficient to elucidate the internationalisation of Brazilian firms. This is because what explains their overseas activity is not market constriction but the experience of firms and the large-scale capitalisation they underwent in Brazil before but mostly during the civil-military dictatorship (1964–1988). Hence, these firms were involved in various economic sectors in the domestic market and, because of their size and technical expertise, were able to execute similar works overseas.[41]

Indeed, we fully agree that domestic 'market constriction' does not explain companies' 'overseas activity' – this is precisely one of Marini's arguments. But having wrongly attributed to him the idea that Brazilian firms only expand because of this, Pedreira Campos then fails to explain where this necessary "experience and large-scale capitalisation" come from, what kind of national or foreign companies have it, and what factors enable them to do business abroad. He ignores the central tenet of Marini's dependency theory – that labour super-exploitation in dependent and peripheral countries is a social, economic, and work-organising regime that, among other things, helps capital overcome problems of realisation and obstacles to profitmaking.[42]

Apart from misinterpreting Marini by reducing his explanation for Brazilian companies' foreign expansion to domestic 'market constriction,' the author

---

39 DIEESE, "Remessas de lucros e dividendos," 12.

40 Ibid., 14.

41 Pedro Enrique Campos, "The Transnationalisation of Brazilian Construction Companies," in *Brics: An Anti-Capitalist Critique*, Ana García and Patrick Bond, eds. (London: Pluto, 2015), 159. This chapter is a shorter version of Pedro Henrique Pedreira Campos, "O processo de transnacionalização das empreiteiras brasileiras, 1969–2010: uma abordagem quantitativa," *Tensões Mundiais World Tensions* (Fortaleza) 10, no. 18–19 (2014): 120.

42 For a more detailed discussion of this point see Martins, *Globalização, dependência e neoliberalismo na América Latina*, especially Chapter 6.

also ignores the efforts he made to explain the nature and characteristics of sub-imperialism in a number of his writings. It cannot be overstated that for Marini sub-imperialism involves not just corporations but all Brazilian capital (whether or not allied to foreign capital) which flows abroad in a relentless drive to find markets, investment opportunities, surplus value and profit usually spearheaded by the state.

Marini challenges the argument that thanks to middle class and state-driven domestic demand capitalism in general and Brazilian capitalism in particular will never face problems in realising commodity production. He does so without denying the central role played by manufacturing exports in mitigating such problems, and instead revisits Marx's explanation of the cycle of capital in *Capital* Volume II in order to show that commodity production must resolve itself through its realisation on the market. This argument is made at a high level of abstraction, but at a concrete level it accepts that capitalism will sooner or later encounter problems realising commodities. That is why for Marini it makes no sense to counterpose outflow abroad to the demand generated by the middle classes or the state[43] because both these types of demand are subject to structural limits.

For Salama, the 'third demand', a prominent feature of the realm of circulation, is a result of the antagonism between the income of some layers of workers who are able to consume 'luxury goods' and others who are excluded from such consumption. Therefore, he says,

> ... a *third* [level of] *demand* can be seen as emerging from this dual process – one that is halfway between that of the very rich and that of the very poor. This demand is largely directed at the consumer durables sector. Added to that of the richest 10%, it reduces the contradiction at the level of realisation of the commodities produced, and allows for greater capital valorisation in this sector... But the 'third demand' is caused not only by a recomposition of industrial employment. It is also partly caused by unproductive workers.[44]

In terms of income distribution, it is true that a state policy of redistributing this 'third demand', which is created as a function of the middle classes, can effectively offset difficulties in realising and valorising capital on the market. But Salama forgets that however much the contradiction is held in check, sooner or later it will burst out even more forcefully, causing serious problems for

43 Marini, "La Acumulación capitalista mundial y el subimperialismo," 29.

44 Pierre Salama, *El proceso de subdesarrollo* (Ciudad de México: ERA, 1972), 213.

realising not only value but also surplus value and commodities in general. This is largely because the economic and material basis of the income derived from the third demand comes from either the redistribution of workers' wages or from a portion of the surplus value extracted by the capitalist class. It is not a third source of income different from that derived from the two antagonistic classes: labour and capital (wages and surplus value).

For Marini, therefore, this type of demand does not resolve the issue at all. In his essay on the circuit of capital in the dependent economy,[45] he showed that when faced with such constraints on demand, capitalism, especially Brazilian capitalism, necessarily goes overseas to invest its capitals and extract surplus value from the productive processes it invests in. It does so in response to the fall in workers' real wages caused by super-exploitation, the limits on middle and upper class consumption, and the problems of realisation those limits create in the sphere of luxury goods production, which is precisely where the highest concentration of investments is to be found and where extraordinary profits are made, i.e. of an order made by big international capital and transnational companies.

So expansion abroad is hardly just a choice that employers make, based on their "… experience and large-scale capitalisation". These factors of course do play a part and should always be taken into account, but serious problems of realisation are what really drives overseas expansion, and these problems are ultimately caused by the very cycle of production and reproduction of capital under conditions of structural dependency.

The other aspect limiting demand is labour super-exploitation itself. It forces capitalist enterprises who are in a position to do so to turn their attention to the domestic market for luxury consumer items and then, or alternatively, to foreign markets. Companies from a country like Brazil can make extraordinary profits abroad because of their monopolistic position compared to the likes of Peru or Bolivia, whose relatively lower level of development is expressed through their lower organic composition of capital.

The following quote from Marini sums up his general argument regarding the cycle of capital in dependent economies:

> …we could say that the cycle of capital in the dependent economy is characterized by a series of particularities. Amongst them, the role played by foreign capital in the first phase of circulation, both in the form of money and of the commodity, as well as in the fact that production determines transfers of surplus value (which will become visible in the second phase

45 Ruy Mauro Marini, "El ciclo del capital en la economía dependiente," 55.

> of circulation), fixes extraordinary surplus value and develops it on the basis of the super-exploitation of labour. Both facts lead quickly to the concentration of capital and to monopolization, while the structure of production becomes divorced from the consumption needs of the masses. The distortion in income distribution originating from this dynamic in the second phase of circulation energizes the sector best able to sustain the development of industries producing sumptuary goods, compounding this distortion to the extent that such industries expand their production and demand more market space. The limits against which this second phase of circulation hits, both in the transfer of surplus value abroad and by the deformation of the internal income structure, lead it to search for the realization of part of its commodities on the world market, with which the circle of dependency of the capitalist cycle comes to a close abroad.[46]

As this definition of dependency and the cycle of capital shows, sub-imperialist expansionism cannot simply be explained by the narrowness of the internal market, because that market itself depends on the general state of production, the organic composition of capital and the country's insertion in (and influence upon) the global division of labour.

Having explained how dependency works and how the limits on production and internal markets for luxury items are compounded by labour super-exploitation, Marini arrives at a definition of sub-imperialism as

> ...the form assumed by the dependent economy in the age of monopolies and finance capital. Sub-imperialism implies two basic components: on the one hand, an intermediate organic composition of national productive systems on the world scale and, on the other hand, the exercise of a relatively autonomous expansionist policy not only accompanied by a greater integration in the imperialist productive system but also maintained within the hegemonic framework exercised by imperialism on the international scene. Put in these terms, it seems to us that, independently of the efforts of Argentina and other countries to reach the sub-imperialist rank, in Latin America only Brazil fully manifests a phenomenon of this kind.[47]

---

46 Marini, "El ciclo del capital," 55. Translation from Adrián Sotelo, *The Future of Work*, 91.

47 Marini, "La acumulación capitalista mundial y el subimperialismo," 37, translation from "Subimperialism implies…" in Luce (2015), 33.

Conclusion

Dependency theory provides a broad framework for understanding how sub-imperialism is constituted under concrete historical conditions in Latin American capitalist social formations at the intermediate level. This is the level of analysis at which dependency is located as a theory and also as a subject of study. It is at this level that we can understand how 'intermediate powers' are historically constituted in the international context without separating them from their (dependent) economic cycles, their specific structures and class struggles, or the State's characteristics in relation to capital accumulation and reproduction and the social conditions in which domination and exploitation take place.

As we have seen, several countries both in and outside Latin America share features of sub-imperialism, but only Brazil is constituted as a state and an economic system actually based on those features. This ultimately distinguishes it from both the dominant imperialism of advanced capitalism (US, UK, Germany, France, Japan, Italy) and from other countries on the dependent periphery of capitalism and indeed the vast majority of the world's underdeveloped countries, which lack the conditions or means, or have not been through the processes necessary to constitute themselves as sub-imperialist. Instead, they end up being dominated and controlled by the classic imperialist powers and by sub-imperialist bourgeoisies, capitals and ruling classes which are socially, economically, politically and militarily capable of harnessing their productive apparatuses, investments and exports towards obtaining huge returns from capital's exploitation of labour. They are also capable of making up the value and surplus value they transfer to the imperialist centres, given that they are countries whose core condition is essentially one of dependence on imperialist productive systems and cycles, the dynamics and contradictions of the world market, and an international division of labour largely designed, imposed and managed by transnational capitalist corporations which operate across the world in strategic partnership with dependent bourgeoisies or, as Gunder Frank called them, *lumpenbourgeoisies*.

CHAPTER 5

The United States and Brazil: Antagonistic Cooperation

Along with Egypt, South Africa and Israel, Brazil is often described as an emerging power because of its technological, economic, financial, trade-related, diplomatic and military advances in recent years. This also holds true for Iran, Nigeria and Argentina. But without denying this reality, it is equally true that however many similarities such countries and systems share with the 'classic imperialisms'—those which in Gunder Frank's words might have once been undeveloped but never underdeveloped[1]—they have failed to break out of dependency and are not in any kind of strategic conflict with imperialism. Instead the lines in the relationship between imperialism and sub-imperialism are blurred by an 'antagonistic cooperation' which ties the dependent country's own cycle of capital to the dominant economy of the advanced centre.

The Marxist theory of dependency and Marini in particular provide a broad framework for understanding how sub-imperialism is constituted in its totality in Latin American capitalist social formations under concrete historical conditions at the intermediate level. As we saw earlier, this is the level at which dependency is located as a theory and as a subject of study, and it is precisely at this level that we can really understand the relationship of antagonistic cooperation between a country like Brazil and the United States.

Imperialism and Sub-Imperialism

For Marini, the specificity of the historical behaviour and dynamic of capital accumulation (both national and foreign) in dependent capitalist countries lies in the conditions of labour super-exploitation under which that accumulation takes place, along with the fact that

> … foreign monopolies are invited to participate in the exploitation of Brazilian workers and the profits made from trade expansion, meaning such a policy is implemented through an unrestricted alliance with foreign capital.[2]

1 André Gunder Frank, "The Development of Underdevelopment," *Monthly Review* 18 (1966): 18.

2 Marini, *Subdesarrollo y revolución*, 193–194.

 | DOI 10.1163/9789004319417_007

This confirms the thesis that in general capitalism cannot just reproduce itself and subsist in and on the edges of its national-territorial spaces, but *necessarily* has to find ways of expanding beyond them. But once again the problem here is how to explain *why* not all countries can expand via capitalist investment beyond their own borders, and the actual *reasons* why countries like Brazil, which are sub-imperialist rather than imperialist, export their power and capitals—including those allied with dominant foreign capitals—in order to appropriate part of the surplus value produced by local workers in 'less developed' countries and regions.

The main argument of both Marx's *Communist Manifesto* and Lenin's *Imperialism: the Highest Stage of Capitalism* is that it is in the nature of worldwide capitalist expansion to create a truly global market. Otherwise such expansion is left with no means of reproduction and so becomes unviable. Hegemonic imperialism has of course always acted by extending and deepening its grip throughout almost the entire world, be it the United Kingdom in the 19th Century; the United States in the 20th and 21st Centuries, or China, also in the current century. But in contrast, however much a dependent country (Brazil, Argentina, Mexico) expands, it does so at most in and on the edges of its own regional space and in some other continents such as Africa, but never like the great powers on a truly global scale.[3] Capitalism's own intensive and extensive development has meant that any new expansion nowadays is relative and limited to local or regional spaces, and can never match the way powers such as the United States or United Kingdom exercised global imperialism historically.

Marini called this phenomenon *sub-imperialism* as a way of characterizing the structural and geopolitical behaviour of 'emerging' and 'intermediate' countries in dependent and underdeveloped areas—in Latin America notably Brazil—in relation to the organic composition of capital worldwide and in the context of the global division of labour. These countries operate in economic and geopolitical spaces and systems on capitalism's periphery but without breaking from it. One of their characteristics is precisely that after going through a period of industrialisation, the most complex and advanced stage of which came in the post-WWII period, they reached a point where they were hegemonised on a structural level by monopolies and finance capital and yet still were unable to overcome dependency and their subordination to the laws, mechanisms, institutions and political-economic cycles of the hegemonic countries of advanced capitalism. In synthesis, Marini argued that

3 See Paul Kennedy, *Rise and Fall of the Great Powers* (New York: Random House, 1987) and *Preparing for the Twenty-First Century* (USA: Random House, 1993).

> The concept of sub-imperialism comes out of defining these intermediate stages. It seeks to describe how the dependent economy is influenced by the law which dictates that increasing productivity (and therefore the organic composition of capital) increases super-exploitation. Of course the concept does not account for the problem in its totality.[4]

Contemporary sub-imperialism has been the subject of much writing and research, particularly into Brazil's position regionally and internationally.[5] So what is Brazil today and what role does it play at these two levels?

For Marini, sub-imperialism, also referred to in terms of 'privileged satellites' or as Gunder Frank described Brazil, "junior partner[s] to the United States",[6] was a question of economic and strategic-political dimensions. Its methodology therefore required consideration of a series of issues, starting with the historical and current expansionism of Brazil as described by Severo Salles in *Lucha de clases en Brasil* [Class Struggle in Brazil]. Brazilian capitalism's increasing dependence on this foreign expansion and the different modes it has assumed in Latin America and beyond also deserved attention in Marini's view.

He observed that sub-regional expansion was led by the Brazilian state through the Brazilian Development Bank (BNDES) and targeted countries like Bolivia and other continents such as Africa. But this phenomenon was far from fully developed during his time and he could not possibly have known its future magnitude or strategic importance. In the light of the current world economic crisis and the particular contradictions facing Brazil it certainly needs to be examined in more depth.

To understand sub-imperialism Marini used a concept he called *antagonistic cooperation*. The term reflects the relationship between an imperialist country (the United States) and a sub-imperialist country (Brazil), in which there is a degree of conflict between powerful national bourgeoisies but without leading

4 Marini, *Dialéctica de la dependencia*, 99.

5 The number of thematic studies of sub-imperialism has grown considerably. See Mathias Seibel Luce, "La expansión del subimperialismo brasileño," *Rebelión*, 4 December 2008, http://www.rebelion.org/noticia.php?id=76977. Poliana García Temístocles and Marisa Silva Amaral, *O capitalismo dependente o Brasil contemporâneo: ¿cooperação ou subimperialismo na América Latina?* (*unpublished*, PDF); Gabriela Fernandes Feliciano Murua, *Subimperialismo: entrada dependente da economia periférica à fase imperialista do capitalismo* (Universidade Federal de São Paulo, Escola de Filosofia, Letras e Ciências Humanas / Guarulhos-SP, March 2014; *unpublished*, PDF).

6 Gunder Frank, *Latin America: underdevelopment or revolution*, 396.

to a breakdown in relations or open confrontation. Instead inter-bourgeois cooperation and collaboration prove more the rule than the exception in relations between sub-imperialist bourgeoisies and their counterparts in the US and other dominant centres of power.[7] Antagonistic cooperation characterised the friction between the US and Brazil over human rights and nuclear energy during General Ernesto Geisel's government (1974–1979), which ended in an agreement between Brazil and West Germany to build a nuclear plant.[8] For the Brazilian military, antagonistic cooperation implied a geopolitical and military ideology which, for Marini and Pellicer

> ...dominated the Higher War College, a nucleus of military technocrats who had taken power along with Castelo Branco. Their thinking is most accurately reflected by a book written by one of their number, General Golbery do Couto e Silva [who Salles describes as an "éminence grise of the 1964 coup and the regime that followed"].[9] Called *Aspectos geopolíticos do Brazil*, (Río de Janeiro, Biblioteca del Ejército: 1957), it argues that as Brazil's geographical location does not allow it to break free from North American influence, it should instead ally itself with the US, demanding in return that the US recognises that "the quasi-monopoly of rule (in the South Atlantic) should be exercised by Brazil exclusively."[10]

In his book, do Couto e Silva outlines the doctrine of the *barganha leal* or loyal bargain. This is

> ...part of the theory that, because of its geographic position, Brazil cannot escape North American influence. In such a situation, [do Couto e Silva] said, no alternative remains but to "consciously accept the mission of associating ourselves with the policy of the United States in the South Atlantic". The counterpart of this 'conscious choice' would be the recognition by the United States that 'the quasi-monopoly of rule in that area should be exercised by Brazil exclusively'. The expression 'quasi-monopoly' results from the impossibility of denying the designs which the argentine bourgeoisie is also harbouring in this sphere.[11]

7 Marini, *Subdesarrollo y revolución*, 77.
8 Cf. Salles, *Lucha de clases en Brasil*, 86.
9 Ibid., 26.
10 Marini and Pellicer de Brody, "Militarismo y desnuclearización en América Latina," 5–6.
11 Ruy Mauro Marini, "Brazilian interdependence and imperialist integration," *Monthly Review* 17 (1965): 20.

This doctrine was spread by

> ... the Higher War College, which in Brazil has helped promote the doctrines of the North American military establishment and systematically formulate policies that mirror the interests of big transnational business moguls and their Brazilian partners.[12]

The Higher War College was established in 1949 by Law 785/49 as an Institute of Superior Studies in Politics, Defence and Strategy attached to the Brazilian Ministry of Defence. It embodies the interests of Brazilian military power, the United States and its supranational investments, and transnational corporations. Ultimately, therefore, interdependency does not exist, only the dependency of a subordinated country which nonetheless enjoys relative autonomy from the imperialist State. The cross-class and inter-bourgeois alliances this engenders then allows the sub-imperialist country to expand beyond its frontiers unhindered and, without upsetting the imperialist powers and their fundamental strategic interests, lay claim to resources and the value/surplus value produced by labour exploitation and benefit from the capital accumulation process thus generated.

Has this condition changed to the extent that countries like Brazil no longer depend on the foreign capital of the transnational corporations of imperialist powers like the US, France and Germany? We think not. What marks them out as sub-imperialist is that as states they are relatively autonomous from imperialism. This boosts their bargaining power with the powerful corporations that represent international capital worldwide. Since Lula's time in office, if not earlier, this condition has been expressed by Brazil's attempt to pursue a two-dimensional relationship of 'cooperation-domination' with Africa which is relatively autonomous from the centre:[13]

> In relation to Africa, Brazilian diplomacy presents two façades: one which is cooperative, as with initiatives like Universidade da Integração Internacional da Lusofonia Afro-Brasileira (Unilab) and knowledge transfer

12 Mike Burgess and Daniel Wolf, "Brasil: el concepto de poder en la Escuela Superior de Guerra," *Cuadernos Políticos* 20 (1979): 90.

13 Maurício Gurjão Bezerra Heleno and Mônica Dias Martins, "Cooperação ou dominação? A política externa do governo Lula para a África," in *Tensões Mundiais World Tensions* (Fortaleza) 10, no. 18–19 (2014): 140.

> programmes, and another which is dominant, as shown by Brazil's interest in expanding its political influence and the predatory activities of Brazilian companies in African countries.[14]

What is *new* about contemporary Brazilian sub-imperialism compared to that of the 1960s and 1970s is the state's dynamic and central role in promoting foreign expansion with BNDES as its springboard. Created in 1952, the bank is a federal public body linked to the Ministry of Development, Industry and Foreign Trade. Its mission is to provide financing for the country's development, exports, technological innovation, environmental development and modernization of public management. In addition, it finances the expansion of both public and private national companies abroad.[15] As Cecilia Vuyk notes,

> Through its different lines of credit BNDES represents one of the most important ways the Brazilian state supports the expansion of Brazilian capitals. Not only was the law regulating BNDES amended in 2003 so as to enable it to finance the expansion of Brazilian monopolies abroad through BNDES Limited,[16] but in June 2011 the Brazilian government opened a new line of credit (BNDES Exim)[17] to support the export of Brazilian

---

14 Bezerra Heleno and Dias Martins, "Cooperação ou dominação?," 128.

15 On this topic See Claudio Katz, "América Latina frente a la crisis global," in Hugo Fazio *et al.*, *La explosión de la crisis global. América Latina y Chile en la encrucijada* (Santiago de Chile: LOM Ediciones, 2009), 43–68.

16 "The office opened in London in November 2009 (BNDES PLC) is the realization of the Bank's arrival to one of the main financial centers in the world, representing one more step of the institution's expansion efforts outside Brazil. The purpose of the office is to increase the Bank's visibility in the international financial community and effectively support Brazilian companies undergoing the internationalization process or those searching for opportunities in the international market. In addition to becoming a point of reference and support for Brazilian companies that already have global presence, the office in London is the bridge between international investors and the great investment opportunities offered by Brazil, which is largely investing in infrastructure, the sophisticated industrial sector and agribusiness with incomparable competitiveness in global terms." Taken from http://www.bndes.gov.br/SiteBNDES/bndes/bndes_es/Navegacao_Suplementar/Menu_Filiais/subsidiaria_londres.html.

17 "BNDES-exim provides Brazilian producers of goods and services with an important source of financing for trading with the rest of the world. Among BNDES-exim's efforts, the increasing support of Brazilian companies trading in South America has been emphasized, in response to their strategy to strengthen commercial and financial ties across the continent," from BNDES, el Banco de Desarrollo de Brasil (no author), http://www.bndes.gov.br/SiteBNDES/bndes/bndes_en/Institucional/The_BNDES_Abroad/Foreign_Trade/.

> products and contribute to regional integration, i.e. the expansion of Brazilian capitals in favour of sub-imperialist integration and economic annexation.[18]

The dynamic role of the Brazilian state is indicative of its regional presence and influence. It also suggests an implicit agreement with the US to allow it to play such a role as long as doing so does not lead in the strategic long term to 'disloyal competition' with the empire. In fact despite friction between the two countries at certain historical conjunctures, not even during Lula's administrations was there any danger of the kind of conflict that might cause the two countries to break off relations. So Marini's 'antagonistic cooperation' is an accurate term to use because it expresses how there can be different moments of both friction and continuity but without necessarily any rupture.

Antagonistic cooperation does not mean that a country might at some point end or overcome its relationship of structural dependency on the dominant centre. As Marini noted,

> Reproducing on a global scale the antagonistic cooperation practised internally, these regimes become extremely dependent on their hegemonic centre – the United States – whilst continually clashing with it as they seek to reap greater rewards from the restructuring processes they are immersed in.[19]

And it was precisely during historical moments of reorganization and/or restructuring in the central capitalist countries, even around the time of major confrontations of the kind that triggered the two World Wars, and the world capitalist crisis of the 1930s, that 'endogenous' processes such as import substitution-based industrialisation took off at the national level – like in some Latin American countries in the post-war period – just as national private and state capital were becoming powerful enough to venture abroad, tailoring their investments to their own interests.

The specificity of sub-imperialist expansion lies in the objective possibility of appropriating surplus value from other countries where sub-imperial capital invests or intervenes. But it is somewhat limited by the peculiar and contradictory nature of the world economy and a very hierarchical global division

18 Cecilia Vuyk, *Subimperialismo brasileño y dependencia del Paraguay. Los intereses económicos detrás del golpe de estado de 2012* (Asunción, Paraguay: Cultura y Participación para el Cambio Social, 2014), 134.

19 Marini, *Subdesarrollo y revolución*, 20.

of labour monopolised by imperialism's economic and political power and huge transnational corporations, which are able to influence and shape public policy in their own interests.

All in all, sub-imperialism is limited in its attempts to expand, not only by its organic composition of capital, its place in the hierarchical global division of labour and its place in the division of the world into imperialist capitalist countries and dependent and underdeveloped countries; but also by the spatial and temporal limits to territorial expansion and the global reproduction of capital which affect any country's attempts to conquer new territories, be they imperialist or sub-imperialist.

The *antagonistic cooperation* characterising relations between Brazil and the United States is therefore subject to the vicissitudes and overdeterminations of a global economy which is both shrinking geographically and is suffering a far-reaching structural and systemic crisis. As for resolving the contradictions, the dynamics of the crisis mean that the hegemonic imperialist countries will only strengthen their control over their dependent counterparts. Only countries like Brazil, and perhaps Mexico and Argentina, are in a position to deal with their own crises and contradictions by transferring them to relatively less developed countries, productive systems and labour forces, such as those of the Andean region, the Caribbean, Central America, or in some cases the Southern Cone itself.

Conclusion

Almost two years after a cooling of bilateral relations because of leaks showing that US intelligence agencies had been spying on Dilma Rousseff's government, the Brazilian president paid a business visit to the United States (29 June–1 July 2015). The press headlines were clear about its purpose: "Dilma in search of investment", "president in reconciliation with the US", "loss of trust between the two countries overcome", "bilateral relations restored". Rousseff declared that "this trip (…) stands as a re-launch of our bilateral relations" that would definitively overcome the "loss of trust" affecting the two governments, while Obama stated that they were "focussed on the future" and that in his view "this visit marks one more step in a new, more ambitious chapter in the relationship between our countries."[20]

20 "Remarks by President Obama and President Rousseff of Brazil in Joint Press Conference," The White House, Office of the Press Secretary, East Room, 30 June 2015,

In general the visit was seen as marking the end of a diplomatic crisis which had blown up at a particularly difficult time for the South American country. In 2013 Brazil was hit by severe economic crisis and a corruption scandal over the diversion of funds from PETROBRAS – the country's largest public company. Interestingly, 5 days before President Rousseff's official visit to Washington the Brazilian Senate approved two defence agreements with the US which had originally been signed in 2010 but were kept on hold ever since. The first one reactivated the *Defense Cooperation Agreement* (DCA), which had been denounced in 1978 by Brazil's military dictatorship of the time because of Washington's attempts to prevent it from receiving nuclear technology from Germany. The second was the *General Security of Military Information Agreement* (GSOMIA), which established rules to protect secret data and stop it from being shared with third countries. According to Brazilian daily *O Estado de São Paulo*, the reason Rousseff decided to get the agreements ratified by Congress after years of delays was to signal a "fundamental change in her government's position regarding defence cooperation with the US".[21]

Having gone through Brazil's lower house (the Chamber of Deputies), the agreements were approved by the Senate. Significantly, this happened just as Defence Minister Jacques Wagner was also setting off for the US in order, according to the Brazilian Foreign Ministry, to secure greater military cooperation between the two nations. Once in Washington he met U.S. Defence Secretary Ashton Carter to get support and assistance for the exchange of military technology within the institutional framework of Defence Cooperation. According to *O Estado de São Paulo* the ratification of the agreements was intended to pave the way for "more trading of secret information, more military exercises, a closer relationship between the two Armed Forces and more opportunities to buy and sell military equipment".[22]

Seven issues were discussed during President Rousseff's visit: (a) the environment, (b) trade, (c) visas (with an agreement that in 2016 Brazil would join the Global Entry programme) (d) defence, resulting in the two agreements on Defence Cooperation and Military Information Security, with an emphasis on

---

https://www.whitehouse.gov/the-press-office/2015/06/30/remarks-president-obama-and-president-rousseff-brazil-joint-press.

21 "Brasil e Estados Unidos vao desenvolver projeto na area de defesa," 29 June 2015, http://www.defesa.gov.br/noticias/16131-brasil-e-estados-unidos-vao-desenvolver-projeto-na-area-de-defesa.

22 "Brasil e Estados Unidos vao desenvolver projeto na area de defesa."

the two-way flow of information, goods, services and technologies, (e) social provision and (f) education.[23]

Obama also used the meeting to express his view that Brazil was more a global than a regional leader:

> Well, I'm actually going to answer in part the question you just asked the President. We view Brazil *not as a regional power but as a global power*. If you think about the preeminent economic forum for coordinating between major economies—the G20—Brazil is a major voice in that. The negotiations that are going to be taking place in Paris around climate change can only succeed with Brazil as a key leader. And the announcements that have been made today about their goals on renewable energy is indicative of Brazil's leadership. Brazil is a major global player. And I told President Dilma [Rousseff] last night that the United States, as powerful as we are and as interested as we are in solving a whole range of international issues, recognizes *we can't do it alone*.[24]

Of course ultimately only he could tell us what he meant by "global power" – whether one more power among many (India, China, Russia), something akin to the power of the United States, or a condition similar to that of countries such as France, Germany or the UK. For many observers the visit also restored Brazil to its traditional status as the U.S.'s 'backyard', and the way the Brazilian Congress voted through agreements at Washington's insistence was typical of a powerful country imposing its agenda on another country as a prior condition of any 'bilateral negotiations'. That is how we should interpret Obama's description of Brazil as a global power and not as just one of many 'regional powers'.

Furthermore, in expressing how the US sees a country like Brazil, its second largest trading partner after China and largest investment destination, terms like 'global power' and 'indispensable partner' do not mark any departure from the language that as a superior imperialist country it has historically used to describe its relationship of 'antagonistic cooperation' with a sub-imperialist country it seeks to dominate. This is even more apparent when it comes to defence, an area in which Brazil is trying to reduce its trading deficit with the US while strengthening the Defense Cooperation Agreement and institutional

---

23 See "Joint Communique by President Barack Obama and President Dilma Rousseff", The White House Office of the Press Secretary, accessed August 31 2016, https://www.whitehouse.gov/the-press-office/2015/06/30/joint-communique-president-barack-obama-and-president-dilma-rousseff.

24 "Remarks by President Obama and President Rousseff" (author's italics).

framework for bilateral cooperation as well as the GSOMIA, which will help consolidate the bilateral flow of information, goods, services and state-of-the-art technology between the two countries. The two governments also agreed during the visit to restart their Defence Cooperation Dialogue (DCD) meetings, the first of which had in 2012 identified "new opportunities" for bilateral and global cooperation. They also underlined the importance of their respective private sectors collaborating on joint defence projects with the strategic objective of "strengthening relations in strategic sectors".[25]

Summarising, we have argued that Brazil is undoubtedly an intermediate, sub-imperialist power which exercises its regional influence through Mercosur, through its foreign investments, and through the expansion of its companies abroad with the state's full backing. But as in Chapter 3 we would also argue that Brazil cannot in any way be considered a global power resembling the great powers of contemporary imperialism.

Evidently one of the main aims of US geopolitical strategy is to isolate Latin America, and Brazil especially given its power and influence, from Russia and China. These two contradictory powers on the global map of inter-state relations have both experienced frictions with the US: Russia is currently the target of US/EU sanctions (in principle economic) as a consequence of the political, military and strategic conflict in the Ukraine; US aims regarding China on the other hand have been described in the following terms:

> It is true that Russia and China continue to be nuclear powers, but the leading military power is the United States, which as with the Soviet Union in the 1980s, is making the most of its superiority and is trying to withdraw from secondary conflicts (Iran, Afghanistan) in order to focus on trapping Beijing in the Sea of China through its military bases and multiple treaties with governments in the region, and threatening Russia by redoubling aid to the chauvinistic and reactionary Poroshenko government in the Ukraine.[26]

This can also be seen by the conflicts in Syria and Iraq, whilst in Latin America it is most apparent in Venezuela, Ecuador and Bolivia. There progressive governments seen as capable of challenging North American hegemony in the region have been targeted by a conservative right which has used every means available to bring them down, its sometimes violent tactics including food boycotts, currency and financial speculation, targeted assassinations,

25 The White House Office of the Press Secretary, "Joint Communique".

26 Guillermo Almeyra, "China, Rusia, Estados Unidos, Unión Europea," *La Jornada*, 6 September 2015, http://www.jornada.unam.mx/2015/09/06/opinion/018a1pol.

paramilitary attacks on strategic objectives (in Venezuela), border disputes such as the one between Colombia and Venezuela and also between Venezuela and Guyana over the Esequibo region, and 'soft coups' carried out by organised right wing forces.[27]

The present work highlights the difference between Brazil's neoliberal state and the 'social' government of a neo-developmentalist type it exists alongside—albeit one stuck within the boundaries of dependent capitalism. This difference is the key to understanding why so far neither the expansion of foreign investment by Brazilian companies nor its relationship with the United States have led to Brazil becoming fully aligned with the US, unlike the governments of Mexico, Colombia, Peru and more recently Argentina following the election victory of the neoliberal right headed by President Mauricio Macri.

This means that with President Rousseff removed and right wing forces winning the next elections in Brazil, Latin America could face a rather difficult and complex scenario in which Brazil ends up aligning itself more closely to North American geopolitical interests. In such circumstances it would maintain a relationship of 'antagonistic cooperation' but one less plagued by contradictions and tensions. This would of course serve US policy interests by making it easier for it to counter the influence of progressive governments and to bring them down even – although not necessarily through an old-style coup d'état but simply at the point where such governments lose support and legitimacy in the eyes of the people.

Conditions in this scenario would also be much more favourable for U.S. private sector investment in the region. This would tend to weaken or substitute institutions developed in recent years which promote Latin American integration, such as MERCOSUR, CARICOM, UNASUR, CELAC or PetroCaribe. Such bodies might even be dissolved in order to resurrect old projects such as the Free Trade Area of the Americas (FTAA) whilst at the same time ploughing ahead with so-called bilateral Free Trade Agreements (FTA). If all this comes to pass, it will mark the definitive breakup of the Latin American unity project which popular forces and the left have fought so hard for in recent years.

27 Since Honduran President Manuel Celaya was brought down in June 2009 and Paraguay's Fernando Lugo was removed following a political trial in June 2012, there have been 'soft coups' in Argentina, Venezuela, and Bolivia. The most recent one to take place was in Brazil, where constitutional president Dilma Rousseff was removed from office for 180 days for having allegedly committed a "crime of responsibility". During this period a political trial was set to determine whether or not she could return. See my articles "Apuntes para una comprensión de la coyuntura histórico-política en curso [I], Las nuevas derechas y la contrarrevolución latinoamericana," *Rebelión*, 23 May 2016, http://www.rebelion.org/noticia.php?id=212538. And "Brasil en la encrucijada," *Rebelión*, 27 June 2016, http://www.rebelion.org/noticia.php?id=213860.

CHAPTER 6

Brasil Potência vs. Sub-Imperialism

In this chapter we discuss three different theoretical approaches to the question of sub-imperialism versus *Brasil Potência* – the notion of Brazil as a great power. In doing so we address two major claims: that Brazil has acquired the status of a developed country; and that the PT's policies of the last fifteen years have turned Brazil into a 'middle class' society by taking 30 million-odd people out of the impoverished favelas and dropping them *ipso facto* into the ranks of the middle classes, who as a result now make up the majority of the population.

The *Brasil Potência* Myth: From a Dependent to a Middle Class Nation?

Without breaking the ties of structural dependency, Brazil has historically done more to promote its own development, industrialisation and economic growth than any other Latin American country. Between 1945 and 1994 this growth was driven by a 'secondary export' model of capital reproduction. But since the early 1990s this has been replaced by a 'primary extractivist' model based on the production of basic and semi-manufactured goods for the world market. It was under this second model that the value of Brazilian exports rose during the first Lula government from US$60.4 billion in 2002 to US$137.5 billion in 2006.[1]

In recent years attention has been focussed on Brazil's economic development and performance and its relationship on the one hand to the country's class structure – as expressed by rising average social wages and income redistribution in favour of the poorest in society – and on the other hand to its heightened influence in nearby Southern Cone and Andean countries. There Brazilian companies have operated and invested on a significant scale, especially as a result of the Initiative for the Integration of Regional Infrastructure in South America (IIRSA). Corporate and state media, intellectuals, public authorities and PR professionals have all promoted the idea of Brazil as the first real and almost paradigmatic example of a country which has 'abandoned' its underdeveloped and dependent condition to become a developed country

1 Flynn, "Between Subimperialism and Globalization," 15.

 | DOI 10.1163/9789004319417_008

and a world power in direct competition for hegemony with old imperialisms such as the United States.

Various authors have expressed such ideas. Zibechi, for example, puts forward three propositions: (a) that "US hegemony has eroded to unimaginable levels before the economic and financial crisis of 2008";[2] (b) that Brazil is now a "middle class society"[3] and (c) that Brazilian capitalism is now "no longer dependent" or just a "medium-sized centre of accumulation" or "sub-power,"[4] but an 'emerging power' which has overcome its peripheral condition and is now heading towards world power status: "I think Brazil's rise to the status of a global power is an irreversible and conflictual process".[5]

To take this last point first, there are actually real barriers preventing the Brazilian military and bourgeoisie from realizing their imperialist dreams of a *Brasil Potência*. Salles lists the most important of these:

> In keeping with Marini's theses, I believe it highly improbable that Brazil can become a leading world power. The most advanced capitalism is concentrated at the system's centre; the social relations in that space, the breadth of its markets, the critical mass of state-of-the-art technology, the concentration of units of capital…the imperialist power located there… these are all major obstacles to entering the big league.[6]

As for to the claim that US imperialism is 'declining', this really is a weak and highly questionable assertion. Zibechi argues that

> When Marini formulated the thesis of sub-imperialism four decades ago, US hegemony had not yet begun to decline and the capitalist system had not yet entered into global crisis.[7]

---

2 Zibechi, *The New Brazil*, 235.

3 Ibid., 235. Against this thesis see Marcio Pochman, *O mito da frande classe média. Capitalismo e estrutura social* (São Paulo: Boitempo, 2014).

4 Ibid., 238.

5 Ibid., 2.

6 Salles, *Lucha de clases en Brasil*, 133–134.

7 Zibechi, *The New Brazil*, 233. The concept of 'hegemony' has its own history and has been given different meanings by different authors. For Anderson the term originated in Russia as "gegemoniya," until Gramsci "… extended the notion of hegemony from its original application to the perspectives of the working class in a bourgeois revolution against a feudal order, to the mechanisms of bourgeois rule over the working class in a stabilized capitalist society" (p. 20), synthesised in the dual notion of coercion-consent under a system of state domination. That meaning was the result of a transformation whereby the original meaning

But although the US is not the same unilateral power among capitalist nations that it was in the 20th Century and now has to face other nuclear powers such as China, India and Russia, it has nevertheless maintained its *supremacy* in the international system of capitalist nations, and its hegemonic weight as the centre of the global capitalist system should not be underestimated.[8] Although it is no longer the driving force behind capitalism, it nonetheless now more than ever needs to stay in the driving seat if it is to preserve its leadership of the global economy and its system of world domination.

That said, it must be stressed that the relationship between the theory of sub-imperialism and the question of US 'hegemony' (in decline or otherwise) is not a mechanical one. The status, autonomy and genesis of the theory of sub-imperialism are quite unique, particularly at a conceptual level and at a certain level of abstraction with its own categories and internal concepts. Marini's version of sub-imperialism thus remains relevant today whether or not US hegemony is in decline, changing only in its degree of intensity. However, that is not to deny that it has certainly been *modified* by changes to global capitalism over the last four decades. For example the Brazilian state has been strengthened by factors such as the BNDES, the impact of science and technology on productive systems and capital reproduction, and the now simultaneous nature of global financial transactions.

Turning to Zibechi's 'middle class' society, this is a controversial claim which even came up during the 2014 presidential debates between Aécio Neves and Dilma Rousseff, although the figures brandished created more heat than light. For Pochman, Brazil's combined economic growth and improved income distribution gave a new impetus to 'social mobility' in the 2000s, notably through a rise in the number of jobs with above-average wages. This brought around 20% of Brazil's population into the mass consumer market. He concludes that

---

of hegemony, which was "… to define the relationship between the proletariat and peasantry in a bourgeois revolution, was transferred by Gramsci to describe the relationship between the bourgeoisie and proletariat in a consolidated capitalist order in Western Europe." Perry Anderson, "The Antinomes of Antonio Gramsci," *New Left Review* I / 100 (1976): 44. The idea was later used in analyses of the world capitalist system to study the relationship between empires and hegemonic cycles and financial crises. It is important therefore to be clear about the sense in which the term is being used, as Zibechi is in his discussion of the 'decline' of US hegemony. See also Carlos Eduardo Martins.

8 There is an interesting discussion of US global hegemony in Claudio Katz, *Bajo el imperio del capital* (Buenos Aires: Ediciones Luxemburg, 2011). See in particular Chapter 11: "El declive norteamericano en discusión," 177–192.

> Like in the advanced capitalist countries in the post-WWII period, a significant layer of the working class was incorporated into the consumption of durable goods, such as televisions, stoves, fridges, sound systems, computers, etc. But this important social change did not however go on to constitute a new social class, and neither did it lift the new consumers into the middle class...It was fundamentally about the recomposition of the working class at a new level of consumption. However in the face of the general movement of transnational monopoly capitalism towards consolidation, in which each country plays a part in the production chain, the social structure is changed significantly.[9]

For João Sicsú, consumption in Brazil has been driven by the working class and not, as media propaganda would have it, the so-called middle class:

> The consumers of the domestic market are workers. In recent years there has been a huge expansion of the working class – that which 'drips with sweat' and suffers on public transport every day. *It is wrong to say that the expansion of the domestic consumer market is down to the emergence of a new middle class.* The middle class is made up of doctors, lawyers, administrators, psychologists ... professionals who are not capitalists and do not exert their physical strength every day producing goods and providing services ... The growth of the domestic market is based on millions of individuals, men and women, who sell their labour power and receive a salary. Most of them earn less than three minimum wages: construction workers, small traders, drivers, street cleaners, maids, motorcycle couriers, etc. They are the new Brazilian consumers. People who emigrated to the southeast by bus and now fly back to the northeast to visit their relatives. In 2003, the Brazilian consumer market was supported by 45.2% of the population, representing income classes A, B and C (79.2 million people at the time). The purchasing power of income classes D and is low and moreover irregular. By 2011 the percentage of the population supporting the consumer market had increased to 63.7% (equivalent to more than 122 million Brazilians) ... So more than 42 million entered income classes A + B + C in the period 2003–11. But most of them did not enter the middle class, just income classes that can consume on a regular basis. This move reflects the expansion of the working class. In 2003, Brazil had

9 Marcio Pochman, *O mito da frande classe média. Capitalismo e estrutura social* (São Paulo: Boitempo, 2014): 71. Translated from Portuguese to Spanish by the author and into English by the translator [Translator].

> 29.5 million formal workers. In 2012, this number increased to nearly 48 million. In addition to the number of formal workers, the number of informal and self-employed workers also increased.[10]

In highly stratified class societies such as Brazil, sociological functionalism creates its own optical illusion. Where there are simply pockets of 'upwards social mobility' á la Weber, it sees the 'middle class' society that neoclassical thinkers have always dreamed of, especially as a way to end the social and political antagonism between labour and capital once and for all. This dream has been typical of liberal ideologies throughout history, which use it to try and justify the 'legitimacy' of class society under capitalism.

Finally, we return to the claim that Brazil is no longer a dependent country. This proposition clearly deserves much greater scrutiny because the figures comparing its GDP to that of the advanced countries and the other BRICS give no indication of the reliability of the source data, let alone any evidence of having overcome the essential characteristic of the *cycle of capital in the dependent economy* described by Marini and summarised by Vania Bambirra:

> … capital accumulation passes through the exterior with the importation of machinery; once machinery begins to be produced internally (only in certain countries and with many limitations in advanced technology sectors like electronics and nuclear energy, which are monopolised by the more developed countries), it is still controlled directly by foreign groups. Even when the dependent economy begins to meet the needs for machinery in sector II (which certainly also ends up being controlled to a large degree by foreign capital), it remains dependent on the technology-capital of sector I of the developed capitalist countries.[11]

In Diagram 1, the cycle of capital would also need to reflect technological development and finance capital, including the fictitious capital which generates *fictitious profits*[12] and the effect of the latter on the Brazilian economy. In theory structural dependency could be 'overcome' by manufacturing the means of production and consumption internally. This could be achieved by integrating the sectors which make them into the internal space of the dependent country.

---

10 João Sicsú, "Quem são os novos consumidores dez anos depois," *Carta Capital* 14 (2013), http://www.cartacapital.com.br/economia/quem-sao-os-novos-consumidores-dez-anos-depois. Italics added.

11 Vania Bambirra, *Teoría de la dependencia: una anticrítica* (Ciudad de México: Era, 1978), 28–29 cited in Adrián Sotelo, *The Future of Work*, 74.

12 Carcanholo, *Capital, essência e aparência*.

Capital Accumulation in Dependent Countries I	Advanced Capitalist Countries	Capital Accumulation in Dependent Countries II
Sector I National (public and private+foreign capital)=100	Capital accumulation	Sector I national (public and private)=80
→→→→→	→→→→→→	→→→→→
Sector II National (public and private+foreign capital)=100		Sector II national (public and private)=80

Note: Our diagram shows that there are two sectors in dependent countries. Sector I consists of the means of production in which national and foreign private capital participate, sometimes combined with State capital. This also occurs in Sector II, which consists of the means of consumption. Next, the arrows show that capital accumulation originating in the dependent country must continue 'abroad' (the world market) and in the advanced capitalist countries, with the hegemons keeping part of the value and surplus value produced by labour power in the dependent and underdeveloped countries. Foreign trade plays a fundamental role in this process, with 70% of it controlled by transnational companies and international capital. In this hypothetical example, it can be seen that the total value falls from 100 in the first movement to 80 in the second -the advanced country retains 20% for its own capital accumulation.

DIAGRAM 1 *Structural flow of dependency*

The dependent country would then be much less dependent on imports from the industrialised centres of advanced capitalism. But this is a far cry from what currently happens in underdeveloped and dependent countries. The literature shows that not even countries like Brazil, Mexico and Argentina managed it during the heyday of Latin American industrialisation between the end of WWII and the 1980s. Instead, these countries have since undergone a process of *de*-industrialisation accompanied by a real crisis of capital accumulation and reproduction whose social and political repercussions are now being felt across almost the entire region.

Capital-Imperialism or Sub-Imperialism? The Thesis of Virginia Fontes

Virgínia Fontes[13] agrees with the theory of imperialism as set out by Lenin and understood in the work of authors such as Gramsci, so we start here with those understandings of imperialism which she disagrees with before examining her concept of capital-imperialism and its relevance to Brazil. The two interpretations of the theory of imperialism which Fontes critiques were both very popular during the 20th Century. One identified imperialism with capitalism, and in doing so obscured the essential differences between the two. The other,

13 Virginia Fontes, *O capital-imperialismo* (Rio de Janeiro: Editora UFRJ, 2010), 359 for example.

which we might call an 'analysis of the world-capitalist system', ended up identifying imperialism with just one country – the United States. Fontes criticises these understandings because "by being either far too broad or restrictively narrow, the definition of the concept loses its sharpness as a mode of the capitalist expansion wherein it originated".[14] Instead she places the emphasis elsewhere:

> To speak, then, of capital-imperialism is to speak of the expansion of a form of capitalism that was already imbued with imperialism but was born under the shadow of the atomic bomb and the Cold War. This form exacerbated the concentration of capitals whilst tending to lock them together in conglomerates. Capital's internal domination is derived from imperialism, but under capital-imperialism it requires and is complemented by external expansion. This external expansion is not just mercantile in nature or based solely on the export of goods or capital, but also drives the expropriation of entire populations of their conditions of production (land), their rights, and the very environmental and biological conditions of their existence.[15]

Concretely, capital-imperialism constitutes a specific category which took shape after the Second World War and is characterised by a 'disorderly and unequal' expansion towards colonial and semicolonial countries, as well as by the specific forms adopted by US imperialism.[16] Fontes uses the concept to understand the new determinations or "substantial changes in its behaviour"[17] that affected the global imperialist system after WWII and are similar to those we describe in Chapter 2. She argues that imperialism was originally linked to the political and economic form associated with colonialism, whereas capital-imperialism emerged, albeit to differing degrees, in 'secondary' or 'peripheral' countries (such as Brazil, Argentina or Mexico), "…[taking] root locally in social, economic and cultural life".[18] She adds that we have since seen

14 Fontes, *O capital-imperialismo*, 148. This and all subsequent citations from this source translated from Portuguese to Spanish by the author and into English by the translator [Translator].

15 Ibid., 149.

16 Ibid., 150–151.

17 Ibid., 154.

18 Ibid., 208. For Fontes there is a conceptual and analytical difference between *colony*, which she identifies with imperialism, and *dependency*, which she identifies with capital-imperialism.

> ...new capital-imperialist tendencies emerge which *originated in* secondary countries and express the interests of the central countries. The former would include what are today called the emerging countries of Brazil, Russia, India and China (the BRICS), along with others like Mexico, South Korea, etc.[19]

Ultimately Fontes' critique extends to any understanding of imperialism, ECLA's included, which sees the political and economic system of domination known as capitalism as somehow 'external' to so-called Third World or (to be more precise) dependent countries. But although her criticism is justified, not all authors shared this 'exogenous' view of imperialism as an 'external factor'. Unlike authors associated with ECLA and Latin American communist party orthodoxy, who did, dependency theorists and above all Marini systematically conceived of imperialism as a structural factor internal to the functioning of the cycle of capital in dependent economies. For Marini therefore, overcoming imperialism, i.e. anti-imperialist struggle, was essentially the same as an anti-capitalist struggle. In this sense he parted company with the kind of reformist, stage-based notions of struggle advocated at the time by most Latin American communist parties, arguing that "imperialism permeates dependent economies and societies completely, representing a factor that constitutes their socio-economic structures, their State, their culture".[20] Elsewhere he observes that "The end product of dependency cannot therefore be more dependency: its destruction has to involve putting an end to the relations of production that go with it."[21] That is to say, capitalist relations of production.

Fontes places Brazil in the capital-imperialist club in recognition of the profound changes to capitalism under the rule of monetary capital or the most concentrated form of capital that has further entrenched capitalism and its subsequent relations, referring of course to finance capital.[22] Brazil has thus been integrated as a subaltern country into the international circuit of the division of labour, but with monetary capital dominating its internal dynamics it has been integrated, she claims, as a subaltern capital-imperialism within the dominant capital-imperialism.[23] This is because it is at an advanced stage of industrialisation and capital monopolization, with the state acting as the main driver of capital accumulation. Furthermore, the state is relatively autonomous from the huge pressures exerted by particular capitalists and has

19 Ibid., 209. Italics added.

20 Marini, *América Latina: dependência e integração,* 90.

21 Marini, *Dialéctica de la dependencia*, 18.

22 Fontes, *O capital-imperialismo*, 303.

23 Ibid., 304.

found effective ways of containing popular demands[24] – something this kind of capitalism excels at:

> Brazil's current situation seems to be the result of new processes which incorporate backward countries into capital-imperialism whilst sharpening old contradictions, such as the lack of popular support internally owing to the poverty suffered by many Brazilians, and a unique popular sensibility which responds with anti-imperialist sentiments to a cultural onslaught exemplified by North American fads.[25]

The 1980s marked a turning point for Brazil, when traditional commodity exports were accompanied by greater direct investment abroad aimed at extracting surplus value through the exploitation of labour power. This took place in the context of qualitative changes in three directions: (1) the appropriation of raw materials in other Latin American countries, (2) the exploitation of labour power in other countries, and (3) domestic policies designed to take the edge off social struggles and pressures.[26] For Fontes these changes embody the characteristics of Brazilian secondary or subordinate (for us, dependent) capital-imperialism.

She then looks at labour super-exploitation. For Marini this was the defining characteristic of dependent capitalism and sub-imperialism, without which they would be rendered meaningless. However she very much misinterprets Marini's thesis before going on to criticise it. She begins by rightly acknowledging that unlike Furtado, Cardoso, Sonntag and Singer, Marini never denied the existence of capitalist development in Brazil. She then sets out two claims: (a) that labour super-exploitation derives from the existence of the *latifundio* and the failure to introduce "radical agrarian reform",[27] which is a far cry from what Marini argued in his main writings; and (b) that this phenomenon, along with rising migration flows and declining wages, has "truncated the law of value",[28] leading to workers being "doubly" exploited. This helps the bourgeoisie with capital accumulation because it means they can grab part of the worker's consumption fund while at the same time ensuring value is transferred to the dominant capitalist centres. In this way sub-imperialism plays a triple role: it exploits labour power at home and abroad; it accumulates aliquot shares of

24 Ibid., 307.
25 Ibid.
26 Ibid., 339.
27 Ibid., 351.
28 Ibid., 352.

surplus value, and it transfers value/surplus value abroad, sealing its condition of structural dependence on the imperialist centres of advanced capitalism.

Fontes also interprets super-exploitation, erroneously in our view, as "essentially" resting on two fundamental determinants in Marini: the "violation of the law of value" (Fontes uses the word "truncation") and the "precariousness of the internal market", which leads to workers being "doubly" exploited.

There are two points to make here. With regard to the "violation of the law of value", super-exploitation is not caused by the existence of the *latifundio,* the absence of agrarian reform, or the increased migration and wage cuts that follow as a result. These factors serve only to exacerbate super-exploitation, mainly by increasing the amount of open unemployment and underemployment as well as informal employment. This growth in the industrial reserve army and both open and disguised unemployment fulfils at least three inter-related purposes: (a) it increases labour exploitation, (b) it increases competition between workers and (c) it reduces salaries, which weakens people's purchasing power and therefore the internal market itself.

It is worth emphasising that the *super-exploitation* of the labour force is a *regime* which dialectically articulates the methods of production and exploitation suited to extracting absolute and relative surplus value. It is an *eminently* capitalist category which operates under conditions of structural dependency and is found in production and the social organisation of work, including the Toyota-ist regime prevalent today. Marini himself describes what constitutes the essence of Latin American dependency in the following terms:

> In developing its market economy as part of the world market, Latin America ended up reproducing internally the relations of production which were present in the very origins of the formation of the world market and which determined its character and its expansion. But this process was marked by a profound contradiction: required to support capital accumulation based on the productive capacity of labour in the central countries, Latin America did so via accumulation which relied on the super-exploitation of workers.[29]

Secondly, 'double exploitation' does not exist for Marini. Instead he refers to a *social regime of labour super-exploitation.* As noted, in the first instance this regime *articulates* Marx's two fundamental *types* of labour exploitation: absolute surplus value and relative surplus value. Marini then a*dds* another type, which takes place under the specific structural conditions of dependency: that

29 Marini, *Dialéctica de la dependencia*, 49.

of the worker being paid at less than the social value of his/her labour power. He concludes that

> ...the three mechanisms identified—the intensification of work, the extension of the working day, and the expropriation of part of the labour necessary for the worker to replenish his/her labour power – engender a mode of production solely based on increasing the exploitation of workers rather than developing their productive capacities.[30]

Contrary to what some critics have claimed, this does not in any way mean that the productive capacity of workers, which is related to the production of relative surplus value, is not developed in the dependent economy. Rather it *is* developed, but only in subordination to (ever intensifying) super-exploitation. The theory of super-exploitation does not claim that dependent countries are unable to transform themselves into specifically capitalist countries, because super-exploitation as a category is part of the capitalist system and closely related to relative surplus value. Marini raises this point when he writes that

> ...impacting on a productive structure based on increasing the exploitation of workers, technical progress enabled the capitalist to intensify the rhythm of labour, to elevate the worker's productivity while, at the same time, maintaining the tendency to pay him or her at a lower rate than his or her real value,[31]

Likewise, he notes elsewhere that

> ... once an economic process based on super-exploitation has started, something terrible is set in motion, and when the dependent economy decides to increase productivity through technological development, its cruelty, rather than being mitigated, actually becomes more pronounced.[32]

Marini observes that in this specific mode of production and exploitation "... the essential characteristic is provided by the fact that the worker is refused the conditions necessary to replenish his or her spent labour power".[33] This

30 Ibid., 40. English translation taken from Adrián Sotelo, *The Future of Work*, 45.
31 Ibid., 71–72.
32 Marini, "Las razones del neodesarrollismo," 4.
33 Marini, *Dialéctica de la dependencia*, 41.

means that in reality "...work is remunerated below its value, and is therefore equivalent to super-exploitation".[34]

In concrete, everyday terms, the key to understanding and quantifying super-exploitation is the concept of the average wage:

> ...labour super-exploitation, which as we have seen means that s/he is not remunerated at the value of his/her labour power, also reduces workers' purchasing power and limits the possibility of realising those commodities. Super-exploitation is reflected in a salary scale where the average is below the value of labour power. This means that even layers of workers who are remunerated at a rate above the average value of labour power (skilled workers, technicians, etc.) find that their wages are constantly subjected to downward pressure by the *regulating role* of the average salary based on the overall salary scale.[35]

To summarise so far then, labour super-exploitation is neither a reflection of nor a product of the *latifundio*-based economy and the possibility of agrarian reform. Nor is it what Cardoso and Paul Singer have described as a 'precapitalist' category.[36] Instead, as Marini states:

> The important point to make here is firstly that super-exploitation does not equate to surviving primitive modes of capital accumulation, but is *inherent to capital accumulation and grows in correlation to the*

34 Ibid., 42.

35 Ruy Mauro Marini, "El ciclo del capital en la economía dependiente," 53, (italics added).

36 Singer gets in a real theoretical muddle and misrepresents Marini's arguments in order to make them fit his own version of them. He concludes that a worker's subsistence originates in non-capitalist modes of production – specifically what he terms "simple commodity production" (p. 202) – and that the "exclusion of the working class in 'undeveloped' countries only applies to 'new products'. This is a result, in his view, of 'import substitution'. It remains totally unclear whether these imports are 'capitalist commodities' or durable consumer goods like refridgerators, TVs, stoves, electrodomestics (pp. 204–205). But worse lies ahead in the form of the contradiction that arises when Singer is asked "... how was the working class supposed to integrate into the internal market if between 1958 and 1969 its real average income dropped by 10%?" To this he replies: "... Because consumption shrank not only in relation to food but also clothes, health care, personal care products and services and even domestic cleaning products. In the final analysis, for the working class to acquire certain services and 'new products' it must eat less and take less care of its health, personal hygiene and housework." See Paul Singer, *Economía política del trabajo, elementos para un análisis historico-estructural del empleo y de la fuerza de trabajo en el desarrollo capitalista* (Ciudad de México: Siglo XXI, 1980): 209.

> *development of the productive power of labour.* To believe otherwise is to admit as capitalism approaches its pure state, it becomes ever less exploitative a system and manages to satisfy the conditions necessary to resolve its internal contradictions indefinitely.[37]

Along with labour super-exploitation, Fontes also addresses the issue of Brazil's internal market.[38] She argues that for Marini this market remains incomplete, because whilst some production is geared towards luxury consumption, most goods are produced for external markets. Here, she continues, the expansion of Brazilian or joint capitals bears the stamp of super-exploitation twice over, and the narrowness of the internal market meant Brazilian as well as foreign and joint capitals had to expand into Latin America. In doing so they turned Brazil into a platform for the export of foreign capital and its Brazilian partners to other countries in the region and further afield. According to Fontes, Marini did acknowledge this trend, which paralleled the expansion of Brazilian capital-imperialism in the 1960s. But the situation changed in the 1970s when the financial system was consolidated under the military dictatorship, leading to a consumer credit boom which altered the structure of popular needs and consumption patterns. She accuses Marini and others of failing to recognise that at this point import-substitution industrialisation started to prioritise the internal market, thus changing the very conditions of that market except during periods of crisis. She does however then go on to assert that despite these differences with Marini and the need to 'update' his work, his 1977

37 Marini, *Dialéctica de la dependencia*, 98. This is Singer's argument when, starting from the false premise that for Marini capitalism is "incapable" of integrating the working class into the internal market (p. 199) and systematically confusing surplus value with absolute surplus value, relative surplus value and wage cuts (p. 200 et seq.), he makes the following kind of assertion: "The historical experience of recent decades tends to suggest that capitalism in undeveloped countries is very limited in its ability to produce relative surplus value, and is therefore *incompatible* with rising real wages… The more capital accumulation again effectively develops the productive forces in undeveloped countries – as it does, albeit with the support of international monopoly capital – the more sector III tends to expand out of all proportion. This inevitably has an impact on workers' living standards," *Economía política del trabajo,* 225. So for Singer and assorted developmentalists and neoliberals, capitalist development translates in both developed and underdeveloped countries as the 'improvement' of workers' living conditions and welfare. Apart from prettifying and humanising the system in question, this flies in the face of the empirical evidence for the historical development of capitalism, and the reality of low wages, flexibility, precarity and informal employment experienced by the working class of the advanced capitalist countries today.

38 Fontes, *O capital-imperialismo*, 357 *et seq.*

essay *La acumulación capitalista mundial y el subimperialismo* [World Capitalist Accumulation and Imperialism] remains highly relevant. This is because it highlights a new factor: Brazil's relative economic autonomy when it comes to its politically driven export of capital, a process which once underway tends to widen *inequality* between countries, altering their status relative to one another and forcing the dominant country to find political forms more suited to its imperialist expansionism.[39]

Bringing to mind Gramsci's well-known dichotomy of domination and subordination, Fonte also argues that Brazil's current imperialist expansion is a clear sign of capital-imperialism's dual condition of dominance and subalternity. Although the language is different, this is in fact the same as the dual condition present in Marini's category of sub-imperialism. She still however criticizes the concept of sub-imperialism[40] for supposedly failing to account for the substantial changes favouring capital concentration in Brazil or the way the reconfiguration of the state has favoured such a tendency. She also charges sub-imperialism with failing to acknowledge the influence of capital-imperialist expansion on the totality of the country's internal social relations or the potential for worldwide inter-imperialist tensions after the fall of the Soviet Union and with the rise of Chinese imperialist expansion.

Obviously Marini did not anticipate these developments because they had yet to occur when he first formulated the concept – a point Fontes ignores. Instead she claims that 'sub-imperialism' as a concept involves the use of two critically important concepts: 'limits on the internal market', and 'super-exploitation' as a structural foundation of sub-imperialism in the periphery. So any analysis that seeks to explain the actual process at work needs to account for the specific forms of capital penetration that take place globally under the dominance of money capital.

Finally, she argues that the fusion of capitals of varied origin means that excess labour must be valorised and value extracted in a different way, and moreover we need to grasp the specific forms adopted by capital-imperialist policy, concluding

> ...I consider that for almost half a century we have been in a new phase of imperialism, one which integrates multiple dimensions of social life and which we can call capital-imperialism. Today Brazil occupies a subaltern position in the unequal group of capital-imperialist countries. As the last one to the table, and amidst tension and instability, the country finds

39 Ibid., 358.

40 Ibid., 359 *et seq.*

> itself in a heady rush to concentrate capitals, leading to dramatic social crises at every step of the way.[41]

In sum, as a means of understanding so-called 'developing' countries, Fontes' capital-imperialism thesis certainly makes for an interesting proposal. Of equal interest are the factors she highlights for this purpose: the role of imperialism in 'developing' countries; the concentration and centralization of capital, and the role of monetary capital (money) in determining the nature of capital-imperialism in peripheral countries. But her thesis takes a step backwards when it criticizes Marini without taking a holistic view of the method and theory which uphold a theory of dependency that is inserted in the dynamics and contradictions of a global capitalist economy where the imperialist countries rule supreme. Furthermore the capital-imperialism thesis fails to articulate, on the one hand, the core mechanism and law at the heart of Marini's theories: the cycle of capital built on the super-exploitation of labour power and its contradictory and unequal relations in each dependent socio-economic formation in capitalism; with, on the other hand, absolute and relative surplus value and their close link to capital accumulation and reproduction both in times of crisis and in times of recovery and growth.

'Local Capitalism' vs. Sub-Imperialism

Rolando Astarita sets out to evaluate Marini's theory of sub-imperialism only to dismiss it in favour of his own theory of what he calls "local capitalism".[42] We shall briefly review and then critique his arguments, revisiting the theory of sub-imperialism. We reassess its relevance in the light of Brazil's current context of high domestic inflation, economic slowdown, and increased dependency on commodity exports (especially to China), all taking place amidst corruption and rising anger, especially among the middle classes, at the impact of the capitalist crisis on living and working conditions – an impact which social-populist PT governments had hitherto managed to somewhat cushion.

Astarita highlights the fact that Marini's theory of sub-imperialism achieved prominence at a time of industrial diversification (notably into manufacturing)

41 Ibid.

42 *Rolando Astarita* [*Blog*]; "Brasil, armamentismo y nacionalismo," blog entry by Rolando Astarita, 4 April 2012, http://rolandoastarita.wordpress.com/2012/04/11/brasil-armamentismo-y-nacionalismo/.

and the internationalization of capital. These developments in the 1960s and 1970s "...led to the capitalist countries forming a tiered, pyramidal hierarchy, and to the rise of medium capitalist powers." For Marini, labour super-exploitation is a structural phenomenon which forms part of the functioning of the cycle of capital in dependent economies, and without it the cycle cannot be explained. In Brazil super-exploitation reduced the internal market whilst stimulating exports and expansion into the world market, notably to the Southern Cone – Brazil's immediate area of influence – and the Mercosur countries, which receive 40% of its exports. Hence for Astarita

> ... a relatively autonomous expansionist policy was pursued at the same time as Brazil was becoming more integrated into the global system of production under the hegemony of imperialism. Brazilian sub-imperialism was not just the expression of an economic phenomenon, but also of the political project of the military technocrats who had taken power in 1964. It was also a response to the rising tide of class struggle in Latin America. So Marini emphasised the ideological intentionality of a Brazilian military state intent on making Brazil a centre from which imperialist expansion would spread to the rest of Latin America.[43]

But although sub-imperialism largely took shape during the military dictatorship (1964–1985) and counter-insurgency state, it actually continued into the post-dictatorship, civil rule and the formal democratization of Latin America's political systems, and right up until the present day[44] in which a group of 'progressive' governments are in power on the continent.[45] Sub-imperialism certainly did not "run out of steam" and end with the dictatorship,

---

43 Ibid.

44 Agustín Cueva describes thus the historical cycle in the Latin American democratization process that followed the dictatorships: August 1979 saw the 'constitutional return' in Ecuador, to be followed the next year by Peru and then Bolivia in 1982. The next year it was the turn of Argentina, where economic crisis and the Falklands War (1982) helped bring on 'democratization'. Then in 1985 the process came to Brazil with the 'indirect election' and Uruguay with its 'direct election'. In 1989 the 35 year Stroessner dictatorship ended in Paraguay (pp. 263–264). And finally, Chile embraced 'democracy' with Patricio Aylwin Azóca's victory in the presidential elections on 11 March 1990. See Agustín Cueva, *El desarrollo del capitalismo en América Latina* 14th ed. (Ciudad de México: Siglo XXI, 1993).

45 On this point see Adrián Sotelo, "Encrucijadas, límites y perspectivas del ciclo progresista en América Latina," *Rebelión*, 25 September 2015, http://www.rebelion.org/noticia.php?id=203714.

as Astarita and other authors have suggested.[46] But neither did some kind of 'imperialist Brasil Potência' emerge along the lines of the classic North American, British or German imperialisms dreamt of by military officers and would-be monarchs like President Collor de Mello (March 1990–December 1992), who was forced out of office on charges of corruption.

Astarita finds both "strengths and weaknesses" in Marini's sub-imperialism. Among the strengths, he says the theory went beyond a "deep-rooted [view] on the left" in the 1960s and 1970s – without saying which left he means – "which saw the military dictatorship in Brazil as nothing more than Washington's puppet". Marini certainly did resist such an analysis, arguing that

> The evolution of the social sciences in Latin America in recent years—despite often repeating old mistakes—has been sufficient to invalidate a thesis that I have done my best to counter here: that Brazil's military regime was just a product of the *deus ex machina* represented for some by US imperialism.[47]

Applying the principles of contradiction inherent to dialectical thinking, Marini forged his theory of sub-imperialism with new elements found neither in Lenin's imperialism nor in the more general theoretical principles discovered and applied by Marx. He did this partly because he was studying a *sui generis* dependent capitalist social formation (that of Brazil and other Latin American countries), and partly because he needed to verify how the general laws of capitalism both affect and adapt to such a formation. But crucially, his analysis

46 The lengthy military dictatorship consisted of three different conjunctures or stages: the first lasted from the coup d'etat in April 1964 until 13 December 1968, when Institutional Act No.5 was passed. The second, lasting from December 1968 until early 1974, saw a "rise in State terrorism… culminating in the creation of a State that disappears people (*Estado desaparecedor*)". The third phase ran from 1974 to March 1985 and consisted of a process in which "…power was centralized and the state of emergency institutionalized, along with a change in the balance of forces between the fundamental social classes and between dictatorship and liberal democracy", Salles, *Lucha de clases en Brasil*, 30. Institutional Act No.5, a decree passed by the dictatorship on 13 December 1968, gave the Executive the following powers: "(1) to close the country's legislatures; (2) to remover elected members of the executive and legislative branches; (3) to suspend citizens' political rights for up to 10 years; (4) to dismiss, transfer, retire, or remove officials from all branches of government; (5) to suspend judges' permanent guarantees of unremovability and job security; (6) to suspend without prior consultation a series of public freedoms by means of a state of emergency," Ibid., 64.

47 Marini, *Subdesarrollo y revolución*, VII.

shows that after industrialisation the Brazilian economy, like most others in Latin America, created its *own,* dependent, cycle of reproduction. This new cycle was not just a mechanical outcome of the influence undeniably brought to bear by international capital and monetary and financial institutions like the IMF and World Bank:[48]

> From that moment on—[when the dependent economy becomes a capital-producing centre: ASV]—the phenomena of circulation present in the dependent economy stop being mainly *problems of circulation of the industrial nation to which the dependent economy is subordinated* and increasingly become *problems of realisation encountered by the dependent economy's own cycle of capital.*[49]

It is worth recalling that Marini's method starts with an analysis of the global economy and its impact on dependent countries. He then goes on to address dependent countries' *own* cycle in relation to the global economy. Having thus stepped down to the level of historical-concrete analysis (i.e. social formation – the very level at which the theoretical study of dependency is located), he describes the form and modus operandi of the general laws of capitalism in conditions of structural dependency, asserting that (a) contrary to the standard ECLA position, they actually operate in such a way that the development of the productive forces does not overcome but rather reinforces labour super-exploitation and (b) in the context of the process of capital production in the dependent economy, the *type of socio-economic formation* is determined by the combination of methods of exploitation (absolute surplus value, relative surplus value and super-exploitation), depending on which of these methods predominates.[50]

What Marini does then is to draw out the dialectical relationship between the cycle of capital in the dependent economy—which is unequal and contradictory in each Latin American social formation—and the specific forms assumed by super-exploitation. So while in some dependent economies capital might predominantly exploit labour through absolute surplus value (essentially by extending the working day and extra hours); in others it will do so through relative surplus value (by increasing both productivity and the intensity of work), and in yet others through cutting real wages. But what we find in reality is a 'virtuous combination' best suited to the more developed

48 Marini, "Estado y crisis en Brasil," 78.

49 Marini, *Dialéctica de la dependencia*, 85.

50 Ibid., 93 *et seq.*

economies with a higher capital composition such as Brazil, Argentina and Mexico, whose systems of production and labour organization usually feature an *interaction* between labour, technology and science.

In the final analysis it is this dual emphasis which explains both the domestic balance of forces between labour and capital and the different levels of development in each of the dependent countries. Neither can be explained, as Astarita maintains, by "differential relations of economic power", because these relations themselves need explaining, as does the methodological, conceptual and analytical content of the concept of "local capitalism".

Among the "weaknesses and problems" Astarita identifies there are those which "entail a Leninist understanding of imperialism". But he fails to clarify what this means and what exactly those weaknesses consist of. He also claims that the meaning of sub-imperialism and the sense in which it should be understood are unclear because the drive to conquer new markets and defend the interests of capital is characteristic of capital generally. This is an obvious point and one that is beyond discussion – Marini was no doubt aware of it and Lenin too. But it does not solve the underlying problem.

Astarita also misinterprets the Leninist theory of imperialism by assuming that imperialism operates under "different laws" to those of competitive capitalism because the "surpluses" (or surplus values?) it obtains from looting and racketeering in its colonies (which, note, "were not capitalist") are solely for its own gain, thus providing the basis for capital accumulation in the centres and "de-accumulation" in the periphery. In fact Lenin sets out very clearly the dialectical relationship (quantitative *and* qualitative) between the similarities and differences between competitive capitalism and imperialist monopoly capitalism, noting for example that

> Half a century ago, when Marx was writing *Capital*, free competition appeared to the overwhelming majority of economists to be a "natural law". Official science tried, by a conspiracy of silence, to kill the works of Marx, who by a theoretical and historical analysis of capitalism had proved that free competition gives rise to the concentration of production, which, in turn, at a certain stage of development, leads to monopoly. Today, monopoly has become a fact.[51]

As we saw in Chapter 1, what Lenin did was to weld together the categories of competition and monopoly and bring them up to date without disassociating

51 Vladimir I. Lenin, *Imperialism, the Highest Stage of Capitalism* (Moscow: Progress Publishers, 1977).

them in any way. It should not be inferred from what he says above, as Astarita does, that the laws of imperialism differ from those of competitive capitalism because they are based only on colonial or semicolonial theft and pillage rather than capital-labour relations, because that is evidently not the case. For Lenin, as for Marx himself and Marxists such as Mattick, Lukács and Mészáros,[52] *capital-labour relations* in their broadest sense underpin, conceptually speaking, any theorization or dialectical analysis of capitalism in either its competitive or imperialist monopoly stage. The difference is that Lenin located his analysis in the far more complex historical conjuncture of the post-1860 period. He takes all the capitalist relations of production, circulation, exchange and consumption bound up with the rise and consolidation of monopolies and finance capital (still prevalent today) and ties them together with the dual movement of concentration and centralization of capital which benefits imperialist and sub-imperialist countries. But competition in no way disappears at the monopoly stage of imperialism. As Mattick notes in his disagreement with Baran and Sweezy over their theory of monopoly capital, "... monopoly, in this sense, always remains competitive, for a non-competitive monopoly capitalism implies the end of market relations such as sustain private-property capitalism."[53] And citing Marx, he adds:

"When capital is still weak," Marx pointed out, "it tends to lean on the crutches of past modes of production. As soon as capital feels itself strong, however, the crutches are thrown away and capitalism moves in accordance with its own laws of motion. But as soon as it begins to feel itself as a barrier to further development and is recognised as such, it adapts forms of behaviour through the harnessing of competition which seemingly indicate its absolute rule but actually point to its decay and dissolution."[54]

The theory of imperialism (see Chapter 3) anchored in competition and monopoly is what inspired Marini's analysis of sub-imperialism in Latin America

52 See György Lukács, *The Ontology of Social Being,* vol. 3: Labour (London: Merlin Press, 1980) and István Mészáros, *Beyond Capital: Toward a Theory of Transition* (London: Merlin Press, 1995). For a condensed version of the latter see István Mészáros, *The Structural Crisis of Capital* (New York: Monthly Review, 2010). See also Paul Mattick, *Crítica de los neomarxistas* (Barcelona: Ediciones Península, 1977).

53 Paul Mattick, "Monopoly Capital," in Paul Mattick, *Anti-Bolshevik Communism* (London: Merlin Press, 1978), 188.

54 Ibid., 188. In his essay Mattick references the German edition of the Grundrisse directly: *Grundrisse der Kritik der Politischen Oekonomie* (Berlin, 1953), 544. At the time he originally wrote it (1966) the Grundrisse had not yet been published in English. For the first published English language translation of the extract see Karl Marx, *Grundrisse* (London: Allen Lane / New Left Review, 1973), 651. [Translator].

and particularly of Brazil as a dependent country inserted in global capitalism's cycle of reproduction. As he himself commented,

> The Leninist theory of imperialism (...) is an obligatory point of reference in the study of sub-imperialism. It should not be invoked to prevent such a study from being conducted, because, among other reasons, it is the Leninist theory of *imperialism*, not *sub-imperialism*.[55]

In this sense looting, racketeering, robbery, dispossession and war, along with what might be called 'more objective' economic laws (monopolies, capital concentration and centralization, competition, the falling rate of profit, imports/exports, monetary and financial systems, fictitious capital), are all processes and instruments which play a vital role in the dynamics of imperialism as a global economic capitalist system. To suppose otherwise would mean accepting that the longer capitalism and imperialism continue their course the less they resort to these methods of expropriation and appropriation of the labour power and resources of the oppressed nations which make up the dependent world, not to mention all the imperialist wars taking place across the world.

How does one interpret, for example, the privatization of natural resources and raw materials which *ipso facto* strip dependent and underdeveloped nations of what they have, as their people look on impotently? Where do the proceeds of this end up once transnational capital has converted them into value and surplus value as part of global capital's cycle of reproduction, with imperialist capital and transnational companies at the helm? This process brings to mind Eduardo Galeano's fascinating book *The Open Veins of Latin America,* in which he exposes the history of pillage and how underdeveloped and dependent peoples have been robbed of their natural resources by imperialist countries right up until the present day. Likewise, it recalls David Harvey's important and polemical theory of *capital accumulation via dispossession*[56] whereby huge transnational companies privatize not just citizens' assets but also those of entire nations, with the backing (including military support) of their bourgeoisies and the imperialist states.

According to Astarita, neither Lenin's classic theory of imperialism nor Marini's theory of sub-imperialism can be applied in any shape or form to Brazil because

---

55 Marini, *Subdesarrollo y revolución*, XVI.

56 Harvey, *The New Imperialism*. For a critique of Harvey see Chris Harman, "Theorising Neoliberalism," *International Socialism* 117, December 2007, http://www.isj.org.uk/?id=399.

> Brazil's relations are typical of those established between capitalist countries at different levels of development. For instance Petrobras and Brahma exploit their Argentine workforces to the same extent as other capitals, whether native or foreign. And Argentine, Brazilian and North American capitals do the same to the Brazilian working class.

But to take another example, one not unfamiliar to critical thinkers, this fails to explain why, if 12 million undocumented Mexican workers are being super-exploited, abused and murdered by *gringo* bosses in the United States whilst working hours far in excess of the national average, North American workers in Mexico are not suffering to the same extent, given that they are presumably exploited by Mexican bosses and capitals? And if our compatriots in the US send home remittances that total a third of all foreign currency entering Mexico after oil and tourism revenues, why do "undocumented North American workers" who are "work[ing] in Mexico" not send home similar amounts to save their families from hunger and poverty? The absurdity of these examples is immediately apparent. They are unimaginable because what we actually have in Mexico is not "local capitalism" but dependent capitalism subordinated to the imperialist economy and its cycle of capital, which became even further entrenched when the asymmetric, unfair and Pan-Americanist North American Free Trade Agreement (NAFTA) took effect in 1994, just as the EZLN rose up to denounce it and present their own demands to the state and national and international public opinion.

The common denominator shared by all capitalist countries is without doubt the exploitation of workers' labour power by capital. This is the source of the value, surplus value and profit extracted by capital using all the means at its disposal, which today include semi-slavery in Brazil and feudal servitude in Mexico. But at the same time, extracting value by seeking out other markets and productive systems is not a means available to all capitalist countries, and certainly not to most dependent and underdeveloped countries (or to be more precise, their 'lumpenbourgeoisie').[57] That is why 'local capitalism' cannot be considered a core characteristic of dependent Latin American capitalism, and certainly cannot be drawn upon to obscure the sub-imperialist ambitions of countries like Brazil for example Brazil, which currently commands the imperialist forces of occupation which were stationed in Haiti under UN cover and to precious little protest from the Brazilian people or the PT government of the time.

57 See André Gunder Frank, *Lumpenbourgeoisie: Lumpendevelopment; Dependence, Class and Politics in Latin America* (New York: Monthly Review, 1974).

So while the ruling classes in dependent, underdeveloped and backward capitalist countries such as Guatemala, Haiti, Surinam, Belize and El Salvador effectively exploit and super-exploit their *own* labour force in alliance with foreign capital, it would be impossible to imagine them doing so in the productive systems of Brazil, Argentina, Mexico, France, the UK or the US. It *is* plausible however to imagine Brazilian capital investing in less developed capitalist countries like Mozambique, Kenya, Nigeria, Bolivia, Peru or Paraguay, as indeed it does. Even in countries ruled by so-called progressive governments, the local labour force is still in effect exploited by the local bourgeoisie and oligarchies acting either alone or in alliance with Brazilian capital, and without any serious contradictions arising between the two.

In keeping with the above and contra Zibechi, Astarita accepts that Brazil will remain dependent for trade, finance and technology on capitalism in the 'developed countries', adding that although Brazil has the sixth largest economy in the world in terms of GDP, it ranks far below the great powers when it comes to GDP-per-inhabitant. The same holds true when measuring its technological capacity. He therefore concludes that "Fundamental changes to the global economy and the direction of technological progress are still decided in the central countries". In other words, *Brazil's capitalist economy is still structurally trapped in a dependent cycle of capital accumulation and reproduction which is subject to the vicissitudes of the global capitalist economy* and the rhythm imposed on it by the hegemonic capitals and companies of US, British, German, French, Japanese and now Chinese imperialism, which has announced that it will be making US$250 billion-odd worth of investments in Latin America in the 2020s.[58]

Astarita concludes from this that Brazil's current position in the global and regional economy cannot be explained by the "Latin American left's traditional theories" (which left?), "influenced" as they are by Marxism-Leninism and in particular the orthodox Marxism of the continent's once pro-Soviet communist parties.[59] But neither, in his view, can it be explained by Marini's theory of sub-imperialism. Rejecting these two approaches, he instead outlines his own, based on the 'local capitalisms' which Marx supposedly described in his writings on India. Apparently referring to *The British Rule in India*, written on 10 June 1853 and published in the *New York Daily Tribune*, no. 3804, on 25 June 1853, in which Marx shows how the British East India Company's systematic pillaging gave rise to an 'Indian capitalism', Astarita argues that this category

58 "China invertirá 250 mil *mdd* en América Latina en la próxima década," *La Jornada*, 8 January 2015, http://www.jornada.unam.mx/2015/01/08/economia/036n1eco.

59 On this see Fornet-Betancourt, *Transformación del marxismo*.

"applies to Latin America" in the form of the states that emerged after most countries achieved political independence in the early 19th Century. These states "participated in the exploitation of labour on an increasingly equal footing with foreign capitals", sharing in the surplus value produced in proportion to their economic power, in circumstances where "Non-economic factors played an ever less significant role. Or to be more precise, they played no greater a role than they would in an advanced country."

The "non-economic factors" relegated in importance here refer to society's superstructure and consist of the State, bourgeois power, class struggle and the legal system. Because for Astarita, what happened in practice in dependent and underdeveloped countries was that these factors ended up existing on an "equal footing" with the superstructures of the advanced capitalist countries, including their international institutions. But given that he applies the category of 'local capitalism' to the whole of Latin America and the Caribbean, can we then assume that the likes of Haiti and Central America, as well as more 'developed' countries like Mexico, are on an equal footing with the imperialist countries when it comes to exploiting labour both at home and abroad? Hardly.

In Astarita, the concept of 'local capitalism' renders sub-imperialism superfluous as a means of "explaining Brazil." For him, the country's arms build-up, heightened influence on international relations as one of the BRICs, and differences with the US on issues such as Cuba, Iran, and global warming are all easily explained by the notion in question and all it entails. But this is to ignore complex historical-structural problems like dependency, and also the particular cycle of money capital, productive capital and commodities and their role in determining the dynamics of underdevelopment and the transfer of value and surplus value to the imperialist centres (described in the MTD as unequal exchange). It also ignores the specific way in which labour power is super-exploited, which consists of systematically blocking the transition from producing absolute surplus value to producing relative surplus value, and the generalization of the latter throughout the productive system. In the Marxist theory of dependency, this is what ultimately explains the *broader reproduction of dependency* and the problems deriving from backwardness and underdevelopment that affect the oppressed workers and peoples of dependent countries.[60]

This is precisely how Marini explains the historical weakness of the dependent bourgeoisie compared to the bourgeoisie in imperialist states and countries, as well as the strength of the State in dependent countries and why it enjoys relative autonomy from the fundamental social classes. These are issues

60 I develop this theme in my book *The Future of Work*. Leiden-Boston: Brill, 2016.

which in contrast cannot be grasped through the prism of 'local capitalism', with its absence of a non-lineal, dialectical understanding of the contradictory and anarchic dynamic of the global capitalist economy in dependent economies.

Our final comment concerns what Astarita identifies as the political consequences of seeing problems from the 'sub-imperialist' perspective. His criticism is not a new one – back during the debates of the 1970s Marini's theory was accused of being 'nationalist' and opening the door to a possible 'confrontation' between the Brazilian working class and, for example, its Bolivian counterpart. Astarita does not anticipate such a terrible scenario, but he does claim that " 'sub-imperialism' also leads us towards a national focus," using this syllogistic argument:

> ...if Brazil is sub-imperialist, and has strong interests in Argentina, then Argentina could be seen as dominated by Brazil (thus raising the task of Argentina's national liberation from Brazil). But then the Paraguayans or Uruguayans would have every right to consider themselves to be exploited or oppressed by Brazilian sub-imperialism, and also by Argentinean sub-imperialism (after all the relationship between Argentina and Uruguay is at least as asymmetric as the one between Brazil and Argentina).

Astarita extends his examples to Europe, noting that some sectors he describes as being on the Greek left had considered theirs to be an imperialist country, but then realised with the onset of the crisis and the imposition of austerity that the real enemy of Greek workers was *German* imperialism. Hence, he surmises, "...the labour-capital contradiction is no longer central". But why, we would ask, should that be the case? After all, whatever their nationality and the origin of the foreign capital exploiting them, all workers have the absolute right not just to consider themselves exploited and oppressed by capital, but to fight against that exploitation. It does not matter whether that struggle takes place in just one country (Brazil, Paraguay, Uruguay, Argentina, Mexico or Greece) and against bourgeoisies of different nationalities, or across different countries by coordinating on an international scale against global capital.

Astarita draws two overall conclusions. Firstly:

> From the viewpoint I am defending, however, these conflicts can be understood as inter-bourgeois conflicts between countries and states defending capitals with different degrees of economic power. A dispute

> over the price of gas is not a national liberation struggle but a struggle over surplus value (in the form of rent or profit) between fractions of capital dressed in different national colours. When a Brazilian, Finnish, German or North American company agrees with Argentine capital to set up an industrial or trade facility, they discuss and agree their respective shares of future surplus value according to the normal criteria used in any negotiation between exploiters. It is labour that is being exploited here, not a nation.

That is all well and good, but where and when does Marini make that argument? His second conclusion is that

> (…) the key dividing line is not between national colours but relations of production. The same goes for investments in Brazil, and indeed in the vast majority of dependent countries in Latin America. It is from this perspective that Brazil's arms build-up should not be interpreted as an act of 'national liberation' (from US imperialism), nor as a flexing of its 'sub-imperialist' muscles. Instead it simply reflects the relative strength of a capitalism seeking to make its presence felt in the competitive wars taking place across the world.

Again we would have to ask why all 'local capitalisms' do not behave in such a way. What is required here is an adequate explanation of the conditions and mechanisms which permit some (but not all) capitalisms to become more competitive globally – particularly when up against the most advanced countries like the US, UK, France, Germany and Japan.

Returning to Astarita's first main conclusion, there certainly are inter-bourgeois conflicts between rival parties whose unequal economic power is reflected in their relative share of surplus value and wealth, and at the political-ideological level these conflicts can indeed be seen as processes of "national liberation". One such example would be the gas war in Bolivia (September–October 2003). Another would be the Venezuelan government's attempts to shore up oil prices after they crashed in late 2014 and 2015, or its fight against the widespread black market in basic products which is a result of economic sabotage by the pro-coup right and speculative capital.

It is true that capital exploits labour and not a nation in the abstract. But it would be very naive to ignore the fact that the 'nation', with all it implies in real concrete terms and with its multiple determinations – territory, language, culture, population, social classes, ideology, the State, ethnicities, natural resources etc. – is a concrete factor that mediates either directly or indirectly the labour-capital relationship and the way capital appropriates the surplus value and wealth produced by workers. So as Francisco de Oliveira argues, the problem of development or growth – and, I would add, sub-imperialism – is one of internal conflict between social classes[61] more than a conflict between nations, in addition to the conflicts that naturally arise with the global imperialist bourgeoisie.

In any case, the problem does not lie there but in the need to explain the structural and socio-political conditions that determine the differences in levels of economic power (greater, lesser or equal) wielded by different bourgeois fractions, and not just take those differences for granted. For this differentiated and hierarchical political power rests precisely on the international division of labour and how different bourgeoisies across the world correspond to varying levels of organic composition of capital. This is Marini's argument as to why sub-imperialist bourgeoisies, and in particular the Brazilian one, differ as much from the imperialist bourgeoisies as from the bourgeoisies and oligarchies of other, less advanced, dependent countries on the capitalist periphery.[62]

The second conclusion Astarita arrives at refers to the "relative strengthening of a capitalism that seeks to make its presence felt in the competitive wars taking place across the world", and it is of course in the nature of all capitalist bourgeoisies to 'want' to appropriate a greater share of wealth, surplus value and even territory, using force if necessary. But desire is one thing and power is another. This raises the question of whether any 'local capitalism' and its respective bourgeoisie can actually do this. Can Haiti, Guatemala, Belize, or Jamaica? Can Bolivia or Bolivarian Venezuela? Of course not. So once again an explanation is needed as to why some capitalisms, particularly sub-imperialist ones, *can* and why they can even to some extent achieve their goals without getting into an open confrontation with the hegemonic imperialism, while others instead end up subsumed to the designs of said imperialism and indeed to other countries and bourgeoisies in the same dependent capitalist periphery which exploit and dominate them.

---

61 de Oliveira, *Crítica à razão dualista*, 33.

62 Certainly for some analysts this is what happened in Brazil, where after (and even before) the 1930 Revolution "there was never a complete break with the previous historical block led by the coffee bourgeoisie in alliance with the socially backward *latifundistas*," Salles, *Lucha de clases en Brasil*, 38. Note that the reforms and institutions subsequently created, such as employment laws, benefitted both these fractions of the Brazilian ruling class.

Conclusion

For differing reasons, the authors we have discussed in this chapter all dismiss sub-imperialism as a concept or category because for them it fails to adequately explain the reality of contemporary capitalism and of Brazil in particular. They rely instead on their own concepts – capital-imperialism, local capitalism, *Brasil Potência* – to grasp the specific nature of the current moment. But in our view it would be enough to reformulate sub-imperialism and dependency theory so as to recreate a theoretical-conceptual and analytical framework capable of characterising crisis-ridden capitalism in its current neo-imperialist and neo-dependent phase (as described in Chapter 3).

We would not deny that the last two decades has seen new and complex world problems come to the fore, and certainly these were not addressed by sub-imperialism. But the main reason for that was that sub-imperialism as a theory was formulated in a historical period dominated by the military dictatorships of the 1960s and 1970s and by US control of the global capitalist economy, as reflected in its policies towards Latin America and the wider world. That does not invalidate the MTD's hypotheses, concepts, categories, theses and suggestions. It is rather a matter of reworking them and developing new lines of investigation. By doing so we can account for the way the global capitalist system's structural crisis is currently reshaping our countries and societies and for the new forms adopted by the sub-imperialist system (not only in Latin America), in the context of the contradictions in international relations within the two main geopolitical blocks to emerge in recent years: that led by the United States, the European Union and Japan; and the Asian block led by China, Russia, India and others.

CHAPTER 7

Dictatorship, Democracy and the State of the Fourth Power

This chapter aims to clear up the tremendous confusion surrounding the relationship between democracy and sub-imperialism. This confusion has led to the counter-insurgency (national security, military) State being identified only with dictatorships, and these in turn with sub-imperialism. Meanwhile democracy and the democratization process that followed the dictatorships in the mid-1980s is associated with the rise and consolidation of civil and constitutional governments which supposedly left not just the dictatorships but sub-imperialism itself behind. In this version, sub-imperialism is no longer relevant today, and is a mere reminder of a past which has been well and truly superseded.

The Latin American literature on this topic, particularly in the field of political science, has tended to focus on what is perhaps the most frequently discussed and controversial issue in political and academic circles: the nature and characteristics of the State. Here we shall refer back to that discussion in the light of Marini's concept of the *state of the fourth power*,[1] which essentially describes the role of the armed forces during the democratization process and the period that followed once the Chilean military's return to the barracks in 1990 had signalled the end of the dictatorships in Latin America on a formal, institutional level. We then relate democratization and the formal State which emerged in its wake to sub-imperialism, which has remained a key feature of the transnational expansion practised by countries like Brazil.

The State in Contemporary Capitalism

The capitalist State is essentially an instrument of the ruling class and big capital. This is the case regardless of whether the historical form it takes is colonial, land-owning oligarchic, populist, dictatorial, or, as in recent times, democratic. It is also an instrument of the different class alliances which have been forged within the power bloc at different stages of history and under

1 The 'fourth power' indicates a fourth branch of state power alongside the legislative, executive, judicial branches referred to further on. [Translator].

 DOI 10.1163/9789004319417_009

different historical conditions. So it is no surprise that the contemporary State has always used every weapon at its disposal against society's exploited and oppressed classes as part of its unconditional defence of the general interests of global social capital. Intellectuals, political scientists, sociologists, party activists and experts in such matters are all shocked to discover this, but it simply expresses the profound contradiction at the heart of the unequal contest between the social classes. So far the winner in this contest has always been big international capital, which uses structural adjustment and pro-austerity policies to protect its profit rates, its corporations, and the system that reproduces the economic, political and social interests of the ruling classes. The pro-business, neoliberal State hegemonic in today's world reflects this state of affairs. The only limits on this global class policy are those set by capital and the ruling classes, who will resort to anything to achieve their goals, including violence and political repression.

Nowhere can this be seen more clearly today than in the European Union and especially Southern Europe, where the state-imposed austerity that has hit workers and the wider population so hard has included huge tax increases (e.g. VAT); wage and pension cuts; an increase in the pensionable age; mass redundancies; increased working hours; cutbacks in social benefits; attacks on health and education; less availability of mortgage credit; court-ordered evictions, and the liquidation and/or privatization of vital public services such as telecommunications, electricity, and postal services. These calamitous policies would not have been possible had the State not relentlessly and systematically pushed through structural reforms. The clearest example of this are Greece and Spain, where the neoliberal agenda has been applied without a moment's respite or the slightest concession in the face of ever worsening living and working conditions.

The classical Marxists had a general, abstract, conception of the capitalist State as an instrument of domination and subjugation of society's exploited and oppressed classes by the ruling classes – a social minority who use different ideological apparatuses, instruments and institutions such as prisons and military/paramilitary forces, laws, the legal system, schools and the media to retain power and wield it to the extent of determining the daily lives of millions of people.

Unlike in conservative and liberal conceptions of the State, we would stress that as a mode of production, as a social formation and as a form of ideological and juridical-political domination, the capitalist system could not exist without the State continually intervening in the economy and society. One of its key functions is to uphold the established order and get rid of any individuals, forces, social movements or alternative power structures which might threaten that order or even bring it down. So although in certain historical and political moments the State might be relatively autonomous from the social classes or appear to stand outside of them (as in Caesarism and Bonapartism), its historical role remains one of ensuring that the system of capital keeps functioning whatever contradictions and difficulties it must confront. And it does this by reproducing that system's core components, namely private ownership of the means of production and consumption, capital's exploitation of labour, the market economy, and wage labour.

In sum, the State guarantees what István Mészáros describes as *second order mediations in capital's social metabolic mode of control,* which give capital its basic ability to self-reproduce and therefore create value, surplus value, and profit.[2] He defines his *second order mediations* as follows:

a) The predominance of the nuclear family, notwithstanding its disintegration under modern capitalism due largely to the increased numbers of women and children entering the labour market.
b) Alienated means of production and their 'personifications.'
c) Mystifying forms of money, from cocoa beans in ancient Mexico to today's international system of financial speculation.
d) The subordination of consumption and the fetishised needs of production and accumulation.
e) The complete separation of alienated wage labour from the means of production.
f) Various different kinds of national states.
g) An uncontrollable and chaotic world market.[3]

These forms of mediation impose themselves on and finally dominate what Mészáros calls *first order mediations,* namely:

a) The interplay between the regulation of biological reproduction, sustainable population levels and natural resources.
b) The socialist regulation of the labour process to satisfy human needs.
c) Simple, egalitarian exchange relations.
d) The conservation and reproduction of the material and cultural requirements of human society.

2 Mészáros, *Beyond Capital.*
3 Ibid., 108–109.

e) The rational and planned allocation of human and material resources, as opposed to their chaotic and irrational 'allocation' by capital in keeping with its social metabolism.
f) The enactment of rules and regulations based on the principles embodied by these primary mediations.[4]

Mészáros argues that since *second order* mediations have a legal and institutional basis, this converts *first order* mediations into alienated forms of the political State, which is responsible for imposing capital's basic need for self-reproduction on society and individuals through what we would argue is a mixture of coercion and consensus.[5] He concludes that by means of second order mediations—which are entirely capitalist in nature—all the *primary functions* of the social metabolism in general (such as nature, population, family, community, culture, art and leisure) are geared towards a fetishising and alienating system's need to self-expand and subordinate everything to the imperatives of commodity production and capital accumulation and reproduction. Such a political and economic system cannot tolerate any type of production or self-governing, cooperative forms of social and communal organisation that do not play by the 'rules of the game' as written by the market and the (capitalist) State. These alternative forms may well be able to 'coexist' in certain times and spaces with the latter, but sooner or later they will face 'real subsumption' under the State's all-devouring, market-driven conditions. This will be achieved either by 'persuasive', consensus-based methods or, when that no longer works, through physical and mental violence until such alternatives are brought to heel.

Among the second order mediations through which the State achieves overall domination, we would highlight the role of national and international ruling class ideology, and in particular the way it is produced and disseminated by the media. The main purpose of the media is to tame and/or neutralize the class consciousness of the working masses so that they conform to the core values and principles of bourgeois society. It quashes the will for change by making people believe the existing order is 'good enough' to 'resolve' and 'satisfy' their needs and problems. This ideology reinforces the idea of capitalism as eternal, omnipotent and indestructible, as if no other ways of life or working were possible. The media furthermore tries to convince people that human activity is driven solely by competition, the 'creative destruction' wreaked by corporations, Man and nature, individualism, selfishness, racism, and the

4 Ibid., 139 et seq.
5 Ibid., 140.

survival instinct, and that these forces are perfectly compatible with the capitalist order. Finding a solution to humankind's biggest problems is just a matter of time and patience!

This then is the general context for the claim that the crisis of capital, which is actually a product of powerful contradictions and macroeconomic and socio-political inequalities, is a necessary, 'painful' condition of capitalist development. For the system's ideological defenders holed up in the State, the bourgeoisie, the political parties or other power structures, crisis is always a 'necessary evil' which can be managed and overcome. They then use this argument to try and discredit any organised attempt by the subaltern, popular and working classes to fight for an alternative to this endless, systemic crisis.

Alongside pro-capitalist and imperialist institutions such as the IMF, the World Bank, the OECD and the BID, the bourgeois State plays a key role during these ever longer and deeper recurring crises, described in modern parlance as systemic due to the system's inability to function without them. As we have argued elsewhere, capital's current crisis derives from its difficulty in producing enough surplus value for the system to reproduce itself on an expanded scale. Because of this difficulty, financial and human resources increasingly pile up in bank coffers, stock exchanges, property and insurance companies and elsewhere, where they are fictitiously 'valorised'. This has the effect of concentrating and centralizing capital even more into the hands of that 1% of the world population who get richer every day by undermining the living, working and environmental conditions of millions of people.

In the present conjuncture of the global crisis, the State's role has been to allow and indeed exacerbate this situation to the benefit of fictitious capital by applying neoliberal policies which protect the interests of the parasitic classes and weaken the productive cycles and labour processes which produce value and surplus value. Fictitious capital has a nominal money value and its existence is based on documents such as Treasury bonds. At any given moment these documents might be found to lack any real basis in productive activity or material assets. But for a capitalist speculator, wealth in this form is as tangible as the wealth produced by millions of workers, who of course neither own it nor produce it for their own benefit but for that of non-workers i.e. capitalists. This leads us to ask who really gains from such a setup. The answer is that capital in general doesn't really care what it invests in, and only cares about the strategic question of where the most profits are to be made – be that in arms manufacturing, environmental destruction, GM crops, the stock markets or cosmetics.

The current system of neoliberal capitalism is fully designed to achieve this aim in the global economy because fictitious capital, i.e. speculative finance capital, *dominates* other fractions of capital. It is a system which fails to create wealth, productive jobs or incomes for workers, but conversely *is* entirely responsible for capitalism's low rates of growth in its current neoliberal phase and the intensive monopolistic processes of concentration and centralization which make profits for fictitious capital's wealthy owners. And to that end it can rely on the unconditional support of the State.

In sum, the State is far from being a neutral entity or subject in the capitalist system. Rather we might describe it as an integral part of the process of domination and reproduction of the system's core social relations. Following Mészáros, these core relations can be defined as private property, the monopolization of the means of production; capital accumulation and reproduction; conflict between capital and waged labour; value and surplus value production via labour exploitation; the dynamics of supply and demand, the world market; colonialism; underdevelopment, and dependency. In other words, the social relations that historically constitute the contradictory duality of imperialism and dependency.

The Limits of Bourgeois Democracy

The military dictatorships in Latin America finally collapsed in the 1980s, unable in the end to impose the kind of political stability that US interests required. With the revolutionary left destroyed, the popular and working class movements defeated, and a certain layer of intellectuals co-opted by the dictatorships, it was this geopolitical fact which, of all the many complex causes at play, ultimately led to the continent's democratization from the mid-1980s onwards. Agustín Cueva describes the process of democratization as starting with the return of constitutional rule to Ecuador in August 1979 and Nicaragua later that same year, followed by Peru (1980); Bolivia (1982), and Argentina (1983). Then it was the turn of Uruguay and Brazil (1985), Paraguay (1989),[6] and finally Patricio Aylwin's victory in the Chilean presidential elections in March 1990, which marked the end of the cycle of military dictatorships. The democratization process which followed across most of Latin America signified a return to institutional rule. This was expressed by the division of State

6 Agustín Cueva, "Posfacio: los años ochenta: una crisis de alta intensidad (1977–1994)," in *Entre la ira y la esperanza y otros ensayos de crítica latinoamericana*, Alejandro Moreano, comp. (Bogotá: CLACSO / Siglo del Hombre Editores, 2008), 141–142.

power into its legislative, executive and judicial branches: a typically liberal arrangement that has been the norm ever since.[7]

Historically there is a correlation between political developments and economic developments on the continent over the whole of this period. The first big populist wave (1930–1945) was accompanied by the first stage of industrialisation under the governments of Lázaro Cárdenas in Mexico, Getulio Vargas in Brazil, Juan Domingo Perón in Argentina and Luis Batlle in Uruguay. This signalled the end of the old primary export-based economy that had been in place since the mid-19th Century throughout almost the whole of Latin America.

Similarly, the cycle of military dictatorships that emerged from the crisis of populism and took root with the 1964 military coup in Brazil would be accompanied by the second stage of industrialisation, known as the *complex stage*. This stage found its highest expression in Brazil, starting with Juscelino Kubitschek's *Plan de Metas* or target-based plan (1956–1961), and later with the so-called *Brazilian miracle* between 1968 and 1973. Described by Maria da Conceição Tavares as a "conservative revolution", the 'miracle' saw GDP grow by an average of 10% a year.

Although there were differences in the ways individual Latin American countries experienced economic and industrial development after the Second World War, there were also important commonalities. In both Mexico and Brazil, for example, it progressed under a model of capital accumulation and reproduction aimed at the internal market which we might call industrial diversification. In Mexico this model was to suffer from a structural crisis that would last from the mid-1960s until finally drawing to a close in 1982. As Marini put it

> The liberal experiment of the 1960s first required the previous political regime to be brought down and replaced by a military dictatorship based on a new class alliance. The current neoliberal offensive has in turn required the military regime to be dismantled, a process which lasted ten years but which has yet to radically alter the power structures. That would require a new dominant bloc to emerge.[8]

7 See James Petras and Morris Morley, "Los ciclos políticos neoliberales: América Latina 'se ajusta' a la pobreza y a la riqueza en la era de los mercados libres," in *Globalización: Crítica a un paradigma*, John Saxe Fernández, ed. (Ciudad de México: Plaza y Janés, 1999), 215–246.

8 Ruy Mauro Marini, "El experimento neoliberal en Brasil," Ruy Mauro Marini Archive (1992), http://www.marini-escritos.unam.mx/072_experimento_neoliberal_brasil.html.

The new power bloc Marini refers to here would be aligned to a dependent, neoliberal model of capital accumulation. This model became more visible with democratization in 1985 and was consolidated under the José Sarney government (1985–1990). But industrialisation was still predicated on import substitution, and a more openly neoliberal model only took hold under the next set of governments—Fernando Collor de Mello (1990–1992), Itamar Franco (1992–1994) and Fernando Cardoso (1995–2003). Policy then took a neo-developmentalist turn under the PT-led governments of Luiz Inácio Lula da Silva and Dilma Rousseff, although the latter would end up returning to a more neoliberal approach, especially in her second term.

In overall terms then, we would say that the second stage of complex industrialisation in Latin America entered into crisis and by the early 1990s had really exhausted itself, giving way to the growth and expansion of a new model of capital accumulation which we would call productive specialization. This new model is orientated towards the world market and has relied on raw material production, semi-manufactured products and agro-business, whilst operating under the 'social' cover of the neo-developmentalist policies of successive PT governments.

This transition was helped along by various international factors. One of these was the far-reaching global crisis which hit capitalism from 1974–1975 onwards and caused a long depression in the world economy which in our view has continued right up until today. Another contributory factor was the onset of what became known as neoliberalism in the imperialist countries and especially the US and the UK – a tendency that would go on to impose itself everywhere until finally achieving global hegemony. Under neoliberalism, capitalist development would be driven by market forces, financial deregulation and privatization. Meanwhile more and more countries were drawn into world trade – a trend that became known somewhat ambiguously as 'globalization'.

This *epochal transition* would be captured on a political and ideological level by right wing US conservatives writing in the 1970s about changes and mutations in both the world economy and individual countries. *The Crisis of Democracy: On the Governability of Democracies* (1975) by Samuel Huntington, Michel J. Crozier and Joji Watanuki[9] was particularly influential at all levels – politically, ideologically, academically and intellectually. Written as a report for the Trilateral Commission think tank founded by David Rockefeller and Zbigniew Brzezinski in 1973 to foster links between the US, Western Europe and Japan, it introduced a number of ideological concepts. These included 'governability'

9 Published as Michel Crozier et al., *The Crisis of Democracy: Report on the Governability of Democracies to the Trilateral Commission*, (New York: New York University Press, 1975).

and its relationship to the 'crisis of democracy' in the West, and government's (in)ability to satisfy growing 'citizen demands' in the United States, which the authors saw as potentially leading to serious social upheaval not only in the US but also elsewhere in the developed world. Marini drew out the significance of these concepts and their relevance to Latin America:

> The US was worried not just about Latin America but the advanced countries themselves. This concern translated into a search for principles and mechanisms which would make democracies governable as defined by fashionable ideologue Samuel Huntington. In the State Department's version, the idea of 'governable democracy' gave way to that of 'viable democracy', understood as a representative democracy overseen by the military. It should be noted that this model did not represent a real break with counter-insurgency doctrine, in which the Armed Forces' annihilation of the internal enemy and reconquest of a social base should be followed by a third stage of democratic reconstruction.[10]

This was a defining moment because it established the close relationship between democracy and neoliberalism. This relationship was to characterise the new pattern of accumulation – one which for the most part is still with us.

In summary then, the oligarchic-landowning and populist cycles gave way to a cycle of dictatorships, which was in turn succeeded by a democratic cycle. This democratic cycle has consisted of three *waves* since the mid-1980s:

a) The *first wave* consisted of the transition from dictatorial rule to civil rule, and included governments as diverse as those of Alan García in Peru; Raúl Alfonsín in Argentina; Miguel De la Madrid in Mexico; Julio María Sanguinetti in Uruguay, and José Sarney Costa in Brazil.
b) The *second wave* lasted from the late 1980s to the mid-1990s and was represented by presidents Carlos Andrés Pérez in Venezuela; Carlos Saúl Menem in Argentina; Paz Zamora in Bolivia; Luis Alberto Lacalle in Uruguay; Carthe Salinas de Gortari in Mexico and Collor de Mello in Brazil.
c) The *third wave* emerged in the second half of the 1990s. Its figureheads were Alberto Fujimori in Peru; Carlos Saúl Menem in Argentina; Ernesto Zedillo in Mexico; Rafael Caldera in Venezuela; Gonzalo Sánchez de Lozada in Bolivia and Fernando Henrique Cardoso in Brazil.[11]

---

10 Ruy Mauro Marini, "La lucha por la democracia en América Latina," *Cuadernos Políticos* 44 (1985): 3–11, http://www.marini-escritos.unam.mx/018_democracia_es.htm.

11 Petras and Morley, "Los ciclos políticos neoliberales".

We would add a *fourth rupturist wave* represented by the coming to power of Hugo Chávez in Venezuela (2 February 1999) and Evo Morales in Bolivia (December 2005) and described as such because their governments are often described as occupying the 'centre left' of the political spectrum. We prefer to simply call them progressive, although what they have essentially done is pursue developmentalist policies of a markedly national character within the limits imposed by dependent and underdeveloped capitalism. The importance of this new political process lies in the way these governments have broken with neoliberal logic and advocated a 21st Century socialism. Their close links to the popular and social movements of indigenous people, peasants, workers, students and the middle classes has perhaps also led them to stress the popular and nationalist character which distinguishes them from the neoliberals and the right in both its orthodox and heterodox versions. They do not refuse to enter into alliances with big national or foreign capital or even transnational corporations, but in doing so have perhaps exercised a greater degree of spatial and temporal control over a neoliberal paradigm which leaves economic processes to the mercy of market forces and reduces the State's role to one of simply ensuring compliance with neoliberal policies.

Today a fierce contest is raging in Venezuela, Bolivia and elsewhere in Latin America between these progressive governments and the neoliberal right. This contest is an expression of class struggle and social conflict in the region, and both forces have chosen to fight using electoral means. It is well known, however, that official ideologues, social democracy, the political parties and the right all see elections as the 'wheel' that keeps bourgeois democracy turning. Any other kind of mobilization or alternative is seen as 'unviable' and bound to 'fail' from the start. Either that or it will end up falling victim to repression as the State performs its natural duty on behalf of the dominant classes.

To avoid illusions, the population must be aware that bourgeois representative democracy imposes very strict limits on the electoral process in our countries – structurally, politically, ideologically and culturally. Any elections that take place under such a democracy must be *governable, viable,* and *restricted:* they must be *governable* because they cannot deviate from the dominant system's rules (including rules governing the media and other information providers); *viable,* because they must comply with electoral law, and above all *restricted* because they rely on 'representation' by whoever is elected to Congress (i.e. deputies and senators). In no way does the electoral process allow the workers and masses to participate effectively in any kind of direct democracy that might eventually clash with the values and principles of the capitalist system and bourgeois society.

Just because a progressive government takes power is not say that it will automatically satisfy the demands of its supporters in the subaltern classes, or radically break with the oligarchies and the policies pursued under the existing pattern of capital reproduction and domination (although Venezuela might be approaching such a break as it confronts the right's systematic attempts to bring down the Maduro government through a so-called 'soft coup').[12]

The major contradictions currently faced by Bolivia are an illustration of this. Members of the COB trade union federation have demanded that the government raise wages and reverse an earlier increase in working hours. Meanwhile indigenous people have clashed with the government as they try and stop capital going ahead with environmentally damaging projects. As part of this an 'Amazon March' was held to oppose the construction of a highway promoted by President Evo Morales and financed by Brazil which was to cut through a 12.363 km^2 government-protected National Park known as Tipnis. Another example of the contradictions at play is the popular and indigenous struggle in the northern Peruvian region of Cajamarca against the huge Conga open-air gold mining project, which according to movement leaders and local inhabitants affects the city's water supply. Six people were killed and almost a hundred injured in protests after another 'centre left' president, Ollanta Humala, took power on 28 July 2011, only to then take a pro-US, neoliberal policy turn. There have also been anti-government demonstrations in Brazil. These have been justified in so far as they reflect the demands of social and popular movements, but are also notorious for having been infiltrated by a right wing seeking to bring down the government by impeaching the president.

It would be unfair to accuse these movements of the subaltern and oppressed classes, which after all only seek to defend their communal, territorial, environmental, social, cultural, and economic interests against capital's voracity, of 'undermining' the sacred democratic and progressive principles of governments which call themselves 'centre-left' – anti-imperialist even – but leave untouched the foundations of capitalism: private property, capital's right

12 The Venezuelan government and *chavismo* suffered a major setback when the right wing MUD won a majority of seats in elections to the single chamber parliament on 6 December 2015, thus paving the way to a referendum through which it hopes to topple Nicolás Maduro's constitutional and legitimate government and bring back the inevitably neoliberal and capitalist Fourth Republic (1956–1999). Similarly, right wing candidate Mauricio Macri narrowly beat *kirchnerismo* in Argentina's presidential elections on 22 November 2015. Both these developments have prematurely breathed life into the 'end of the progressive cycle' thesis promoted by some intellectuals in respect of Latin America's governments.

to exploit alienated labour, and the perverse dynamic which ties State policies to the development of the market economy.

Furthermore, this fourth rupturist wave still retains the structures of regimes based on charismatic *caudillos* (Lula, Evo, Chávez, Maduro, Kirchner, Correa, Ortega) who go beyond their constitutional role as legitimate rulers to substitute the masses and represent them along corporatist lines. So what is needed is a radical *fifth rupturist wave* of a kind which is no doubt already brewing in Venezuela, Ecuador and Bolivia. This fifth wave should be based not on leaders and political parties who operate in the official sphere of the State (as with previous waves) but on the masses and their class organizations of workers, peasants, indigenous people, and indeed all the class fractions and segments that suffer under the political and ideological yoke of the State and capital. To differentiate it from the previous one, we would call this fifth wave socialist-democratic. It would need to act strongly and carve out the space required for a direct democracy in which the vast majority of the population can participate. It would also need to be decidedly anti-imperialist and anti-capitalist in character if it really is going to manage to build a new society of a kind which acts as an antipode and a counterweight to capitalism and social inequality.

From the Counter-insurgency State to the Democratic State

We shall now move the discussion in this chapter on to a more concrete level of analysis in order to clarify two concepts used by Marini to understand the relationship between the State and sub-imperialism. The military dictatorship in Brazil created a counter-insurgency state or *estado desaparecedor*[13] as Severo Salles puts it. With the onset of democracy after 1985 this gave way to a *state of the fourth power*: a concept which, admittedly, Marini did not develop sufficiently beyond the work he did on it in the 1980s as he saw the democratization processes getting underway. He defined the state of the fourth power as one in which the Armed Forces exercise

> a role of vigilance, control and leadership over the entire state apparatus. This structural and functional characteristic of the state will come about, of course, only as a result of the total enslavement of the state apparatus by the armed forces (beyond the parliamentarian democratic characteristics that the state might display) and as a result of the militaristic legal

13 In other words, a state that 'disappears' its citizens. [Translator].

> order which will be imposed on all political life, in particular national security laws.[14]

This is how Marini interpreted the constant pressure and blackmail applied by the military in Latin America and in Chile and Brazil especially in order to maintain its institutional status, influence and control over state affairs as its condition for accepting the regional transition to democracy that began in the mid-1980s.[15] Of course in Brazil a key part was played by the implicit commitment of the political bureaucracy and state officeholders to a blanket amnesty for the military as a *sine qua non* of their return to the barracks, despite citizen demands that the state accept responsibility for the dictatorship's crimes.[16] So instead of a rupture, a peaceful, conservative transition was negotiated in which

> Economic policy did not change; the Armed Forces continued ability to intervene in politics was to be progressively and partially reduced over time; responsibility for State terror was not attributed to anyone, and the 'bionic' senators (indirectly elected and therefore virtually appointed) took part in the Constituent Assembly of 1987–88.[17]

This commitment is still in place: even though the dictatorship's brutal human rights violations were documented in the National Truth Commission (CNV)'s official report, published on 10 December 2014, Brazil remains the only Southern Cone country which *de jure* has yet to judge the crimes in question, which are in fact *crimes against humanity*.

Created in May 2012, the Commission was tasked with investigating and clarifying the circumstances surrounding the human rights violations committed by the military dictatorship between 1964 and 1985, identifying the perpetrators, and enforcing the "…right to memory and historical truth, and promote national reconciliation". One of its specific objectives was to review the 1979 Amnesty Law (ratified by the Brazilian justice system in 2010). To do this it spent 31 months collecting 1121 testimonies and dozens of expert opinions, holding 80 public hearings across the country, and carrying out hundreds

14 Ruy Mauro Marini, "The Question of the State in the Latin American Class Struggle," in *Contemporary Marxism* 1 (1980): 7.

15 See Marini, *América Latina: dependência e integração*.

16 Severo Salles, *Ditadura e luta pela democracia no Brasil. O inicio da distensão política (1974–1979)*, (Salvador, Brasil: Quarteto Editora, 2003), 131.

17 Salles, *Ditadura e luta pela democracia no Brasil*, 134–135.

of investigations. Its 4,000-word, 300-page report was the first of its kind, and examines these rights violations and crimes against humanity in the context of a society racked by corruption and impunity. It describes the intimidation, torture and elimination techniques used by the State against the largely communist and leftist opposition during the dictatorship, and the still incomplete figures so far show 434 deaths or disappearances in 21 years of military rule, compared to 30,000 in Argentina and 3,000 in Chile. Unsurprisingly the military reacted to its publication by discrediting it and denying the accusations made. The Superior Military Tribunal, accused by the CNV of having given legal cover to the excesses of the dictatorship, declared on 16 December 2014 that the report was "untrue, unjust and wrong", and assured that what happened during the 21 years of the military regime was "…quite the opposite" of what the report claimed.[18]

This is the context in which a commitment was made to the military caste in the 1980s that as a condition of any 'peaceful transition' to democracy they would be granted an amnesty and protected as an institution from any judicial proceedings that might end in imprisonment. This commitment still stands today. As Marini went on to comment:

> This marked the beginnings of a strategy which would be applied across the board in the 1980s, when military ideology and democratic restoration combined to demand an immediate solution.[19]

The US's disastrous defeat in Vietnam, the Carter administration's promotion of 'human rights', and the effects of the Falklands War (2 April–14 June 1982) all played a decisive part in bringing *overseen, restricted* and *governable* democracy to Latin America. The armed forces did not lose any of their influence on the State apparatus as a result, but instead went from directly exercising State power to operating under the wing of civil institutions whose formal constitutional powers are embedded in the executive, legislative and judicial branches of the State, which had been asphyxiated under the bloody dictatorships:

> So the thing to do now is to carry out a political "opening" which can preserve the essentials of the counter-insurgency state [which consist of] the institutionalization of big capital's direct participation in economic management and the subordination of the powers of the state to the armed

18 See SCA-TUCA, "Informe Final de la Comisión Nacional de la Verdad de Brasil," 10 December 2014, http://www.cnv.gov.br.

19 Marini, *América Latina: dependência e integração,* 22.

> forces, through the state organs which have been created, particularly the National Security Council (...) – things are moving towards a state of four powers, or more precisely, a *state of the fourth power*, in which the armed forces will exercise a role of vigilance, control and leadership over the entire state apparatus.[20]

From the US State Department's perspective in relation to Latin America, this led to the concept of 'viable democracy', which "promoted a democratic-representative regime overseen by the Armed Forces (...) which did not constitute a real rupture with counter-insurgency doctrine":[21]

> Washington has begun to devise a new approach to Latin America, expressed by the idea of 'viable democracy'. The concept's vagueness hides its conviction – so often voiced by the continent's Geisels, Videlas and Pinochets – that the peoples of Latin American are not yet ready for 'full democracy'. But it also points to a political solution which stops short of 'full democracy' and is translated into an institutional regime which does what it can to respect basic democratic freedoms and enjoys a certain level of social support. With this qualification, the North American recipe is closer to the practices of the Brazilian military than to those of their Argentine, Chilean, Uruguayan colleagues... Euphemisms aside, 'viable democracy' means restricted democracy: an attempt to institutionalize counter-revolution in Latin America.[22]
>
> [Thus...] until the mid-1980s, political life in Brazil was characterised by the military's efforts to retain the initiative and control the liberalization process. By doing so they sought to achieve institutional restructuring of a kind that would formally guarantee their role as the *fourth power* of the State. This power would be wielded by the military's corporatist bodies and the intelligence services, the highest expression of which would be the National Security Council. Similar proposals inspired the Chilean Constitution of 1980, as well as those unsuccessfully put before a plebiscite by the Uruguayan military in 1982, and the partly successful demands made by the Argentine military shortly before they gave up power.[23]

---

20 Marini, "The Question of the State", 6–7 (italics in the original).

21 Marini, *América Latina: dependência e integração*, 23.

22 Ruy Mauro Marini, "¿Hacia una 'democracia viable' en América Latina?" *El Sol de México*, 16 December 1976.

23 Marini, *América Latina: dependência e integração*, 24.

Marini went on to add that

> An analysis of events shows that only in Chile was the state of the fourth power fully realised, although far from ensuring political stability it has actually become a source of ongoing institutional conflict.[24]

As we have seen, the Brazilian counter-insurgency state (also described as a 'national security state') lasted the time span of the dictatorship, from the military coup d'état up until a second phase which began with democratization, when it was transformed into a state of the *fourth power*. Sub-imperialism on the other hand has remained a constant during both historical periods. Diagram 2 illustrates the contrast:

1964→ 1985 1985→→→→→ 2015

Dictatorship--Democracy

Counter-insurgency State **State of the Fourth Power**

S U B - I M P E R I A L I S M

DIAGRAM 2 *Sub-imperialism in Latin America*

As Luce notes, sub-imperialism is a particular form taken by the dependent economy that goes beyond the regime that ruled Brazil's during its technocratic-military dictatorship. Moreover, it is a feature not just of Brazilian reality but that of other countries "that took on the condition of sub-imperialist socio-economic formations", such as South Africa and Israel.[25]

Conclusion

In this chapter we have looked at the nature of the capitalist State and the main way(s) it reproduces capital and upholds the social structures that reproduce

24 Marini, *América Latina: dependência e integração*, 24–25. The last paragraph cited is not in Marini's article "La Lucha por la Democracia en América Latina," *Cuadernos Políticos* 44 (1985): 3–11, but was added to *América Latina: dependência e integração*, by which time the Chilean process had advanced further.

25 Luce (2015), 42, footnote 7.

the social relations at the heart of the system. In doing so we have shown that the State generally serves as a means by which the ruling class furthers its interests through public policies consistent with the logic of value and surplus value production in order to maximise profit rates and the profitability of capital in general. We also noted that there are differences between State and government, with the latter able to assume the form of different types of political regime. Thus it can be shown that historically Latin America has experienced the colonial State, the landowner State, the populist State, and finally military dictatorships or the counter-insurgency State. In the current period the democratic State has prevailed, but as we have shown this has not meant the end of sub-imperialism. Neither has the state of the fourth power disappeared, but has rather taken on different forms in different Latin American countries.

Having differentiated the type of State that existed during the period of dictatorships from the kind which emerged with democratization, it remains clear that sub-imperialism is a feature of both periods which is underpinned by the model of capital reproduction THAT LASTED FROM THE END of WWII until the early 1990s and went hand in hand with industrialisation and State policies directed at industry, trade, tariffs, subsidies, taxation and incentives for internal consumption. It was a model powered by internal markets based on high-end consumption and, to a lesser extent, by manufacturing exports for the world market.

Finally, we noted that sub-imperialism in the sense Marini intended the category to be understood has been a constituent part of both military rule and the democratic State prevalent throughout Latin America today. At the same time, we acknowledge that not all the democratic countries can assume the sub-imperialist condition. This is an issue we look at in the next chapter, where we argue that to understand the contemporary and regional situation we need to re-engage with sub-imperialism as a category in the context of its regional and extra-regional insertion and in relation to the United States, as determined by the expansionist dynamic described by Marini in his writings on the subject.

CHAPTER 8

Sub-Imperialism and the Contemporary Capitalist Crisis

The survival of sub-imperialism as a political regime and model of capital reproduction depends on the global capitalist economy and the relations of production and domination in the advanced countries and above all the core imperialist powers of the US, UK, Germany, France and Japan. In this chapter we review the different models of capital reproduction present throughout the history of dependent Latin America. In doing so we aim to shed light on the specific characteristics of the Brazilian model as the country has developed into a producer and exporter of raw materials and mineral products which also depends heavily on the dynamic of Chinese imports.

Latin American Models of Reproduction

Historically speaking Latin America has been host to four different socio-economic formations, each corresponding to a particular pattern of capital reproduction. These are:

Socio-economic formations		Capital reproduction
A dependent colonial-exporter formation (1521–1850)	←→	Colonial (1700s–1850)
A dependent capitalist-exporter formation (1850–1930–1950)	←→	Primary goods exporter -first wave (1850–1945)
A dependent capitalist-industrial formation (1950–1982)	←→	Industrial diversification for the internal market (1945–1982)
A formation based on a dependent neoliberal pattern of reproduction specializing in production for export under the hegemony of fictitious capital (1982–2015)	←→	Dependent neoliberal model -product specialization and external demand (1982–2015) - Secondary -exporter -manufacturing export-based; Brazilian model (1945–1994) and Mexican model (1982–2015) - Primary goods exporter -second wave: primary export-based; Brazilian model (1994–2015)

DIAGRAM 3 *Economic formations and patterns of capital reproduction in Latin America*

 | DOI 10.1163/9789004319417_010

Generally, only the largest countries – Brazil, Mexico, Argentina – have experienced all of these patterns of reproduction, while Chile, Colombia and Peru have experienced them to a lesser degree. Other than the colonial formation, which was subordinated to the expansion of European empires (Spain, Portugal, England and France), all the other formations have been characterised by 'cumulative mechanisms of dependency' (decapitalisation due to repatriation of profits to imperialist countries; balance of payment deficits; access to loans and financial 'aid' offered by foreign capital, and foreign debt).[1] These mechanisms have facilitated the penetration of the Latin American economy by foreign capital along with three of dependency's defining features: dependency on the world market (the export–import dialectic); dependency on manufactured imports of tools, machinery, and processed raw materials from the advanced countries; and finally, control and ownership of new technology patents by foreign companies whose business interests dictate their conditions of use.[2]

This has all resulted in a huge decapitalisation of dependent economies which has been relatively offset by the greater level of decapitalisation and growth of foreign debt that took place elsewhere in the 1970s and 1980s. At the same time, it led to an increase in super-exploitation as a means of counteracting falling profit rates, further making an impact on the balance of payments of value/surplus value transfer to the industrialized centres.

Alongside this, several Latin American countries including Mexico have made the transition from a model of dependent industrialisation based on import substitution and the internal market to one based on super-exploitation and low wages. In Mexico and Central America this new model has been dominated by the export-driven *maquila* industry. In the Southern Cone countries on the other hand, industrialisation has mainly given way to a reprimarised agro-export model based on primary products (food, raw materials and minerals). As Boron puts it, "…whereas *progresismo* once looked to industry, today it is about extractivism, primary products and exports"[3] and now encompasses the sale and export of nature itself, in the shape of unprocessed raw materials and food and energy products which end up in industrialized countries to the detriment of underdeveloped and dependent ones.

We are faced then with a paradox. In the 1990s Latin American states took a major turn towards neoliberalism and restructured their economies and

1 Vania Bambirra, *Teoría de la dependencia: una anticrítica* (Ciudad de México: Era, 1978), 29.

2 Vania Bambirra, *El capitalismo dependiente latinoamericano*, 100–105.

3 Borón, *América Latina*, 172.

production. This involved a process of de-industrialisation, leading to a new primary export-based pattern of capitalist reproduction which prioritised extractivism and the agrobusiness economy.[4] But this new world market-facing model, fuelled by privatizations and structural reforms, made barely any impact on the region's integration into the global economy, as shown by the fact that Latin American and Caribbean exports rose by a mere 1.8% over 20 years as a share of world trade, from 3.8% in 1985–1989 to 5.6% in 2005–2009.[5]

De-industrialisation widened the gap between the growth of the productive apparatus and capital accumulation—whether or not technological development took place. Working class consumer needs and demand became restricted to branches and sectors of production run by micro-enterprises and small businesses producing mostly low grade consumer goods with little technological input. Demand was generally met by precarious and informal markets geared towards satisfying nothing more than subsistence needs. Meanwhile the numerically much smaller privileged classes—just 5–10% of the population depending on the country and its level of development—turned to luxury consumption, financial speculation, and the lucrative sectors represented by the black market, drug trafficking and the casino economy. This state of affairs mirrors Marini's classic characterisation of the dependent economy:

> ... because it was so highly concentrated in luxury goods production, technological development ended up posing serious problems for realisation. These problems have been addressed through State intervention (by enlarging the bureaucratic apparatus and freeing up access to production subsidies and credit for luxury consumption), as well as inflation, with the aim of transferring purchasing power from the lower to the higher sphere of circulation. This has meant cutting real wages even further in order to have enough surplus to carry out this transfer of income. But the more workers' spending power is limited, the less chance there is of stimulating any technological investment in production geared towards

4 Between 2000 and 2010 soya exports made up 40% of Brazil's total exports. Most of that went to China, which in turn imported almost a third of its iron ore from Brazil. James Petras, "Brasil: o capitalismo extrativo e o grande salto para tras," in *Observatório das Nacionalidades, Tensões Mundiais World Tensions* (Fortaleza) 10, no. 18–19 (2014): 307. Available in English online at http://www.globalresearch.ca/brazil-extractive-capitalism-and-the-great-leap-backward/5343624.

5 José Durán Lima and Alessia Lo Turco, "El comercio intrarregional en América Latina: patrón de especialización y potencial exportador," in María I. Terra and José D. Lima, (coords.), *Los impactos de la crisis internacional en América Latina: ¿hay márgen para el diseño de políticas regionales*?, Red Mercosur de Investigaciones Económicas, Serie Red-Mercosur 18 (2010): 101.

> mass consumption. So it is no surprise that while the luxury goods industry continues to grow at high rates, industries reliant on mass consumption (the so-called 'traditional industries') tend to stagnate and even go backwards.[6]

The conclusion Marini draws from this makes up one of his central propositions, one that is still relevant today:

> *Production based on the super-exploitation of labour thus once again engendered its own mode of circulation, at the same time separating the productive apparatus from the consumer needs of the masses.* The stratification of this apparatus into so-called 'dynamic industries' (making luxury goods and the capital goods needed to produce them) and 'traditional industries' reflects how the structure of production has adapted itself to dependent capitalism's own structure of circulation.[7]

So what does a dependent socio-economic formation look like under neoliberal capitalism? We would highlight five key features:

a) The weakened bargaining power of national governments vis-a-vis transnational corporations and international financial and monetary bodies. The kind of bargaining power enjoyed in the past at least helped ameliorate the effects of greater structural dependency on imports and on what remained of import 'substitution'. This power clearly depends also on the kind of government in office and its political approach to economic and foreign policy. In recent times for example, progressive governments in Bolivia, Ecuador and Venezuela have pursued a path of greater sovereignty and less dependency anchored in so-called 21st Century Socialism,[8] which, along with other policies, has guided a process of Latin American integration, representing what Marini described as a *latinoamericanismo renovado* or renewed Latin Americanism. This intense process of political, economic, social and cultural integration and unification

6 Marini, *Dialéctica de la dependencia*, 73.

7 Ibid., 74. Italics in original. We should also note that Marini's theory of dependency provides the theoretical and methodological elements needed to produce a specific theory of the dependent state which recognises its essential role as one of maintaining and reproducing dependency and its economic cycle, which as we have seen is characterised by luxury consumption, the world market and labour super-exploitation.

8 See Hugo Chávez Frías, *El socialismo del siglo XXI*, (Caracas: Ministerio del Poder Popular para la Comunicación y la Información, Colección Cuadernos para el Debate), 2011.

began with the creation of the Caribbean Community Market (CARICOM, 4 August 1973), followed by MERCOSUR (26 March 1991); the Central American Integration System (SICA, 13 December 1991); PETROCARIBE, created by president Hugo Chávez on 29 June 2005; the Union of South American Nations (UNASUR, 17 April 2007) and the Community of Latin American and Caribbean States (CELAC, 23 February 2010). To this list we could also add genuinely alternative media such as TELESUR (24 July 2005), which began broadcasting in Venezuela on 9 February 2007. But in keeping with the theoretical and political premises of Marini's thought, the process will have to go much deeper and much further before it can truly achieve the kind of economic and political integration envisaged in the original Bolivarian ideal, one that enables the peoples of Latin America to

> ...build new political and legal superstructures, with a capacity to negotiate, resist and apply the pressure required to be an effective presence in the face of already existing superstates or those that are emerging in Europe, Asia and America itself.[9]

b) In abandoning industrialisation as a 'development strategy' devised and championed by developmentalists and neo-developmentalists, Latin American countries redrew their 'economic road map' of the world market in order to head in a 'more profitable' and sustainable direction. They did this in two ways. One drew on natural resources, food products, and agro-industry (the South American and Andean extractivist model), and entailed causing serious harm to the environment and the wealth it harbours. The other way, more typical of Mexico and Central America, was based partly on manufacturing goods for export in maquiladoras usually run by US-based transnational corporations; partly on tourism, and partly on the foreign currency earned from the remittances sent home by thousands of undocumented workers selling their labour power in the US and Europe. All these activities remain crucial to Mexico and Central America's dependent model of capitalist accumulation and reproduction, and particularly to El Salvador and Guatemala given their high levels of emigration.

c) Maquilas and the export of labour have thus come to embody the 'growth strategies' pursued by governments and by the private interests (both national and foreign) who dictate the direction Latin America must take in order to keep up with the demands made by the extreme version of globalization which supposedly every country in the world 'must pass through' if they are

9 Marini, *América Latina: dependência e integração*, 146.

to prevail in the global division of labour and inter-capitalist competition between companies, capitals and nations.

d) Greater dependency in trade, finance, technology, science, the military, culture and every other area, with the subsequent loss of sovereignty that implies in favour of capital and national and foreign private investors. This has especially affected Mexico and Central America, the countries most dependent on the United States.

e) The structural and political impossibility of going back to 'development' and 'social welfare' policies due to the logic of the dependent neoliberal model of capitalism in both its 'primary exporting' and 'manufacturing exporting' versions and said model's 'social subjects' (national and foreign investors, speculators, drug traffickers, the comprador bourgeoisie, and State technocrats). This is because the process of easy profit-making essentially takes place abroad and relies upon the dynamics of world markets as well as the place of any given Latin American country in the global division of labour created and controlled by the imperialist powers and transnational corporations.

Here Brazil is an example of an intermediate formation, where the government has intervened to alleviate crises (like the global crisis of 2008–9) by freeing up credit, raising wages and stimulating the internal market whilst on the external market it continues with its global strategy of *sub-imperialism* and its heavy reliance on China. Under the PT it has also pursued neo-developmentalist policies, although with the most recent economic crisis they were increasingly sacrificed in favour of neoliberal adjustment policies.[10] In short, there have been two sides to Brazilian policy in recent years: an attempt to fight poverty and unemployment up to a certain point but without affecting or confronting the interests of big national and foreign capital operating in the country.

One visible consequence of the dependent insertion of Latin America under its own unique cycle of capital and the accumulative mechanisms of dependency referred to earlier has been 'reprimarisation'. This is the process whereby primary production (raw materials, food, agro-industry) has become tied to natural resource-based manufacturing in a world market which has been successfully monopolised and centralised by transnational corporations. This has had implications for Latin America:

> After dropping to around 52% of total exports in the early 1980s and then to a low of 26.9% in the late 1990s, raw materials regained their relative

10 See Giovanni Alves, *Trabalho e neodesenvolvimentismo. Choque de capitalismo e nova degradação do trabalho no Brasil* (Bauru, Brasil: Projeto Editorial Praxis, 2014).

> share of total exports, to 42% in 2011. Conversely, industrial products, which had gained a larger share towards the end of the 1990s, fell in relation to total exports over the past decade. Much of this had to do with the positive terms-of-trade shock in South America during much of the past decade, consisting of rising prices for many of its export commodities. The heavy slowdown in the Latin American and Caribbean region's manufacturing exports worldwide over the past decade contrasts with the performance of its raw material exports. The latter have gained relative share [sic] at the expense of exports of low-, medium- and high-tech manufactures, which grew much more slowly than in the 1990s. This reflects the slowing growth shown by exports from engineering- and labour-intensive manufacturing sectors.[11]

The Mexican and Central American modality of accumulation (D1), closely tied to the US economic cycle, is showing ever stronger signs of crisis and exhaustion, especially when it comes to the maquila industry at its heart. The second modality (D2), which still dominates the Southern Cone economies, is currently the more dynamic of the two and depends heavily on the going price of raw materials and basic products made from natural resources. For example, exports from Brazil, Argentina, Chile, Bolivia and Peru are mostly limited to a mere handful of raw materials and primary goods, with oil, copper, iron, soya, coffee, sugar, fish, meat, fruit and gas representing around 42% of the total in 2011.[12]

After taking hold in Latin America outside of Mexico and Central America (particularly Costa Rica), this latter modality has entered into decline since the prices of some of these products began to fall. One reason for this fall has been the slowdown in the Chinese economy and consequently in Chinese imports as the Chinese state has tried to respond in the last two years by pursuing policies aimed at developing its internal market and increasing relative wages and purchasing power, thus seeking to halt a trend that has already triggered not only the first devaluation of the yuan since it was initially devalued in 1994, but also a fall in the stock market which hit economies worldwide, among them the Southern Cone countries and especially Brazil.

---

11 ECLAC, *International Trade and Inclusive Development: Building Synergies* (Santiago de Chile: United Nations, 2013), 57, http://www.cepal.org/en/publications/37040-international-trade-and-inclusive-development-building-synergies.

12 See ECLAC, *Latin America and the Caribbean in the World Economy 2011–2012: Continuing Crisis in the Centre and New Opportunities for Developing Economies* (Santiago de Chile: United Nations, 2012), 15, http://repositorio.cepal.org/bitstream/handle/11362/1187/1/E1200770_en.pdf.

Indeed the world prices of primary products have plummeted across the board. In 2014 oil fell by 9.1%, along with coal (–17.1%), copper (–6.4%) and iron ore (–28.4%).[13] In the same year the value of Chinese imports overall rose by just 0.5%, as this table shows:

TABLE 1 *Increase in value of Chinese imports (percentages)*

2002–2011	2013	2014	2015–2019*
22.6	7.3	0.5	9.3

* Economist Intelligence Unit forecast.
Source: Economist Intelligence Unit, "China cambia prioridades", La Jornada, 3 March 2015, 26. Available online at http://www.jornada.unam.mx/2015/03/03/economia/economist.pdf.

As we can see, having grown by 22.6% a year between 2002 and 2011, the average rate of increase in the value of Chinese imports slowed to 7.3% in 2013 and 0.5% in 2014. The same figures show that the average increase of 9.3% predicted for the 2015–2019 period is well below the historical average. This slowdown has especially affected Brazil's soya and iron ore-dominated exports, which in 2014 fell by 4.8% or 51.7 billion dollars. In the same year exports from Argentina, Peru and Venezuela fell by 13.8%, 2.5% and 13.7% respectively. Chile on the other hand saw a slight increase of 1.6%, mostly accounted for by copper, while Mexican imports rose by 9.3% and Uruguayan imports by 6.6%.[14]

On top of this Latin American exports to the European Union have gone into decline as a result of the crisis afflicting Europe in recent years. This trend is expected to continue into the long term, and the EU's terms of trade with Latin American governments continue to be subject to negotiation.

The 2008–9 crisis was centred above all on the United States. Its impact on Latin America translated as a fall in export income, direct foreign investment, and migrant worker remittances, as well as a big drop in tourism.[15] This impact was uneven: the countries most immediately affected were those most locked into a subordinate relationship with the US economy like Mexico and Central America, which had been applying neoliberal public policies since the

13 Economist Intelligence Unit, "China cambia prioridades" *La Jornada*, 3 March 2015, http://www.jornada.unam.mx/2015/03/03/economia/economist.pdf.

14 Ibid.

15 Carlos Marichal, *Nueva historia de las grandes crisis financieras. una perspectiva global, 1873–2008* (Ciudad de México: Editorial Debate, 2010), 312.

1980s. In contrast, Argentina, Brazil and Chile all had sufficient central bank reserves to be able to fund anti-cyclical measures. Argentina for example was able to withstand the crisis thanks to the debt moratorium it had agreed with creditors in 2002. In Brazil averted the worst effects of the crisis were averted by exports, notably to China, and by the stability of local banks. Additionally, its internal market and consumption levels were kept buoyant by federal and state government social programmes such as *Bolsa Familia* (Family Subsidy), *Programa Ingreso Ciudadano* (Citizen Income Programme) and *Acción Joven*. Chile, for its part, increased public spending, invested in infrastructure and set up social funds, albeit on a limited scale.[16]

Mexico, on the other hand, maintained its ultra-neoliberal, conservative policies and reaffirmed its unconditional and dependent subservience to the US – evident ever since the FTA took effect in January 1994 – whilst transferring the crisis onto the workers and embarking on the extreme neoliberal programme of structural reforms, above all privatizations, imposed by the PRI government and political parties in 2012–2015.[17]

This resulted in a double bind: on the one hand de-industrialisation deepened (in contrast to the previous period). At the same time growth rates contracted so much that not enough value or surplus value could be produced, and super-exploitation was intensified in a bid to counteract this trend. But the end result was negative because investment rates were still too low to either reinvest properly in the process of accumulation and capital reproduction (expanded reproduction) or, even more importantly, to start tackling structural unemployment by creating new jobs. The corollary of all this was seen in the flow of capital into the coffers of speculative fictitious capital. This caused an even greater contraction of the productive cycle, thus further centralizing capital and strengthening the multinationals.

Neoliberal capitalism has shown itself to be incapable of responding to the global crisis by reactivating and revitalising the economy through positive long term policies focussing on employment, productivity, social spending and economic development. This is a problem even for progressive governments, many of whom have watered down their efforts to implement anti-poverty social programmes, defend national sovereignty, and combat inflation and currency devaluations. Clearly, however, there are substantial differences between governments. Some are openly neoliberal and pro-US, like the Mexican one. There are also 'centre-left' governments which maintain

16 Marichal, *Nueva historia*, 213 *et seq*.

17 See my book *México (re)cargado. Dependencia, neoliberalismo y crisis* (Ciudad de México: FCPyS / Editorial Itaca, 2014).

> ... ambiguous relationships with the United States, tolerate democratic victories and utilise large-scale social programmes (Brazil, Argentina). Alongside these two more or less pro-establishment types of administration, a new type of reformist government has emerged that not only pursues popular goals but mobilizes the masses in confrontations with imperialism and the local dominant classes (Venezuela, Bolivia).[18]

The gap between the two kinds of 'centre-left' government described here has widened with time, especially in the case of a Brazil currently immersed in a deep structural crisis, endemic corruption, and a right wing campaign to discredit the current government. The first clear indication of this campaign came with the *sui generis* coup d'état against the constitutional president Dilma Rousseff: having been democratically elected with over 55 million votes, on 12 May 2016 she was suspended from office for 180 days to allow a 'political trial' to proceed against her for having committed an alleged 'crime of responsibility'. The Senate eventually voted to remove her for good in its final verdict on 31 August 2016.

At the same time, the crisis has also strengthened the transnational and ideological discourse so beloved by global capital around the 'structural reforms' being promoted in a macroeconomic and political context in which average global economic growth rates are contracting. Thus for IMF Managing Director Christine Lagarde the global economy has 'taken off' following a deep recession, but the recovery is still weak (Table 2). She therefore 'suggests' that governments draw up plans to stimulate economic growth, claiming this might help the unemployed millions in the macroeconomic context of weak growth shown by this table:

TABLE 2 *GDP growth in selected regions and countries, 2007–2014 (percentages)*

	2007–2010	2011	2012	2013	2014
World	1.8	2.8	2.3	2.2	2.8
Developed countries	0.3	1.5	1.3	1.1	2.0
-United States	0.3	1.8	2.8	1.9	2.5
-Japan	0.0	−0.6	1.4	1.5	1.4
-Eurozone	0.2	1.6	−0.7	−0.4	1.2

18 Claudio Katz, "The Singularities of Latin America" in *Socialist Register: The Crisis and the Left*, Leo Panitch, Greg Albo, Vivek Chibber eds. (Pontypool, UK: The Merlin Press, 2012), 205.

	2007–2010	2011	2012	2013	2014
Developing countries	5.9	5.9	4.7	4.6	4.7
-China	10.8	9.3	7.7	7.7	7.3
-India	8.1	7.3	4.7	4.8	5.0
Latin America	3.0	4.3	2.9	2.5	1.8
Russian Federation	2.4	4.3	3.4	1.5	n/d

Source: For 2007–2010 data, United Nations Department of Economic and Social Affairs, *World Economic Situation and Prospects* 2014, (New York: United Nations, 2014), http://unctad.org/en/PublicationsLibrary/wesp2014_en.pdf. For 2011–2014 data, "Regional Integration and Value Chains in a Challenging External Environment," in Economic Commission for Latin America and the Caribbean (ECLAC), *Latin America and the Caribbean in the World Economy, 2014* (Santiago de Chile, United Nations, 2014), 11, table 1, http://repositorio.cepal.org/bitstream/handle/11362/37196/1/S1420692_en.pdf.

For a representative of global capital to make such a statement tells us only that the road to hell is paved with good intentions. Unfortunately for workers, any attempt to reduce unemployment or improve living conditions under global capitalism will always be overridden by the adjustment and austerity policies imposed by big capital, as Greece, Spain, Italy and France have found out. In this light, World Bank president Jim Yong Kim's claim that extreme poverty in the world can be reduced by the year 2030 sounds highly implausible, especially as it would mean lifting a million people out of poverty every week. His good intentions fail to even explain by what means poverty would be reduced aside from the disastrous measures which have impoverished millions of workers over the last three decades, including in the advanced European countries and in particular southern Europe.

These neoliberal reforms clearly do not impinge upon the interests of big capital and much less on those of the speculative capital which dominates the cycle of reproduction and siphons off profits. While that remains the case they will continue apace to the detriment of the workers who make up most of humanity. That is why the IMF has not altered what it euphemistically calls 'structural reforms' in the slightest. Instead it invariably points to the 'cause' of the problem as lying in the long term slowdown of the global capitalist economy, especially now that it has spread to 'emerging' economies like China and India:

> Global economic activity strengthened in the second half of 2013 and is expected to pick up further in 2014, led by a faster recovery in the advanced economies. World output growth is projected to increase from 3 per cent in 2013 to slightly above 3½ percent in 2014 and nearly 4 percent in 2015. Activity in the advanced economies will be driven by a reduction of fiscal

> headwinds, except in Japan, and still highly accommodative monetary conditions. Meanwhile, the momentum of growth in emerging market economies is likely to remain subdued, reflecting tighter financial conditions and homemade weaknesses in some cases. Risks around the outlook have diminished somewhat, but remain tilted to the downside, (…)[19]

In other words the IMF, founded at the Bretton Woods conference in July 1945, agrees with many economists of both a Marxist and non-Marxist persuasion that the global capitalist economy is only showing marginal growth and is in permanent danger of falling into recession. It is therefore in a situation of what might be described as structural semi-stagnation.

Another source of instability it points to is the impact of falling commodity prices on exporter countries such as those in Latin America and the Caribbean, which rely heavily on imports from China and other industrialized countries. Its figures show that growth rates in Latin America fell from 7.5% in 2010 to 2.9% in 2011 and 0.9% in 2012, and from 9.2% to 8.0% and 2.0% respectively in the

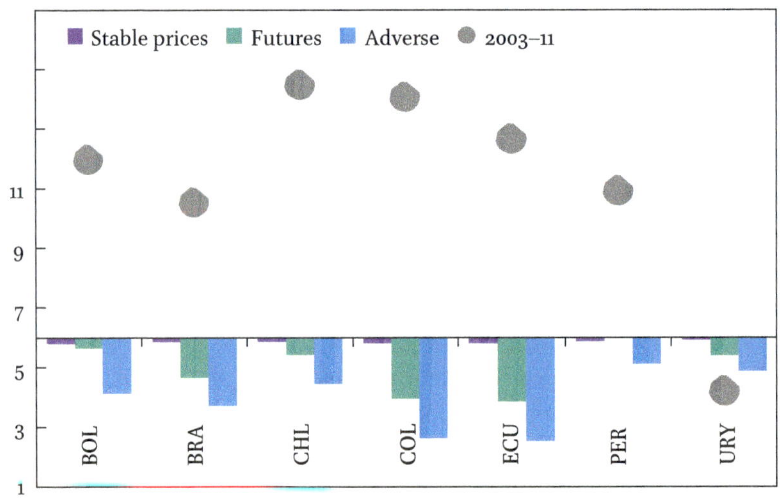

FIGURE 1 *Selected Latin America: Projected NCPI growth under alternative scenarios, 2014–2019 (average annual growth rate; percent)*
Note: NCPI = net commodity price index.
Source: IMF staff calculations. Source: "Regional Economic Outlook: Western Hemisphere – Rising Challenges", available online at http://www.imf.org/external/pubs/ft/reo/2014/whd/eng/pdf/wreo0414.pdf, April 2014, Figure 4.8, 53.

19 IMF, *Regional Economic Outlook, April 2014: Western Hemisphere: Rising Challenges,* (Washington D.C.: International Monetary Fund, 2014), https://www.imf.org/external/pubs/ft/reo/2014/whd/eng/pdf/wreo0414.pdf.

Caribbean.[20] The current global economic climate has meant Southern Cone countries (Brazil, Argentina, Peru) have been hit particularly hard by this trend.

According to international foreign trade bodies, raw material and energy prices entered a long cycle of decline in 2012, affecting both producers and consumers. Figure 1 shows the contrast between this period and the long price boom of 2003–11:[21]

According to the IMF, the price of raw materials from Latin America and the Caribbean declined for 12 consecutive months between 2013 and 2014, with metals continuing to fall until March 2014 (−15%). It predicts that this trend will continue because "... supply is increasing while demand growth from large emerging markets is expected to slow,"[22] affecting exporters of raw materials and agricultural products. It concludes that:

> CPI forecasts using current prices of commodity futures suggest that the peak of the ongoing commodity super-cycle has passed. The current market-based outlook for 2014–19 is characterized by a sharp decline in NCPI growth rates across LAC, with an annual growth rate (averaged over time and across economies) about 6½ percentage points lower than during the commodity boom – and actually negative for most countries.[23]

By the end of 2014 the price of oil had fallen sharply. This mainly affected oil-dependent nations such as Mexico, whose federal budget absorbs over 30% of the foreign currency earned from oil sales. Between 2 June and 18 December 2014 alone the price of oil for export sank by 47% from US$D102.41 to $48.43 a barrel:[24] a loss of 62 billion pesos or 4 billion dollars according to Mexican company PEMEX,[25] leading the government to cut social spending. But oil is not the only product to experience such a decline in price. Metals and agricultural products have also been hit by speculative capital moving into apparently

20 IMF, *World Economic Outlook: Slowing Growth, Rising Risks, September 2011*, (Washington D.C.: International Monetary Fund, 2011), 181 (Table A3), http://www.imf.org/external/pubs/ft/weo/2011/02/pdf/text.pdf.

21 Ironically, FAO figures show a counter-tendency occurring during this long commodity price boom: the doubling of food prices between 2000 and 2010, with cereal prices almost tripling (cited in Borón 2014, 67).

22 IMF, "Rising Challenges," 14.

23 IMF, "Rising Challenges," 51.

24 "Precio del petróleo, segundo obstáculo para el crecimiento: Banxico," *El Universal*, 19 December 2014, http://www.eluniversal.com.mx/finanzas-cartera/2014/banxico-petroleo-pib-1063035.html.

25 "Quita Pemex beneficio laboral," *Reforma*, 18 March 2015.

more lucrative markets in the financial sphere of fictitious capital, encouraged by the prospect of the US Federal Reserve raising interest rates.

The Bank of America – Merrill Lynch claims that the price of raw materials has in fact already collapsed. In a survey of fund managers with a USD604 billion total portfolio, it found that as the respondents moved their money into more profitable vehicles such as investment funds, the more "they [were] increasing their cash reserves whilst their reserves in commodity-based vehicles [were] diminishing" whilst also helping raise the value of the US dollar.[26]

IndexMundi uses World Bank data to show that in the first half of 2014 the price of raw materials plunged by an average of 30%, agricultural products by 13% and metals by 10%. For investment banking and securities firm Goldman Sachs, the stronger dollar combined with the lower growth forecasts for China in the last two years (Table 1) will further depress the world price of raw materials, with negative consequences likely for most countries with commodity export-based models of reproduction.[27]

The Capitalist Reproduction Model and Brazil's Trans-Latin Companies

Capitalist development in Brazil really took off after the 1930 Revolution,[28] a watershed moment in the country's history. Prior to the Revolution the economy had been under the hegemony of the primary or agrarian-exporter sector and rural landowners, but after it this period gave way to a new one of urban-based productive structures controlled by a dominant industrial bourgeoisie.[29] This process was given further impetus by the so-called 'Brazilian miracle' (1968–1973), which the dictatorship used to advertise the country's 'economic success', thus heightening the expectations of foreign investors and at the same time improving the government's image abroad.[30]

Between 1935 and 1985 Brazil's manufacturing sector grew by an average of 10% annually, a figure which speaks to the kind of industrialisation that took place,[31] the bourgeoisie's increasing power over other ruling class fractions,

26 "Colapso de materias primas a nivel mundial empuja el dólar al alza: Merrill Lynch," *La Jornada*, 17 December 2014, http://www.jornada.unam.mx/2014/12/17/economia/024n1eco.

27 Ibid.

28 A classic work on this is Florestan Fernandes, *La revolución burguesa en Brasil* (Ciudad de México: Siglo XXI, 1978).

29 de Oliveira, *Crítica à razão dualista*, 35.

30 See José Serra, *El 'milagro' económico brasileño. ¿Realidad o mito?* (Buenos Aires: Ediciones Periferia, 1972).

31 Petras, "Brasil: o capitalismo extrativo e o grande salto para tras," 302–303.

and the increasing power of global capital. But as noted earlier, this did not lead to a rupture but rather to a strategic compromise between the different bourgeois factions, among whom the industrial fraction was now dominant.

Brazil was also the country which extended its pattern of reproduction (C) the longest, until the early 1990s when it gave way to the D2 modality of reproduction under the Collor and Cardoso governments. Cardoso's *Plano Real* served as a springboard for even more neoliberal policies and a constitutional reform which allowed him to stand for re-election.[32] During his first term in office (1995–1998) trade liberalization and the state's loss of autonomy in economic policy made it harder for national industry to export its products and compete with foreign imports. This led to a balance of payments deficit and greater control by global capital of important branches of industry. The country once again became an exporter of raw materials[33] and "...the world's biggest exporter of meats and second biggest exporter of cereals":[34]

> ...Brazil reverted to becoming a primary commodity exporter, as soya, cattle, iron and metals exports multiplied and textile, transport and manufacturing exports declined.[3] Brazil became one of the leading extractive commodity exporters in the world. Brazil's dependence on commodity exports was aided and abetted by the massive entry and penetration of imperial multi-national corporations and financial flows by overseas banks. Overseas markets and foreign banks became the driving force of extractive growth and industrial demise.[35]

The situation did not change during the Lula and Dilma administrations but in fact worsened, dashing the hopes of leftists and progressives who had naively expected this predatory model of development to be replaced by one more attuned to popular interests. Instead the existing pattern of reproduction became more entrenched in line with the neo-developmentalist policies pursued by PT governments at the helm of a neoliberal state under new global and macroeconomic conditions:

> The post-neoliberal governments of Lula and Dilma did not change the essence of the political metabolism of the neoliberal state established in the 1990s in Brazil, whether in its narrow sense (i.e., political society and bureaucratic-administrative structure), or in its broader sense (i.e., civil

32 Salles, *Ditadura e luta pela democracia no Brasil*, 138.

33 Ibid., 111.

34 Ibid., 124.

35 Petras, "Brasil: o capitalismo extrativo e o grande salto para tras," 302–03.

> society and its socio-metabolism). In the end, imbued with the spirit of Lulism and in the name of governability, the post-neoliberal governments made a pragmatic choice to reproduce the neoliberal state they had inherited from the 1990s; and even worse, to preserve the essence of the oligarchic, bourgeois Brazilian state originating from the military dictatorship.[36]

The 2003–2011 rise in raw material prices coincided with the consolidation of the trend towards productive specialisation in agrobusiness and predatory extractivism during the Lula and Dilma governments, together making extractivist capital the "driving force of the economy".[37] Thus

> Under the administration of President Lula da Silva, Brazilian companies got a boost from an active diplomatic policy that gave them a key role in enhancing relations with Africa. In addition to business missions led by senior officials and financial support from the development banks, there were export promotion and productive development policies.[38]

It ought to be noted however that this 'extractivist model' was different from the one prevalent in Brazil and Latin America during the 19th Century:

> Brazil might be described as having 'reprimarised' but with a major difference compared to before: the exploitation of raw materials now uses very sophisticated processes and is very conducive to technological innovation, especially when it comes to exploiting oil and gas.[39]

As extractivism has intensified, Lulism and the PT carefully avoided any confrontations with either workers and working class organizations like the trade unions, or on the other hand with big national and foreign capital. In this way

> ...As a political style, Lulism combined two 'virtuous' traits: fighting against poverty but without confronting the hegemonic power bloc of capital, i.e. the internal power bloc linked organically in the global sphere to the hegemonic historical bloc of financialised neoliberal capitalism. Lulism is the hegemonic spirit of the social democratic project in Brazil today which aims, within the framework of the neoliberal bourgeois

36 Alves, *Trabalho e neodesenvolvimento*, 150.

37 Petras, "Brasil: o capitalismo extrativo e o grande salto para tras," 306.

38 ECLAC, *Foreign Direct Investment in Latin America* (Santiago de Chile: United Nations, 2013), 76, http://repositorio.cepal.org/bitstream/handle/11362/36861/1/S1420130_en.pdf.

39 Pierre Salama, "Globalización comercial: desindustrialización prematura en América Latina e industrialización en Asia," *Comercio Exterior* 62 No. 6 (2012): 40.

> order, to make a project of income redistribution and combating extreme poverty compatible with not confronting capital.[40]

This explains why the economic and political climate was much more favourable under the Lula governments (2003–2010) than under his successor. Lula enjoyed an average annual GDP of 4.1% and used his government's 'popular mandate' to ensure governability and tackle the problems caused by the 2008–09 global crisis. Notably, even at the height of the crisis income per capita rose and inflation was held at 6%, leaving behind the days of hyperinflation,[41] and in 2006–2008 the economy grew by 5.1% a year before falling 0.3% in 2009.[42] What Dilma Rousseff inherited from Lula then was

> ...a country on track, which after huge hydrocarbon reserves were found off the Atlantic coast appeared to be heading for another stupendous decade in economic and social terms, during which it would consolidate its leadership status in South America. A very different situation to the one the country would confront four years later.[43]

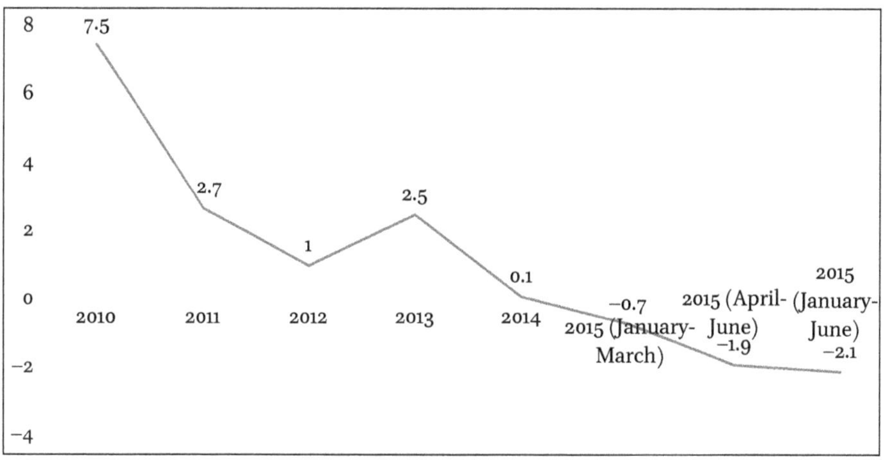

FIGURE 2 *Brazil in recession: GDP performance, 2010–2015 (January–June)*
Source: IBGE, "PIB recua (−1,9%) em relação ao 1° tri de 2015," in http://saladeimprensa.ibge.gov.br/noticias?view=noticia&id=1&busca=1&idnoticia=2973, 28 August 2015.

40 Alves, *Trabalho e neodesenvolvimento*, 152.

41 Andrés Carvas, "Dilma, todo en contra," *Proceso* 1991 (2014), http://www.proceso.com.mx/?p = 391988.

42 DIEESE, "Remessas de lucros e dividendos: setores e a dinámica econômica brasileira," *Nota Técnica* 137 (2014): 15.

43 Carvas, "Dilma, todo en contra."

On the domestic front, IBGE figures (Figure 2) show that during Rousseff's first period in office (2011–2014) GDP increased by an average of 1.6% annually:[44] in 2010 by 7.5%; in 2011 by 2.7%; in 2012 by 1%; in 2013 by 2.5%; and in 2014 by 0.1%. But for the first half of 2015 the figures show a fall of −2.9%, which is when the IBGE officially declared the country to be in recession.[45]

As we have argued, everything pointed to the president's second term (2015–2019) being much more risky and complicated than her first or those of her predecessor. By then, the global economy had slowed down, commodity prices had fallen, domestic inflation was reaching double figures (9.56%), interest rates were at their highest for nine years (14.25%), unemployment was rising, fiscal savings were low, and the national currency had been losing value against the dollar since early 2015. On top of all that, resources had been squandered on sporting events and well-known government and business figures have been tainted by corruption in the wake of the PETROBRAS money laundering scandal. Understandably, the crisis was driving different sectors to take to the streets in protest as discontent spread right across the popular and working classes.

There was evidently a certain contradiction in a supposedly left wing popular government with a (neo)developmentalist agenda not only working with a neoliberal (capitalist) State feeding off a primary-exporter model of reproduction – different from that which existed under 19th Century oligarchic-landowner regimes – but also, until the political trial of President Rousseff, working in close alliance with the parties of the right (mainly the PMDB and PSDB, in a way which typified the particular nature of the power bloc in Brazil).

If the two Lula governments performed well in a context of rising export prices, the situation facing Dilma in her second term was more of a structural nature and characterised by a sharp fall in raw material and energy prices, with have serious repercussions for the national economy and the country's social and political crisis. Globally, IMF data indicates that GDP grew 2.8% in 2014. This was predicted to shrink even further in 2015, creating real difficulties for Brazil throughout 2015 and probably 2016. It would also affect other Latin America and Caribbean countries, including Mexico, albeit in different ways.

Brazil's relationship with China is especially striking. The Chinese colossus has been an extremely dynamic presence on the world market in recent years, posing a real competitive threat to Western imperialist powers and Japan, which have spent the last ten years in a downward spiral of slowdown

---

44 Ibid.

45 ECLAC, *Preliminary Overview of the Economies of Latin America and the Caribbean* (Santiago de Chile: United Nations, 2014), 50, http://repositorio.cepal.org/bitstream/handle/11362/37345/31/S1420977_en.pdf. The 2015 figure is from the IBGE.

and recession. It's emergence as a world power alongside the traditional global powerhouses is relatively new, and it is still hard to determine whether it is in a condition to become a new imperialist centre with its own 'satellite countries' or dependent hinterland which it might actively feed off in order to compete with the imperialisms in crisis. All that can be said is that if this country-empire continues making such huge strides forward in terms of its productive processes and competitiveness then it really will come to represent a new 'centre-periphery theorem' alongside the traditional centre-periphery system which emerged in postcolonial Latin America and the Caribbean and then became more generalised after the Second World War.

This brings us to how much Latin America's dependency on China has increased in the last decade. In 2000 only 1% of its exports went to China. Ten years later that figure had jumped to 8%, with raw materials and manufactures made using natural resources especially prominent. This relationship had been consolidating itself since 2008 as China increased its exports of manufactures, while Latin America's largely commodity-based exports rose to around 60%.[46]

But as noted earlier, Latin America's relationship with China and with international trade generally appears to have suffered from the collateral effects of the aforementioned fall in energy and raw material prices and gradual decline in the rate of Chinese economic growth over the last three years. As a result, all those countries that had been enjoying significant growth rates (Chile, Brazil, Argentina, Peru and Venezuela) are now feeling the effects of a slowdown which, as in the past, will make it harder for governments to implement anti-recessionary policies aimed at reviving the internal market and freeing up credit so as to at least soften the impact of the decline in people's purchasing power.

Faced with so many economic and financial problems, triggered largely by the fall in raw material prices and the contraction of economic growth rates in Brazil and other Latin American countries, it is hard to imagine any serious attempt being made to change the current pattern of capitalist reproduction and alleviate these difficulties by replacing the extractivist dependent primary-exporter model with one based on industry, the internal market and the export of manufacturing goods. Even if such a change were possible it would be a long time coming, and in the meantime governments would be forced to take measures which would seriously undermine living and working conditions.

Given the degree of uncertainty about the decisions that the big companies and capitals which determine the course of the global capitalist economy will make, it is virtually impossible to predict the exact forms the structural

46 Other Asian countries also increased their share of Latin American exports between 2000 and 2010, with the total for Asia's developing countries rising from 3.5% to 15%. ECLAC, *Latin America and the Caribbean*, 51.

crisis will take or the policies governments and international bodies will subsequently adopt in order to protect the interests of big international capital, which is the strategic subject that overdetermines the march of nations, productive processes and markets. What is clear however is that the crisis will have a very damaging effect on those dependent economies which, as we have seen, limit themselves to production for export, be that of manufactured goods from the *maquilas* (Mexico and Central America) or the extractivism of the Southern Cone countries and Brazil's primary-export model.

One way that capital *can* protect business and with it profit rates is to recycle itself *abroad* via the capital flows that fractions of the dependent Brazilian bourgeoisie—allied or not to foreign capital—have generated elsewhere. Here we might recall the Treaty of Itaipu signed by the military governments of Stroessner (Paraguay) and Emílio Garrastazu Médici (Brazil) on 26 April 1973. The Treaty benefitted Brazil and in particular its ruling class by giving it financial, political and military control over Paraguay's Itaipu hydroelectric dam, thus symbolising its increasingly sub-imperialist approach to bringing other countries under the aegis of its mode of capital accumulation and reproduction:

> The treaty establishes that Paraguay cannot freely use its share of the electricity (50%), but must give any unused electricity up to Brazil in exchange for compensation; it also gives priority to employing Brazilians to administer the binational dam and authorises the military invasion of Paraguayan territory in the event of any threat to its security. These requirements have not been amended over the decades, and show how the Brazilian state's political, economic and military control over the dam serves as a means of furthering the growth of its monopolies.[47]

It should be noted that the electricity generated by Itaipu with Brazil as its destination is distributed by Furnas Centrales Eléctricas S.A, a company controlled by state holding Eletrobras, which is also a monopoly. The asymmetrical and unjustly subordinate relationship between Brazil and Paraguay becomes apparent upon looking at land ownership and at production, where there is a clear wage gap between workers from the two countries. In terms of land ownership, 2013 figures show Brazilians own around 12% of Paraguayan land as private property. Meanwhile the hourly rate paid to a skilled Paraguayan worker in the textile industry is about 3.9 US dollars, whereas their Brazilian equivalent earns US$10.11 dollars, a difference of 61%. An unskilled Paraguayan

47 Cecilia Vuyk, *Subimperialismo brasileño y dependencia del Paraguay. Los intereses económicos detrás del Golpe de Estado de 2012* (Asunción, Paraguay: Cultura y Participación para el Cambio Social, 2014), 6.

worker in the same sector earns $2.65 an hour, compared to the $4.24 an hour paid to their Brazilian counterpart, or 37.50% more.[48]

Another important advantage for Brazilian businesses lies in the use they can make of Paraguay's Maquila Law of 3 July 1997 (regulated by the Presidential Decree of 17 July 2000).[49] The law offers tax exemption to foreign companies importing machinery and raw materials as long as the final product is for export. It also provides for a one-off tax of 1% on the import value when the product leaves Paraguay. This explains why 80% of the total capital invested in Paraguayan maquilas is Brazilian – a similar share to that of US businesses in the Mexican maquilas. Thanks to this level of Brazilian investment the sector has grown, with exports from the maquilas rising by 52% between 2013 and 2014 – an increase of over US$260 million.

There are other important reasons behind the expansion of Brazilian companies into Paraguay. These include

a) The availability of cheap labour: although the minimum wage is higher in Paraguay than in Brazil—US$325 a month versus $204.10 respectively based on the exchange rate during September 2015 – Paraguayan businesses do not have to pay into an equivalent of the Brazil's FGTS (Employee's Severance Guarantee Fund) or pay a trade union contribution. Furthermore Paraguayan workers enjoy only 12 days of paid holidays for every five years worked, compared to 30 days for the same length of service in Brazil.
b) Lower taxes: in Paraguay taxes are lower because income tax and VAT are charged at 10% on average. In contrast income tax in Brazil is charged at 25% in addition to three additional taxes which together come to more than 25%: PIS (Social Integration Programme), Cofins (Contribution for the Financing of Social Security), and ICMS (Services and Merchandise Circulation Tax).
c) Lower production costs: especially important given the deep structural crisis and crisis of industrial production currently affecting Brazil's economy. Energy is 50% cheaper in Paraguay than in Brazil, thus making a major difference.[50]

---

48 The figures are from Cecilia Vuyk, *Subimperialismo brasileño*, 11.

49 The Law and the Decree can both be viewed on the website of the Executive Secretariat of the National Council of the Export Maquila Industry (*Secretaría Ejecutiva del Consejo Nacional de la Industria Maquiladora de Exportación de Paraguay*), http://maquila.gov.py/EN/leyes-relacionadas-a-la-maquila.php.

50 Figures taken from Heloísa Mendonça, "Empresas brasileiras migram para o Paraguai atraídas por baixos custos," *El País*, 11 September 2015, http://brasil.elpais.com/brasil/2015/09/10/politica/1441837292_242802.html.

Initiative for the Integration of Regional Infrastructure in South America (IIRSA)

The Initiative for the Integration of Regional Infrastructure in South America (IIRSA) was begun by the Cardoso government before Lula enthusiastically took up the baton. In general terms it is an indication of how much the Brazilian presence has expanded in the region through its role in building infrastructure for the three key sectors: transport, energy and communications.

The project is made up of different regional Integration and Development Hubs:

- Andean Hub
- Southern Andean Hub
- Capricorn Hub
- Amazon Hub
- Guianese Shield Hub
- Southern Hub
- Paraguay-Parana Waterway Hub
- Central Interoceanic Hub
- MERCOSUR-Chile
- Peru-Brazil-Bolivia

Brazil is the hegemonic partner, participating in 8 of these 10 Hubs while other South American countries only participate in two at most. One sign of its dominance is that the MERCOSUR-Chile and Peru-Brazil-Bolivia Hubs together receive over US$57 billion, which is almost 60% of all IIRSA investment. If we add the Capricorn Hub (Chile, Argentina, Paraguay, Brazil), that figure rises to 70%.

To achieve and maintain its hegemony, Brazil uses the BNDES and the Growth Acceleration Program,[51] both of which play a key role in the IIRSA. The government-backed BNDES provides credit on the condition that it is used to purchase and invest in exclusively Brazilian goods and services. This ensures that regional infrastructure integration supports the outflow of Brazilian commodities and capitals. In that way, it uses the IIRSA to guarantee the

51 Alex de Geus, "Las caras de IIRSA: ¿integración regional o interconexión sudaméricana para la explotación de recursos naturales a favor de Brasil y/o del empresariado mundial?" (Universidad Complutense de Madrid, 2011), http://www.academia.edu/2219320/Las_caras_de_IIRSA_integraci%C3%B3n_regional_o_interconexi%C3%B3n_Sudam%C3%A9ricana.

reproduction of capitalist and sub-imperialist expansion in its regional sphere of influence.[52]

However in some countries such as Bolivia and Peru, indigenous and social movements have denounced the environmental damage the project has caused as threatening the very existence of the region's native communities. Atilio Boron concludes that the IIRSA is

> ... a project that did not emerge as a response to the region's social and economic needs, or the demands of civil society, social movements and political forces, but one that was pushed forwards by the IDB [Inter-American Development Bank] with the intention of developing and integrating transport, energy and telecommunications infrastructure and so consolidate Latin America's export-orientated economies within 10 years. With this in mind the aim is to organize South America's geographical spaces around the development of a complex regional system of land, air and river transport, oil and gas pipelines, waterways, sea and river ports, and electrical and fibre-optic lines, to name a few; always and absolutely of course under the logic of neoliberalism.[53]

Here we once again find the neoliberal State promoting and executing important infrastructure, including energy and communications projects, under the essentially capitalist criteria of seeking maximum profits for its investors, who are also supported by international bodies such as the IDB, Andean Development Corporation (Corporación Andina de Fomento – CAF), BNDES and, to a lesser extent, the World Bank.

The Expansionist Dynamic of Brazil's Trans-Latin Companies

There are a number of reasons why trans-Latin companies have expanded. These include

- The difficulties in realising commodities and capitals at home, as explained by Marini in the body of work cited in Chapter 2 of this book.
- The continuous need to look abroad because of internal market saturation owing largely to labour super-exploitation, low wages and problems in realising commodities.

52 Flynn, "Between Subimperialism and Globalization," 20.

53 Borón, *América Latina*, 164.

- The search for access to natural resources and sources of raw materials.
- Foreign investment as a way of maintaining growth: leading companies can only survive by specialising and going global.

Trans-Latin companies use their operative and financial capacity to acquire strategic assets in other countries. This enables them to transform the way they operate, because assets with greater added value and technological content can make processes more efficient. However, "very few have invested outside their country to undertake different activities and thus scale up the value chain; there are virtually no examples of trans-Latins acquiring strategic assets abroad."[54]

Between 2004 and 2013 trans-Latin companies from Latin America and the Caribbean invested US$30 billion a year on average overseas (i.e. outside their countries of origin) – some 100 billion in total.[55] They also significantly increased in number, as Table 3 shows:

TABLE 3 *Developing economies: Presence of largest companies, 2004–2013 (number of companies)*

	2004	2006	2008	2010	2013
Latin America	44	53	66	77	69
Brazil	19	22	31	37	31
Mexico	18	17	18	18	19
Chile	5	6	8	9	9
Colombia	0	2	3	6	6
Venezuela (Bolivarian Rep. of)	0	2	2	4	1

Source: ECLAC, *Foreign Direct Investment*, based on data for several years in the Forbes Global 2000 Leading Companies, available at http://www.fores.com/global2000/list/.

Brazil originally began to expand its foreign direct investment (FDI) in the 1970s as a way to stimulate exports, focussing especially on energy resources. By 1990

54 ECLAC, *Foreign Direct Investment in Latin America and the Caribbean* (Santiago de Chile: United Nations, 2013), 99, http://repositorio.cepal.org/bitstream/handle/11362/36861/S1420130_en.pdf.

55 ECLAC, *Foreign Direct Investment*, 65.

its cumulative FDI stood at over US$40 billion, a figure that other developing economies would only reach many years later. Mining corporation Vale do Rio Doce and some construction and engineering firms began to expand overseas in the 1980s, in some cases to other continents such as Africa. This trend continued into the 1990s, with some companies becoming ever more specialized whilst others started to diversify. Petrobras, for example, invested in the refining, distribution and marketing of petroleum products in Bolivia, and is now the largest company exploiting gas and making lubricants there, as well as owning around a quarter of Bolivia's petrol stations.

Another characteristic of the Brazilian trans-Latins is that they are based in Latin America itself, although as noted the largest among them have also expanded into other continents.[56] Vale is the largest investor in Africa: it now has over US$7,700 billion tied up in nine countries, having acquired mining companies in South Africa, the Democratic Republic of the Congo and Equatorial Guinea. In 2012 the company's coal mining project in Mozambique became fully operational, and it also owns iron ore reserves in Guinea. It has invested heavily in power plants, railways and port infrastructure. Elsewhere, Petrobras runs oil operations in Angola, Libya and Nigeria, and is looking into similar opportunities in Ethiopia and Benin. It furthermore plans to build an ethanol production plant in Mozambique.

Brazilian engineering and construction firms with a presence in Africa include Odebrecht, Andrade Gutierrez, Camargo Corrêa, and Queiroz Galvão. Odebrecht has participated in oil and gas projects, infrastructure projects, residential condominium-building, urban planning and biofuel production. Since 2006, the BNDES has provided US$3.2 billion in loans to develop 65 different projects in Angola, of which 32 were carried out by Odebrecht.[57]

For some authors, it is thanks to its considerable industrial strength that Brazil has succeeded in consolidating its regional presence. Katz comments that

> The expansion of the Brazilian multinationals has awoken certain expectations with respect to the eventual consolidation of an economic driving force for regional development. Yet such hopes will run up against the transnational character of these companies and the conflicts that result from the everyday operation of these firms. Far from displaying

56 Ibid., 77.

57 Ibid., 81.

> more benevolent behaviour than their counterparts in Europe and the United States, these companies spark strong tensions with the region's small countries. These conflicts in turn fuel important internal tensions among the Brazilian elites between those in favour of unmitigated support and those that urge only conditional support for these companies.[58]

It must be stressed that without state backing it is hard to imagine Brazilian companies expanding abroad in such favourable conditions and with the same level of support to help them weather periods of difficulty for internal markets and the effects of financial crises on the import/export cycle. ECLAC describes this support in the following terms:

> Brazil is unique in Latin America because of state backing for FDI in the form of financial support from National Bank for Economic and Social Development (BNDES). The bank's productive development policy, put in place in 2008, aims specifically at positioning Brazilian companies among global leaders in their sectors, targeting the aviation, oil, gas, petrochemical, bioethanol, mining, pulp and paper, steel and meat industries (BNDES, 2008). BNDES can take an ownership stake in Brazilian trans-Latins making new acquisitions, providing financing with performance requirements designed to provide the bank with a share in future profits and granting special lines of credit to certain companies (Sennes and Camargo Mendes, 2009). Since 2005, BNDES has granted financing to several enterprises for overseas expansion, totalling US$5.750 billion.
>
> For example, BNDES purchased 100% of the US$1.26 billion in notes issued by Marfrig to acquire Keystone Foods, as well as a large part of the bonds issued by JBS Friboi in compliance with the guarantees for the purchase of Pilgrim's Pride for US$800 million. The bank currently holds a 20% interest in Marfrig and a stake of nearly 25% in JBS Friboi. BNDES also granted a special loan to Itautec to enable the acquisition of Tallard in the United States, and has opened special lines of credit for leading software and pharmaceutical firms like Prosoft and Profarma respectively (Sennes and Camargo Mendes, 2009).[59]

---

58 Katz, "The Singularities of Latin America," 208.

59 ECLAC, *Foreign Direct Investment*, 83–84.

The data shows that FDI by Brazilian trans-Latins fell from 2009 onwards, reaching negative figures as a result of the difference between capital inflow (i.e. of foreign capital) and outflow. However Brazil remains the largest exporter of FDI in the region, and Brazilian companies continue to pursue an expansionist strategy:

> Brazil has the largest stock of FDI abroad in the region, but for the fourth year running it reported negative FDI outflows in 2014 according to the methodology of the fifth edition of the IMF Balance of Payments Manual. This does not mean that Brazilian companies are abandoning their investments abroad. Indeed, in 2014 Brazilian companies invested US$19.556 billion in capital contributions, which is the highest figure since 2011, but received US$23.096 billion in net loans from subsidiaries abroad. The result is a negative inflow of US$3.540 billion, similar to last year's figure. New investments in 2014 primarily targeted the financial services sector and telecommunications.[60]

Brazilian FDI also declined because a rise in domestic interest rates led companies to finance their domestic operations by borrowing abroad where rates were much lower. As a result, and in contrast with their Mexican and Chilean counterparts, Brazilian trans-Latins' rate of expansion decreased.[61] This trend will probably continue if domestic interest rates and inflation keep rising, economic growth further contracts, and the currency continues to be devalued. All of these factors shrink the internal market and cause job losses and tax hikes, leading to regressive income redistribution and heightened social discontent. If it does continue then it raises the question of what impact the international crisis will have on the situation, given the fall in raw material prices and the slowdown of the Chinese economy upon which the Brazil so now depends.

Conclusion

The most prolonged and advanced process of industrialisation in Latin America began to show signs of having run its course in the late 1990s, when the restructuring of Brazil's production inaugurated a new pattern of capital reproduction – one that was dependent, extractivist and export-orientated. This

60 Ibid., 33.

61 Ibid., 81.

new pattern was experiened in two distinct phases. During the first phase, the price of the raw materials and energy products exported by most of Latin America's dependent economies continued to rise. This benefitted Brazil hugely, as it did other exporters like Argentina and Chile. But in the second and current period these prices entered a downward cycle which now looks likely to be permanent, thus bringing to a final close the economic *boom* experienced during the first decade of the new century following Argentina's economic recovery in 2001–2002.

We have seen that the Brazilian economy grew during Lula's two terms in office but shrank by almost half under Rousseff, who confronted countless difficulties in her second period: an economy bordering on recession, rising inflation, corruption scandals and growing social discontent that had started to engulf the popular classes, including the workers. And given the global capitalist crisis and the political turmoil Brazil is still experiencing at the time of writing, the national situation can be expected to deteriorate even further as a consequence of the neoliberal measures being implemented by the interim right wing government of Michel Temer from the conservative PMDB.

Only a few dependent and underdeveloped countries such as Brazil in Latin America are in a position, economically, socially, politically and militarily speaking, to mitigate internal difficulties by expanding abroad and making productive investments in strategic sectors of the economies they invest in, by setting up plants and production and then reaping the full benefits. The State's unconditional support for these companies ensures their continued expansion, even when their overseas projects trigger protests by social and popular movements because of the threat they pose to communities and the environment. And finally, as we have stated, the difficulties experienced are conjunctural and are by no means in conflict with sub-imperialist capitalism's expansionist tendencies either in Latin America or further afield.

Epilogue

Even in the current era of so-called globalisation, neoliberalism and *pensée unique*, imperialism is still the chief *modus operandi* of the dominant capitalist system worldwide. The classic theory of imperialism identified its core features: the concentration of production and capital; the rise of monopolies; the fusion of banking and industrial capital and emergence of a financial oligarchy; the export of capitals over commodities; the formation of global capitalist monopolies which divided up the world between them, and finally the geographical carve-up of the entire planet by the leading capitalist powers. These features were then restructured in light of the new determinations and relationships now being reproduced across the world by both imperialism's leading representatives, with the United States acting as imperialism's centre, and other powers which have emerged as real players in international relations to challenge US hegemony, i.e. China, India, Iran, South Africa, and Russia.

Imperialism never did dissolve into abstract notions of 'globalization' or 'empire', or fantasies involving 'multitudes', a 'global village', 'the age of access,' and so on.[1] Rather the term *neo-imperialism* captures for us the new features it acquired in the 1980s and 1990s with the fall of the Berlin Wall, the Washington Consensus and the end of the Soviet Union and the socialist bloc. As we have seen, democratization in Latin America signalled the end neither of imperialism as a geopolitical and economic system of global domination, nor Brazilian sub-imperialism, nor the authoritarian neoliberal regimes common in Mexico and elsewhere. Instead it served to restructure them in the post-Cold War period, providing new foundations and characteristics.

For Marini this break was what really marked the difference between a counter-revolutionary (or counter-insurgency) state and a state of the fourth power. In the latter, the Armed Forces returned peacefully to their barracks and were then reinserted into institutional life via the National Security Council and other mechanisms there to ensure their interests were represented and demands heard within the new configuration of political power under civilian governments. Yet even then, with civilian rule, the separation of constitutional powers, and an electoral system that enables citizens to take part in a representative democracy, the institutions of military power remain an active presence

1 See for example Michael Hardt and Antonio Negri, *Empire* (Cambridge, Massachusetts: Harvard University Press, 2000) and Jeremy Rifkin, *The Age of Access: The New Culture of Hypercapitalism, Where All of Life is a Paid-for Experience* (New York: J.P. Tarcher, 2000).

 | DOI 10.1163/9789004319417_011

in economic, social and political life, ready to intervene when called upon to uphold the existing order. What is nowadays called a 'soft coup' is simply the means by which an alliance of the right and supranational forces has fought to re-impose its hegemony and domination of the State and society by overthrowing the progressive Latin American governments that have consolidated their power over the last two decades in countries like Venezuela, Bolivia, and Ecuador. In Argentina and Venezuela this alliance has already gone some way towards achieving its aims, even if developments in those two countries have yet to become a generalised political trend across the region (see footnotes 226, 255 and 331).

Once this process was completed, and with the 'ghost of communism' and 'radical leftism' no longer a threat, formally democratic political systems combining executive, legislative and judicial powers were put in place which were subject to functioning as 'governable', 'viable' and 'restricted' democracies tolerated and overseen by Washington whilst also reflecting the compromise agreed with the military as a *sine qua non* of the 'democratic transition'.[2] Meanwhile, in a parallel and corollary development, the market, globalization and neoliberalism were imposed as the new ideological cornerstones of dependent capitalism and harbingers of macroeconomic growth and development in dependent countries.

We have seen that in Brazil, and especially under PT administrations, this new process saw the neoliberal state continue to thrive whilst *neo-developmentalist* governments tried to contain and reduce poverty among the poorest and neediest in society. But we have also seen how both the global capitalist crisis and the crisis and deceleration of the Brazilian economy itself have now made these policies much harder to deliver, giving way to social austerity and macroeconomic adjustment programmes which have targeted variables such as the balance of payments, exchange rates, interest rates, inflation and social welfare. The crisis has been compounded by problems of corruption and impunity involving government, business and political figures, which have only fuelled social discontent.

The overall picture is completed by the prolonged recession in the developed economies of advanced capitalism, the vicissitudes of the US economy, and the end of the long economic boom in China, where growth in 2015 contracted

2 We would hypothesize that the process set in motion by the Bolivarian Revolution in Venezuela managed to break out of the straightjacket imposed on democracy, and that it is precisely by giving democracy a more radical form that, without breaking with capitalism and dependency, it has still been fiercely attacked by the right wing opposition and Washington, with the latter even threatening military intervention.

to the order of 7%. This was 0.5% less than in the previous three years and the Asian giant's lowest figure for 25 years. Growth was furthermore forecast to fall to 6.8% in 2016. Speaking at the opening of his country's National Assembly on 5 March 2015, Chinese Prime Minister Li Keqiang noted that this had already started to affect the global capitalist economy.[3]

For us, whilst the current world crisis is unfolding at the very centre of the capitalist system, it affects every single society and country. Its dynamic is linked to the ever receding possibility of economic reactivation as structural unemployment grows, labour market conditions become more precarious, and super-exploitation[4] becomes an ever more generalised means of trying to halt and/or reverse the falling profit rates suffered by the big global monopolies.

There is no doubt that the global capitalist economy's significant difficulties in recent years are largely a result of the structural and financial crisis which shook the world in 2008–2009. And despite some weak signs of recovery, these difficulties have continued up until the present, as shown by Figure 3 below:

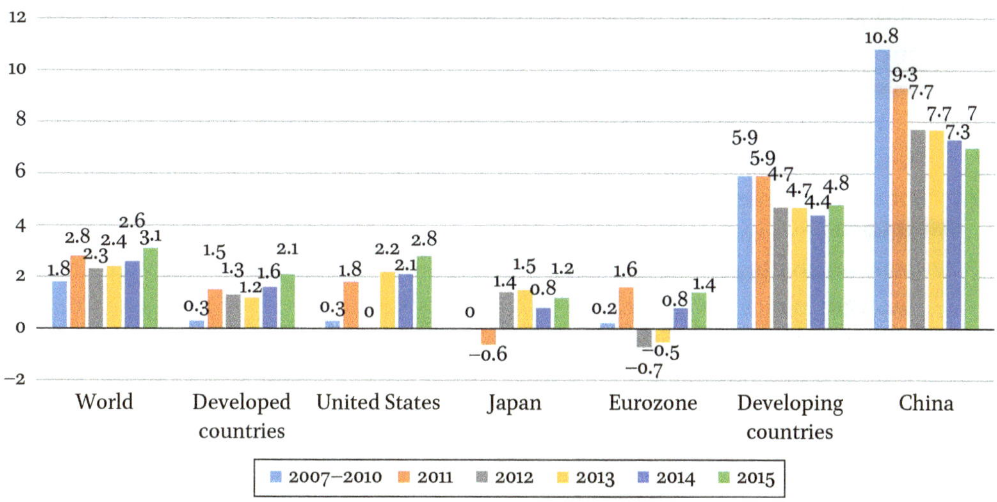

FIGURE 3 *Selected regions and countries: GDP growth, 2007–2015* (percentages)
Source: ECLAC, Preliminary Overview of the Economies of Latin America and the Caribbean (Santiago de Chile: United Nations, 2014), 13, based on United Nations, Global Economic Outlook (New York: Department of Economic and Social Affairs, October 2014), Figures for 2014 are estimates and those for 2015 are projections.

---

3 "China enfría su economía," *Periodismo Internacional Alternativo* (PIA), 6 March 2015, http://www.noticiaspia.org/china-enfria-su-economia/.

4 This issue is examined in Marini, "Proceso y tendencias," 49–68.

Of particular note is the Chinese economy's deceleration from an average yearly growth of 10.8% in 2007–2010 to 7% in 2015.[5] This has had predictably negative effects on foreign trade and especially Chinese imports from the Southern Cone in recent years. In 2014 ECLAC explained this situation in the following terms:

> ... The prices of a number of the region's export commodities, which had begun to fall in 2012, continued to trend downwards—or stood still, in certain cases— in 2014. This was partly the effect of shrinking global demand for these goods, owing chiefly to China's economic slowdown, and partly the effect of an expansion in global supply resulting from earlier investments in the natural resources sector.[6]

Thus a slowdown in Chinese demand and intense commodity speculation explain the country's lower growth. Another reason for this trend has been the Chinese government's strategic decision to prioritise endogenous development based on the internal market and income growth policies, as the Prime Minister announced to the National Assembly in 2015. This does not mean however that China has abandoned its foreign trade policy, which remains a vital component of its development strategy.

Other than in the most dynamic 'developing countries' such as China, India, South Africa and Nigeria, economies elsewhere have performed very poorly, with devastating consequences for the global economy. The severe slowdowns experienced by Japan and the Eurozone (see Figure 3) show no sign of abating in the medium or long term, despite the adjustment and austerity policies imposed in recent years by the Troika of the European Commission (EC), European Central Bank (ECB) and International Monetary Fund (IMF) to 'try' and reverse the trend. Hence it is no surprise that global economic forecasts are being revised downwards on a daily basis. Adding to the gloom, there do not seem to be any prospects of a medium term 'recovery' on the horizon either – only more structural reforms which seek to deal with the crisis and the problems faced by business and global finance capital by attacking the living and working conditions and welfare provision of workers worldwide.

---

5 Furthermore, the National Bureau of Statistics of China has adjusted GDP growth for 2015 downwards to 6.9%. See http://data.stats.gov.cn/english/.

6 ECLAC, *Preliminary Overview of the Economies of Latin America and the Caribbean* (Santiago de Chile: United Nations, 2014), 33, http://repositorio.cepal.org/bitstream/handle/11362/37345/31/S1420977_en.pdf.

At the same time, the global capitalist system needs to grow at a compound rate of at least 3% just to ensure its 'survival'.[7] But ever since WWII it has exhibited a secular tendency to decline. Thus whilst average growth between 1945 and 1974 stood at over 6%, this fell to 5% between 1974–1980, and down again to 3.4% in the 1980s, 1.8% in the 1990s, and stood at or below 0% during the 2000s.[8] By then, the famous 'thirty glorious years' that made up the golden age of capitalism were truly over with no hope of coming back, despite the deluded hopes of the international financial institutions. US average growth, for example, fell from 4.4% in the 1960–1968 period, to 2.5% in 1979–1985. Likewise growth in Japan between the same two periods declined from 10.4% to 4%; in West Germany from 4.1% to 3%; in France from 5.4% to 1.1%; and in the UK from 3.1% to 1.2%. Average growth across all OCDE member states fell from 5.1% to 2.2%.[9]

Alongside this global economic trend, another emerging feature of capitalism has been the ever greater dissociation between the economic cycle and unemployment/underemployment rates. As Marini noted, before 1973 unemployment rates had stabilised at 4% of the workforce. This figure then shot up in the 24 most industrialized countries, hitting a peak in 1983 of 8%, or over 30 million people. But even as these countries came out of recession in the early part of the next decade, unemployment remained at around 6% in 1990 and rose again in the years that followed.[10] Proving Marini's thesis correct, by 2012 it had reached 7.9% in the OCDE countries; 10.5% in the European Union, and 11.4% in the Eurozone.[11] Hence capitalism has only managed to grow anywhere on the back of higher unemployment, wage cuts, greater exploitation, and a huge shift towards flexible and precarious employment.

In view of these trends the IMF realises that capitalism is now utterly incapable of guaranteeing the kind of stable economic growth rates which might fuel a recovery with a social component: one consisting of better wages,

---

7 David Harvey, *The Enigma of Capital and the Crises of Capitalism*, (London: Profile Books, 2010), 126.

8 Kostas Vergopoulos, *Globalização: o fim de um ciclo. Ensayo sobre a instabilidade internacional* (Rio de Janeiro: Contraponto, 2005), 73.

9 David Harvey, *The Condition of Postmodernity* (Oxford: Blackwell, 1989), 130.

10 Marini, "Proceso y tendencias," 55.

11 See Eurostat, July 2012, http://epp.eurostat.ec.europa.eu/cache/ITY_PUBLIC/3-31082012-BP/EN/3-31082012-BP-EN.PDF. International Labour Organization, *Global Employment Trends 2014: Risk of a Jobless Recovery?* Table 1, with forecasts for 2014 and 2015 (Geneva: ILO, 2014), 19, http://www.ilo.org/wcmsp5/groups/public/---dgreports/---dcomm/---publ/documents/publication/wcms_233953.pdf.

productive jobs and in general, a return to the old Keynesian welfare state of the Thirty Glorious Years, that long *boom'*

> ...built upon a certain set of labour control practices, technological mixes, consumption habits and configurations of political- economic power, and that this configuration can reasonably be called Fordist-Keynesian.[12]

In this regard, a team of IMF writers have turned to the concept of 'potential output', which they define as "... the level of output consistent with stable inflation (no inflationary or deflationary pressure)", to make the following observations:

- In recent years potential output growth in both advanced and emerging economies has gone down. In the former this trend has been apparent since the early 2000s at least.
- The current global financial crisis is related to both a reduction in the "*level* of potential output" in advanced and emerging economies and the continual fall in their growth rates.
- In the former, potential growth will probably "increase slightly from current rates but remain below pre-crisis rates in the medium term". The cause of this is to be found in "aging populations" and "the slow increase in capital growth from current rates"
- Potential output growth in the emerging economies is likely to fall even more in the medium term due to "aging populations, weaker investment, and lower productivity growth as the technological gaps between these economies and advanced economies get narrower".[13]

They conclude that

> Reduced prospects for potential growth will raise new policy challenges such as achieving fiscal sustainability. Increasing potential output will need to be a priority in major advanced and emerging market economies.[14]

12 Harvey, *The Condition of Postmodernity*, 124.

13 IMF, "Press Points for Chapter 3: Where Are We Headed? Perspectives on Potential Output," *World Economic Outlook*, (April 2015): 1, https://www.imf.org/external/pubs/ft/weo/2015/01/pdf/sum.pdf.

14 Ibid.

Interestingly, this analysis covers the periods both before and after the 2008–2009 crisis, and in doing so reveals qualitative differences between the structural behaviour of advanced capitalist countries and dependent / underdeveloped countries respectively. Thus in the first period potential growth began to decline in the former just as it started rising in the latter. In both cases this was a result of productivity differentials, with production declining in the advanced countries following a period of growth fuelled by innovations in the field of information technology, whilst growing in the dependent countries because of "structural transformation" and an "expansion of global and regional value chains", which "stimulated technology and knowledge transfers". Nonetheless this did not help our countries overcome the dependent and underdeveloped condition in which they remain today.

In the second period, both advanced and dependent economies have suffered a decline in output and average economic growth rates. For the IMF, economic growth rates declined because of the reduction in potential growth, which is itself related to the global financial crisis:

> In advanced economies, potential growth declined from slightly less than 2 percent in the precrisis period (2006–07) to about 1½ percent during 2013–14, owing to reduced capital growth and adverse demographic factors not related to the crisis. In emerging market economies, potential growth declined by about 2 percentage points during this period, with lower total factor productivity growth accounting for the entire decline.[15]

Output and growth rates are both expected to continue to be lower than in the pre-crisis period, with the average potential growth rate in the advanced capitalist countries forecast to rise by just 0.3% to 1.6% in 2015–20 compared to 1.3% during 2008–2014, which again the report puts down to demographic factors and sluggish investment growth. In comparison, potential growth in the (dependent) emerging economies is predicted to fall from 6.5% in 2008–2014 to 5.2% in 2015–2020. This trend is explained by an aging population, structural limits to capital growth, and a lower increase in total factor productivity as those economies approach the 'technological frontier'. As for Latin America, the IMF estimates that potential growth will fluctuate around 3% over the 2015–2020 period – the region's lowest for 12 years.[16]

---

15 Ibid., 2.

16 "Prevé IMF que América Latina crecerá 3% en los próximos 5 años," *La Jornada*, 23 May 2015, http://www.jornada.unam.mx/2015/05/23/economia/023n3eco.

Overall the organisation sees declining medium and long term potential growth as posing a number of challenges, including how to maintain "fiscal sustainability"; the future course of monetary policy, and, most pressingly, whether to maintain or raise interest rates, especially in developed countries like the United States which have kept them at almost zero.[17] Unsurprisingly, its recommendations for addressing the situation include "structural reforms" to stimulate demand, private investment in infrastructure and other productive sectors, greater labour flexibility to make "human capital" more efficient and productive, and business restructuring, including staff reorganisation and layoffs. All these measures are intended to create the kind of conditions required by crisis-hit markets and inter-capitalist monopoly competition.

What we have described is part of a worldwide strategy which also encompasses the near-global imperial war the US is pursuing across the world – from the Ukraine and Syria to Iraq, Afghanistan and Yemen, as well as via Venezuela-style coup attempts. It is a strategy that also involves generalising the socio-economic regime of super-exploitation as an 'alternative' way for capital to confront the crisis and restore economic growth to the capitalist system, albeit at a much lower level than during the Thirty Glorious Years of Keynesian and Fordist capitalism.

At no other time since the stabilising strategies of neoliberalism and finance capital took hold in the 1980s have modern capitalist crises so needed to restructure the world of work in line with market logic and market conditions. No aspect is left untouched, be it wages, work processes, trade union education, training and qualifications, or the industrial reserve army of labour. Restructuring also means defeating the workers socially and politically, without which neoliberalism cannot really function. The role of the State in this process is a strategic one, its policies seek to raise profit rates, counteract the tendency for accumulation to slow down and — in alliance with Troika-led international monetary and financial bodies — restructure and deregulate the labour force and productive systems.

The austerity policies introduced in the advanced capitalist countries, and renewed in dependent ones in response to falling energy and commodity prices, are the most conspicuous sign of how capitalism has hit its structural and

17 As of 16 December 2015 the US Federal Reserve raised interest rates for the first time since June 2006, from a range of 0% to 0.25% to a new one of between 0.25% and 0.5%. It remains unclear what the impact of this will be on the global capitalist economy in terms of stock market investments, borrowing costs, exchange rates and the adjustments that governments will have to make to counter the negative effects it may have on their fiscal balances and balances of payment.

civilisational limits as a mode of production, life and work based on private property, labour exploitation, the plundering of natural resources, and systems of political domination which uphold the established order. But as we have seen, these policies and strategies have not even helped the State and capital to mitigate the structural and financial crisis of capitalism, let alone unleash a new wave of economic growth similar to that of the post-war period. In Latin America the global crisis has already begun to have a negative impact on key variables such as the balance of payments, employment, wages and inflation, leading to tax hikes, privatizations, and a squeeze on public finances. This has hit living, working and social conditions hard, even in so-called progressive countries like Brazil and Argentina, whose welfare policies had been of some help to people in the preceding years. The problem, as noted earlier, is that the right and business interests have ably exploited the social discontent generated by this economic crisis and the corruption and impunity that have gone with it to promote chaos and opposition to these and other recently elected governments of a similar ilk.

In Brazil the social effects of the capitalist crisis were seen when the *Movement Pase Libre* (MPL) burst onto the scene in June 2013 to mobilize the middle classes against public transport fare rises and the millions poured into staging the FIFA Confederations Cup– popularly dubbed the 'Copa de las Rebeliones' – between 15 and 30 June of that month, a year before the country also hosted the World Cup (12 June–13 July 2014).[18] This excerpt from Marini illustrates the historical similarities between these current day social struggles and those of the past:

> In addition to the inter-bourgeois contradictions currently being shattered by the crisis and the desperation of the working masses whose living standards are again being driven down after receiving a small wage rise which had sparked hopes of a new trend in that direction, the main source of political instability in Brazil right now appears to be the petty bourgeoisie's reaction to the situation. Because of the strategic role it plays in the system of domination, when the petty bourgeoisie becomes an insurgent movement it acts as a spark and prefigures a heightening of class struggle in the country....[19]

---

18 An analysis of these protests can be found in Ricardo Antunes and Ruy Braga, "Los días que conmovieron a Brasil. Las rebeliones de Junio-Julio de 2013," *Herramienta* 53 (2013): 9–21.

19 Marini, "Estado y crisis en Brasil," 83.

The similarity between this description of the social conflict in 1960s Brazil and the conflicts and revolts triggered by the economic crisis and the Rousseff government's neoliberal policies in recent times shows that class struggle always remains a constant of the capitalist system, even if a particular conjuncture within a given historical period is favourable to the masses, such as during Lula's two terms in office.

Developments since Rousseff won her second mandate (2014–2018) suggest that Brazil is currently experiencing not just economic semi-stagnation but a difficult, conflict-ridden phase on a social and political level which holds out little promise for the centre-left government and its public policies. Class conflict, previously obscured from view by social democratic and neo-developmentalist policies, is now increasing in step with the deepening economic crisis, currency devaluation, rising living costs and even problems with the water supply in Sao Paulo, which is Brazil's most populated city in Brazil and the second most populated in Latin America. The situation has undoubtedly been compounded by the corruption and impunity at the country's largest public company, Petrobas, where business owners and top government officials have been exposed and brought to justice amidst a national and international public outcry. The federal police originally launched Operation Car Wash or *Petrolão* on 17 March 2014 to investigate the possible laundering of 10 billion Reales (3.7 billion dollars at the 17 March 2015 exchange rate of 3.35 Reales to the dollar). According to the press by April 2014 46 people were facing charges of organised crime for targeting the country's financial system and money laundering with 30 were already behind bars, including businessman Alberto Youssef and ex-Petrobras director Paulo Roberto Costa. Currently 50 people linked to corruption and embezzlement at the oil company are still being investigated and face possible jail sentences.

As the social and economic crisis has gathered steam, so too has the right wing and media-led movement against the PT government demanding the president's impeachment over the Petrobras scandal that so shook the country.[20] The Brazilian right has learned to exploit social discontent as adeptly as its Venezuelan counterparts by channelling it through social networks such as Facebook. In this way it drew at least a million protestors onto the streets of Sao Paulo on 15 March 2015, with thousands more in almost all of Brazil's other major cities. Their slogans included 'Dilma Out' and 'No to Corruption',

---

20 On 6 May 2016 the Senado voted to impeach Brazilian President Dilma Rousseff in order to secure her removal for her alleged part in 'crimes of responsibility'. Her political trial began on 12 May 2016, and she was removed from office for 180 days pending the Senate's final decision, which came on 31 August 2016 and confirmed her removal.

along with the less common but equally significant anti-communist and even fascist slogans raised by small, angry groups demanding military intervention – a stark reminder of the bloody military dictatorships of the 60s, 70s and 80s in Our America.

Observers identified three main groups with links to business and financial sectors as being behind the demonstrations. VemPraRua.net, formed in September 2013 and sympathetic to the PSDB, is considered the most moderate and did not demand impeachment. Its media profile was raised by the presence of ex-footballer Ronaldo, singer Wanessa Camargo and various actors and actresses on the day of the protest. *Movimento Brasil Livre* (MBL), one of the main anti-Dilma groups, is made up of young liberals and conservatives whose recipe for ending the crisis is a leaner state and the privatization of basic services such as education and health. And thirdly there is *Revoltados Online*, which organized the traditional *cacerolazos* in various cities. Run by 20 people, pro-impeachment and claiming to oppose corruption, it was they who sold the famous 'anti-Dilma kits' with the slogan 'God, Family and Property'[21] – an ominous throwback to the days leading up to the 1964 military coup.

Whatever its political aims and motivations, and without underestimating either the opportunities the situation offers to those fishing in troubled waters or indeed the PT and the government's responsibility for it, this movement should be seen as part and parcel of a global right wing offensive which is also evident in Venezuela, Ecuador, El Salvador, Argentina, Syria, the Ukraine and other countries where local governments have been destabilized by US-backed, right-wing 'local oppositions'. The US has recently re-launched its strategy for re-establishing its hegemony and supremacy in Latin America and the Caribbean and then using that as a springboard to refocus its offensive on China and Russia – without discarding military action. The US needs to overcome these two new and very real rivals if it is to realign capitalism and imperialism with its own geo-strategic interests and those of other countries like Germany and France in Europe.

Contra what is argued in some of the literature on the subject, geopolitics and economics are inseparable, so it is only natural that these global geopolitical developments and the crisis and restructuring of reproduction patterns in Latin America should feed into one another. The region's future prospects in the context of a world capitalist crisis are therefore far from straightforward.

---

21 Central Sindical and Popular-CONLUTAS, "Manifestaciones cuestionan en las calles al gobierno Dilma," *Rebelión*, 17 Marc, 2015, http://www.rebelion.org/noticia.php?id=196556.

In this book we have argued that there are currently two hegemonic patterns of reproduction at work in Latin America. One is the extractivist-dependent-exporter model typical of the Southern Cone. The other is based on industrial manufactures mainly produced by North American transnational corporations using the maquila industry export model. Mexico is the prime example of this second pattern, and Central America to a lesser extent. Prior to the 2008–2009 global crisis raw material and energy prices were continually rising, and it was conceivable then that the reprimarised extractivist model might be able to fuel economic growth in countries like Brazil where it had taken hold. In contrast the Mexican pattern or model of reproduction was by this time already reaching depletion. Mexico therefore considered adopting the primary exporter model, combining it perhaps with the production and export of manufactures, but focussing above all on the production and export of oil, raw materials and other agricultural products. Its plans appeared to receive a major boost from the 'structural reforms' with which government and global capital hoped to kickstart this new wave of 'capitalist development'. The *Mexican moment,* as the global media and business pretentiously called this false dawn of a new era of 'economic development', was supposed to be the envy of the entire world, and the Mexican president waxed lyrical about the panacea represented by the 'new capitalism'.[22] But unhappily for both the local technocracy and global capital, since 2012 not only have Mexico's average growth rates fallen, but a new, long term structural cycle has begun to disrupt and damage Latin American economies across the board.

In those countries where the first pattern of reproduction and accompanying State policies predominate, this new cycle has made it a lot harder to counter the effects of falling global commodity and energy prices by restructuring the economy through a process of reindustrialisation. This is simply because such a process would take several years without any positive short or medium term results, as indeed Brazilian authorities and businesses have recognised in the light of the country's current macroeconomic difficulties. Meanwhile, in those economies characterised by the second pattern of dependent capital reproduction (Mexico and Central America), we find that the declining price of Mexico's chief export, oil, has made it impossible for it to embrace the primary-extractivist model. This is even more the case since international and private national capital benefitted from oil privatisation. Neither has it been possible for Mexico to rely for the production and export of manufactures on a maquila sector dominated by transnational North American corporations.

22 See by this same author *México (des)cargado. Del Mexico's moment al Mexico's disaster* (Ciudad de México: UNAM / Itaca, 2016).

Only 5% of the sector's materials have to be sourced from 'national value chains', so maquilas have become little more than North American economic enclaves where capital accumulation and reproduction only serve to increase business and profitability. This brings us back to Marini's concept of economic annexation, which differs from sub-imperialism in the ways described earlier.

Whilst Mexico is almost entirely dependent on the United States, Brazil enjoys a lot more relative autonomy. It is this autonomy which makes it a sub-power (*antagonistic cooperation*) and able, if not to overcome its historical-structural dependency on the advanced economies (and now China), then certainly to expand its capitals, businesses and products both regionally and to other continents such as Africa where, as we have seen, its presence has grown in recent years. The reality of this expansion is confirmed by the fact that during the first eight months of 2014 Brazil's outward direct investment was positive[23] for the first time since 2010. As seen earlier, this may eventually resolve Brazil's crisis and rising domestic interest rates to some degree; and for capitalist businesses overseas expansion could prove to be the ideal way to offset the fall in profits caused by declining domestic growth rates.

Capital must of course exploit the local advantages a country presents and compensate for any problems encountered by exploiting local workers even more. It is true that some studies[24] show a decline in the rate of exploitation during the two Lula governments and during Rousseff's first term too. But given a combination of falling export prices, rising taxes, rising domestic interest rates and plummeting economic growth rates, it is also likely that current neoliberal austerity policies and the inflationary upturn will lead global social capital to try and counteract the crisis and falling profits by raising average rates of exploitation once again. If this happens it will probably lead to a new wave of job losses and greater labour flexibility and precarity, which will be institutionalised by new pro-capital labour reforms. Indeed, reforms of this kind have already provoked major protests by workers up and down the country. In May 2015 demonstrations were held simultaneously in at least ten states against a new pro-outsourcing law seen as an attack on workers' rights. Furthermore, the CUT, the country's largest trade union federation and which had backed Rousseff's re-election, asked her to veto Provisional Measures 664 and 665 after they were approved by the Senate on 9 June 2015, because by making

23 ECLAC, "Foreign Direct Investment in Latin America Declines 23% in the First Half of 2014," *Press Releases*, 24 October 2014, http://www.cepal.org/en/pressreleases/foreign-direct-investment-latin-america-declines-23-first-half-2014.

24 Eleutério F.S. Prado, "O mau humor do 'mercado'," 17 April 2014, https://eleuterioprado.files.wordpress.com/2014/04/o-mau-humor-do-mercado.pdf.

it harder to apply for sickness benefits, widows' pensions, and unemployment benefit they undermined previous working class gains.[25]

As in the past, the miracle cure offered for the mounting problems of a Brazilian economy afflicted by both a structural crisis and a global crisis of the capitalist mode of production and its core contradictions lies in a combination of luxury consumption, the world market and, above all, state action on behalf of the ruling class and big capital operating in the country. President Rousseff and other top government officials have spoken on several occasions in support of not only changing the course of the current commodity export-centred 'economic model' – in which industrial manufactures only make up around 37% of exports – but also of intensifying overseas expansion as the most realistic way to tackle the national crisis. Again, Marini was not mistaken. It was he who pointed out that this – sub-imperialism – represented the structural 'solution' for a country accustomed to looking abroad to resolve the acute problems of production and realisation encountered by a pattern of capital reproduction such as the current one that is dependent on the world market and the dynamics of transnational corporate investment and profitability.

The Marxist theory of dependency and Marini in particular provide a broad framework for understanding how sub-imperialism is constituted in its totality in Latin American capitalist social formations under concrete historical conditions at the intermediate level. This is the level at which dependency is located as a theory and as a subject of study, as we saw in Chapter 2.

Although several countries both in and outside Latin America share features and characteristics of sub-imperialism, only Brazil is constituted as a state and an economic system on the basis of those characteristics. This ultimately distinguishes it from both the dominant imperialism of advanced capitalism (US, UK, Germany, France, Japan) and from other countries on the dependent periphery of capitalism- indeed the vast majority of the world's underdeveloped countries- which lack the conditions, means, or history of prior processes needed to constitute themselves as sub-imperialist. Instead, they end up being dominated not only by the classic imperialist powers but by sub-imperialist bourgeoisies and ruling classes who possess the social, economic, political and military means to harness their productive apparatuses, investments and exports towards obtaining huge returns on the back of capital's exploitation of labour, and are able to make up the value and surplus value they transfer to the imperialist centres, because as sub-imperialist countries their core

25 See Ministério do Trabalho e Emprego do Brazil, a Previdência Social, *Resumo das Regras nas Medidas Provisórias* no. 664 e no. 665, n.d., http://www.previdencia.gov.br/wp-content/uploads/2015/03/Cartilha-regras-MP-664.pdf.

condition is essentially one of simultaneously depending on imperialist productive systems, the dynamics and contradictions of the world market, and the international division of labour.

Along with the rest of Latin America, Brazil currently faces a marked decline in its chief economic indicators (GDP, balance of payments, higher inflation, lower commodity prices etc.) along with heightening social discontent and the advance of the organised right. Problems of corruption and impunity have only added fuel to this fire. The 2018 presidential elections offer an opportunity, albeit one that is far from guaranteed, for progressive and popular forces to recapture the power currently in the hands of pro-business sectors and the conservative right.

At the same time and unlike in other less developed countries on the capitalist periphery, Brazilian capitalism has the strategic option of combating its long term structural crisis by stepping up overseas expansion through both direct capital investment and the private capital of local companies who are in a position to expand. We have seen that the Brazilian government has so far unconditionally supported this expansion, largely through BNDES, and will do so even more if in the hands of conservative and pro-business parties and groups who will no doubt will further refine the sub-imperialist project on the basis of labour super-exploitation, extra support for a luxury consumer sector geared towards the privileged classes, and, above all, overseas expansion, just as Marini argued in his most important investigations, analysis and theoretical-political predictions.

Bibliography

Aguirre Rojas, Carlos Antonio. *Braudel a debate*. Ciudad de Mexico: JGH Editores, 1997.

Aguirre Rojas, Carlos Antonio, *La escuela de los Anales*. Madrid: Montesinos, 1999.

Aguirre Rojas, Carlos Antonio, Immanuel Wallerstein. *Crítica del sistema-mundo capitalista*. Ciudad de Mexico: ERA 2003.

Alves, Giovanni. *Trabalho e neodesenvolvimentismo. choque de capitalismo e nova degradação do trabalho no Brasil*. Bauru, Brazil: Projeto Editorial Praxis, 2014.

Anderson, Perry. "Las antinomias de Antonio Gramsci." *Cuadernos Políticos* 13 (Mexico), Editorial ERA, July–September 1977: 4–57.

Antunes, Ricardo and Ruy Braga. "Los días que conmovieron a Brasil. Las rebeliones de junio-julio de 2013." *Revista Herramienta* 53 (Buenos Aires) 53, July 2013: 9–21.

Aricó, José. *La cola del diablo, itinerario de Gramsci en América Latina*. Buenos Aires: Siglo XXI, 2005.

Assadourian, Carlos Sempat et. al. "Modos de producción en América Latina." In *Cuadernos de Pasado y Presente* 40 (Buenos Aires), 1973.

Astarita, Rolando. "Brasil, armamentismo y nacionalismo." http://rolandoastarita.wordpress.com/2012/04/11/brasil-armamentismo-y-nacionalismo/.

Bagú, Sergio. *Economía de la sociedad colonial. Ensayo de historia comparada de América Latina*. México: Editorial Grijalbo, Consejo Nacional para la Cultura y las Artes, 1992.

Bambirra, Vania. *Teoría de la dependencia: una anticrítica*. Mexico: Era, 1978.

Beinstein, Jorge. *Capitalismo senil, a grande crise da economia global*. Rio de Janeiro: Record, 2001.

Bernis, Gerard de. *El Capitalismo contemporáneo*. Ciudad de Mexico: Nuestro Tiempo, 1988.

Bezerra Heleno, Maurício Gurjão and Mônica Dias Martins. "Cooperação ou dominação? A política externa do governo Lula para a África." In *Tensões Mundiais World Tensions* (Fortaleza) 10, no. 18–19 (2014): 125–143.

Birch Jonah. "La teoría postcolonial en debate. Entrevista a Vivek Chibber." *Herramienta* 53 (2013): 157–169. http://www.herramienta.com.ar/revista-herramienta-n-53/la-teoria-postcolonial-en-debate-entrevista-vivek-chibber.

Blomström, Magnus and Björn Hettne. *Development Theory in Transition*. London: Zed Books, 1984.

Boron, Atilio. *Empire and Imperialism: A Critical Reading of Michael Hardt and Antonio Negri*. London: Zed Books, 2005.

Boron, Atilio. *América latina en la geopolítica del imperialismo*. Mexico: UNAM, 2014.

Bukharin, Nikolai. *Imperialism and World Economy*. London: Merlin Press, 1972.

Burgess, Mike and Daniel Wolf. "Brasil: el concepto de poder en la Escuela Superior de Guerra". *Cuadernos Políticos* 20, 1979: 89–103.

Carcanholo, Reinaldo. *Capital, essência e aparência*, vol.2. Expressão Popular: São Paulo, 2013.

Cardoso, Fernando Henrique. "Notas sobre el estado actual de los estudios de la dependencia." *Problemas del subdesarrollo latinoamericano*, edited by Sergio Bagú et al, 90–125. Editorial Nuestro Tiempo: México, 1976. Third edition.

Cardoso, Fernando Henrique and Enzo Faletto. *Dependencia y desarrollo en América Latina.* Ciudad de Mexico: Siglo XXI, 1969.

Carvas, Andrés. "Dilma, todo en contra." Proceso 1991, 2014. http://www.proceso.com.mx/?p=391988.

Castro-Gómez, Santiago. "Latinoamericanismo, modernidad, globalización. Prolegómenos a una crítica poscolonial de la razón." Available at: http://www.periodismo.uchile.cl/talleres/teoriacomunicacion/archivos/teoriassindisciplina.pdf.

Central Sindical and Popular-CONLUTAS. "Manifestaciones cuestionan en las calles al gobierno Dilma." *Rebelión*, 17 March 2015. http://www.rebelion.org/noticia.php?id=196556.

Chávez, Frías Hugo. *El socialismo del siglo XXI.* Caracas: Ministerio del Poder Popular para la Comunicación y la Información (Colección Cuadernos para el Debate), 2011.

Chossudovsky, Michel. "The Dangers of a Middle East Nuclear War." *Global Research,* 17 February 2006. http://www.globalresearch.ca/the-dangers-of-a-middle-east-nuclear-war/1988.

Córdova, Armando and Héctor Silva Michelena. *Aspectos teóricos del subdesarrollo.* 4th ed. Caracas: Época, 1977.

Coronil, Fernando. "Naturaleza del poscolonialismo: del eurocentrismo al globocentrismo." In *La colonialidad del saber: Eurocentrismo y ciencias sociales. Perspectiva americana,* edited by Edgardo Lander. Buenos Aires: CLACSO / UNESCO, 2000.

Crozier, Michel, Samuel P Huntington, and Jōji Watanuki. *The Crisis of Democracy: Report on the Governability of Democracies to the Trilateral Commission*. New York: New York University Press, 1975.

Cueva, Agustín. "Posfacio: los Años Ochenta: Una Crisis de Alta Intensidad (1977–1994)." In *Entre la Ira y la Esperanza y Otros Ensayos de Crítica Latinoamericana.* Compiled by Alejandro Moreano. Bogotá: CLACSO / Siglo del Hombre Editores, 2008.

DIEESE. "Remessas de lucros e dividendos: setores e a dinámica conômica brasileira." *Nota Técnica* 137, June 2014.

Durán Lima, José, and Alessia Lo Turco. "El comercio intrarregional en América Latina: patrón de especialización y potencial exportador." In *Los impactos de la crisis internacional en América Latina: ¿hay márgen para el diseño de políticas regionales?* María I. Terra and José D. Lima, (coords.), 101. Red Mercosur de Investigaciones Económicas, Serie Red-Mercosur 18, 2010.

ECLAC. *Latin America and the Caribbean in the World Economy 2011–2012: Continuing Crisis in the Centre and New Opportunities for Developing Economies.* Santiago de Chile: United Nations, 2012. http://repositorio.cepal.org/bitstream/handle/11362/1187/1/E1200770_en.pdfECLAC.

ECLAC. *International Trade and Inclusive Development: Building Synergies.* Santiago de Chile: United Nations, 2013. http://www.cepal.org/en/publications/37040-international-trade-and-inclusive-development-building-synergies.

ECLAC. *Foreign Direct Investment in Latin America and the Caribbean.* Santiago de Chile: United Nations, 2013. http://repositorio.cepal.org/bitstream/handle/11362/36861/S1420130_en.pdf.

ECLAC. *Preliminary Overview of the Economies of Latin America and the Caribbean* (Santiago de Chile: United Nations, 2014), 50. http://repositorio.cepal.org/bitstream/handle/11362/37344/S1420978_es.pdf?sequence=68.

ECLAC. "Foreign Direct Investment in Latin America Declines 23% in the First Half of 2014." *Press Releases*, 24 October 2014. http://www.cepal.org/en/pressreleases/foreign-direct-investment-latin-america-declines-23-first-half-2014.

Economist Intelligence Unit. "China cambia prioridades." La Jornada, 3 March 2015, 26. Available online at http://www.jornada.unam.mx/2015/03/03/economia/economist.pdf.

El Universal. "Precio del Petróleo, segundo obstáculo para el crecimiento: Banxico." *El Universal*, 19 December 2014. Available at: http://www.eluniversal.com.mx/finanzas-cartera/2014/banxico-petroleo-pib-1063035.html.

Emmanuel, Arghiri, Charles Bettelheim, Samir Amin, and Christian Palloix. "Imperialismo y comercio internacional." *Cuadernos de Pasado y Presente* 24, Cordoba (1971).

Emmanuel, Arghiri. *Unequal Exchange: A Study of the Imperialism of Trade.* New York: Monthly Review, 1972.

Esty, Daniel et al. *Working Papers: State Failure Task Force Report.* McLean, Virginia: Science Applications International Corporation, 1995. http://www.researchgate.net/publication/248471752_Working_Papers_State_Failure_Task_Force_Report.

Esty, Daniel et al. *State Failure Task Force Report*: *Phase II Findings*, 1998. http://wilsoncenter.org/sites/default/files/Phase2.pdf.

Eurostat. "Your key to European statistics." http://epp.eurostat.ec.europa.eu/cache/ITY_PUBLIC/3-31082012-BP/EN/3-31082012-BP-EN.PDF. July 2012.

Feliciano Murua, Gabriela Fernandes. *Subimperialismo: Entrada dependente da economia periférica à fase imperialista do capitalismo.* Guarulhos-SP: Universidade Federal de São Paulo, Escola de Filosofia, Letras e Ciências Humanas, March 2014. *Unpublished,* PDF.

Fernándes, Florestan. *La revolución burguesa en Brasil.* Editorial siglo XXI, México: 1978.

Fernández Nadal, Estela. "Los estudios poscoloniales y la agenda de la filosofía latinoamericana actual." *Herramienta* 24: 2003–2004.

Flynn, Matthew. "Between subimperialism and globalization. A case study in the internationalization of Brazilian capital". *Latin American Perspectives* 157, 34, No. 6 (2007): 9–27.

Fontes, Virginia. *O capital-imperialismo. Teoria e história*. Río de Janeiro: Editora UFRJ, 2010.

Fornet-Betancourt, Raúl. *Transformaciones del marxismo.* Plaza y Valdés: México, 2001.

Frank, André Gunder. *Dependent Accumulation and Underdevelopment.* London: Macmillan, 1978.

Frank, André Gunder. "The Development of Underdevelopment," *Monthly Review* 18 (1966).

Frank, André Gunder. *Latin America: Underdevelopment or Revolution.* New York: Monthly Review Press, 1969.

Frank, André Gunder. *Lumpenbourgeoisie: lumpendevelopment; dependence, class, and politics in Latin America*. New York: Monthly Review Press, 1974.

Frank, André Gunder. *El subdesarrollo del desarrollo. Un ensayo autobiográfico.* Caracas: Nueva Sociedad, 1991.

Frank, André Gunder. *Capitalism and Underdevelopment in Latin America: historical studies of Chile and Brazil.* Monthly Review Press: 1967.

Fukuyama, Francis. *State-Building: Governance and World Order in the 21st Century.* New York: Cornell University Press, 2004.

Furtado, Celso. *Subdesarrollo y estancamiento en América Latina*. Buenos Aires: Eudeba, 1966.

Gambina, Julio C. "Economía a Fines del 2011." *Rebelión*, 20 December 2011. Accessed 21 January 2015. http://www.rebelion.org/noticia.php?id=141613.

Germani, Gino. *La Sociología en la América Latina.* Buenos Aires: Eudeba, 1964.

Germani, Gino. *Política y Sociedad en una Época de Transición.* Buenos Aires: Paidós, 1968.

Geus, Alex de. "Las Caras de IIRSA: ¿Integración Regional o Interconexión Sudaméricana para la Explotación de Recursos Naturales a Favor de Brasil y/o del Empresariado Mundial?" Madrid: Universidad Complutense de Madrid, 2011. http://www.academia.edu/2219320/Las_caras_de_IIRSA_integraci%C3%B3n_regional_o_interconexi%C3%B3n_Sudam%C3%A9ricana.

Grossman, Henry. *La ley de la acumulación y del derrumbe del sistema capitalista*. Siglo XXI: México, 3ª ed. 2004.

Harman, Chris. "Theorising neoliberalism." *International Socialism* 117 (2007). http://www.isj.org.uk/?id=399.

Hardt, Michael and Antonio Negri. *Empire.* Cambridge, Massachusetts: Harvard University Press, 2000.

Harvey, David. *The New Imperialism,* Oxford: OUP, 2003.

Harvey, David. *The Enigma of Capital and the Crises of Capitalism*. London: Profile Books, 2010.

Harvey, David. *The Condition of Postmodernity.* Oxford: Blackwell, 1989.

Hayek, Friedrich A. *The Road to Serfdom.* UK: Routledge, 1944.

Helman, Gerald B. and Steven R. Ratner. "Saving Failed States." *Foreign Policy* 89 (1993).

Huntington, Samuel. *The Clash of Civilizations and the Remaking of World Order.* New York: Simon & Schuster, 1996.

ILO. *Global Employment Trends 2014: Risk of a Jobless Recovery?* Geneva: ILO, 2014. http://www.ilo.org/wcmsp5/groups/public/---dgreports/---dcomm/---publ/documents/publication/wcms_233953.pdf.

IMF. *Regional Economic Outlook, April 2014: Western Hemisphere: Rising Challenges.* Washington D.C.: International Monetary Fund, 2014. https://www.imf.org/external/pubs/ft/reo/2014/whd/eng/pdf/wreo0414.pdf.

IMF. *World Economic Outlook: Slowing Growth, Rising Risks, September 2011.* Washington D.C.: International Monetary Fund, 2011. http://www.imf.org/external/pubs/ft/weo/2011/02/pdf/text.pdf.

Kahl Joseph. *Tres sociólogos latinoamericanos.* Ciudad de Mexico: ENEP / Acatlán, 1986.

Katz, Claudio. "América Latina frente a la crisis global." In Hugo Fazio et. al., *La explosión de la crisis global. América Latina y Chile en la encrucijada.* Santiago de Chile: LOM Ediciones, 2009.

Katz, Claudio. *Bajo el imperio del capital.* Buenos Aires: Ediciones Luxemburg, 2011.

Katz, Claudio. "The Singularities of Latin America" in *Socialist Register: The Crisis and the Left.* Edited by Leo Panitch, Greg Albo, and Vivek Chibber, 200–216. Pontypool: The Merlin Press, 2012.

Kennedy, Paul. *Rise and Fall of the Great Powers.* New York: Random House, 1987.

Kennedy, Paul. *Preparing for the Twenty-First Century.*USA: Random House, 1993.

Klein, Naomi. *The Shock Doctrine.* New York: Metropolitan Books, 2007.

Kohan, Néstor. *Fetichismo y poder en el pensamiento de Karl Marx*. Editorial Biblos: Buenos Aires, 2013.

La Jornada. "Colapso de materias primas a nivel mundial empuja el dólar al alza: Merrill Lynch." *La Jornada*, 17 December 2014. Available at: http://www.jornada.unam.mx/2014/12/17/economia/024n1eco.

La Jornada. "China invertirá 250 mil *mdd* en América Latina en la próxima década." *La Jornada,* 8 January 2015. Available at: http://www.jornada.unam.mx/2015/01/08/economia/036n1eco.

La Jornada. "Prevé IMF que América Latina crecerá 3% en los próximos 5 años." *La Jornada*¸ 23 May 2015. Available at: http://www.jornada.unam.mx/2015/05/23/economia/023n3eco.

Lambert, Jacques. *América Latina, estructuras sociales e instituciones políticas*. 2nd ed. Barcelona: Ariel, 1970.

Lambert, Jacques. *Os dois Brasis.* São Paulo: Editora Nacional, 1976.

Lenin, Vladimir I. *Imperialism, the highest stage of capitalism.* Moscow: Progress Publishers, 1977.

Lenin, Vladimir I. *What the "friends of the people" are and How They Fight the Social-Democrats.* Moscow: Progress Publishers, 1970.

Luce, Mathias. "La expansión del subimperialismo brasileño", 4 December 2008. http://www.rebelion.org/noticia.php?id=76977.

Luce, Mathias. "Subimperialism, the Highest Stage of Dependent Capitalism." In *Brics: An Anti-Capitalist Critique*, edited by Ana García and Patrick Bond. London: Pluto, 2015, 27–45.

Lukács, György. *The Ontology of Social Being, Volume 3: Labour*. London: Merlin Press, 1980.

Luxemburg, Rosa. *The Accumulation of Capital.* London: Routledge, 2003.

Marichal, Carlos. *Nueva historia de las grandes crisis financieras. Una perspectiva global, 1873–2008.* Ciudad de México: Editorial Debate, 2010.

Marini, Ruy Mauro. "Brazilian interdependence and imperialist integration." *Monthly Review* 17, no. 7 (1965): 10–29.

Marini, Ruy Mauro. *Sobre el patrón de reproducción de capital en Chile.* Cuadernos de CIDAMO 7, s/f.

Marini, Ruy Mauro. *Dialéctica de la dependencia*. Ciudad de México: Era, 1973.

Marini, Ruy Mauro. *Il Subimperialismo Brasiliano*, Turin: Giulio Einaudi Editori, 1974.

Marini, Ruy Mauro. "¿Hacia una 'democracia viable' en América Latina?" *El Sol de México*, 16 December 1976.

Marini, Ruy Mauro. "Estado y crisis en Brasil." *Cuadernos Políticos* (Ciudad de México) 13 (July–September 1977), 76–84.

Marini, Ruy Mauro. "La acumulación capitalista mundial y el subimperialismo." *Cuadernos Políticos 12* (April–June 1977), 21–39.

Marini, Ruy Mauro. "La cuestión del fascismo en América Latina." *Cuadernos Políticos* 18 (October–December 1978).

Marini, Ruy Mauro. "Las razones del neodesarrollismo (respuesta a Fernando Enrique Cardoso y José Serra)." *Revista Mexicana de Sociología* (Ciudad de México), XL (1978): 57–106.

Marini, Ruy Mauro. "El ciclo del capital en la economía dependiente." In *Mercado y dependencia*, edited by Úrsula Oswald, 37–55. Mexico: Nueva Imagen, 1979.

Marini, Ruy Mauro. "Plusvalía extraordinaria y acumulación de capital." *Cuadernos Políticos* (Ciudad de México) 20 (April–June 1979): 18–39.

Marini, Ruy Mauro. "The Question of the State in the Latin American Class Struggle." In *Contemporary Marxism* 1 (1980): 1–9.

Marini, Ruy Mauro. *Subdesarrollo y revolución*. Siglo XXI: México, 12a edicion, 1985.

Marini, Ruy Mauro. "Geopolítica Latino-Americana." Arquivo Pessoal de Marini depositado no Programa de Estudos de América Latina e Caribe-Universidade do Estado do Rio de Janeiro, ca. 1985. http://www.marini-escritos.unam.mx/066_geopolitica_latinoamericana.html#_top.

Marini, Ruy Mauro. *América Latina: dependência e integração*. Brasil Urgente: São Paulo, 1992.

Marini, Ruy Mauro. "Proceso y tendencias de la globalización capitalista." In *La teoría social latinoamericana. Volume IV, Cuestiones contemporáneas*, edited by Ruy Mauro Marini and Márgara Millán, 49–68. Ciudad de México: El Caballito, 1996.

Marini, Ruy Mauro. *Memoria*. Ruy Mauro Marini Archive. http://www.marini-escritos.unam.mx/002_memoria_marini_esp.html.

Marini, Ruy Mauro and Márgara Millán. *La teoría social latinoamericana,* Ciudad de Mexico: Ediciones El Caballito, 1994.

Marini, Ruy Mauro and Olga Pellicer de Brody. "Militarismo y desnuclearización en América Latina; el caso de Brasil." *Foro Internacional* (Mexico) 29 (July-September 1967).

Martins, Carlos Eduardo. *Globalização, dependência e neoliberalismo na América Latina*. Boitempo Editorial: São Paulo, 2013.

Marx, Karl. *Capital Volume One.* London: Lawrence and Wishart, 1974.

Marx, Karl. *Capital: Volumes one and two*. Ware: Wordsworth, 2013.

Marx, Karl. *Grundrisse.* (London: Allen Lane in association with *New Left Review*, 1973), 651.

Mattick, Paul. *Crítica de los neomarxistas*. Ediciones Península: Barcelona, 1977.

Mattick, Paul, *Anti-Bolshevik Communism.* London: Merlin Press, 1978.

Medina Echavarría, Jose. *Economic development in Latin America: sociological considerations.* United Nations Economic Commission for Latin America, 1963.

Mendonça, Heloísa. "Empresas brasileiras migram para o Paraguai atraídas por baixos custos." *El País*, 11 September 2015. http://brasil.elpais.com/brasil/2015/09/10/politica/1441837292_242802.html.

Mészáros, István. Beyond capital: toward a theory of transition. London: Merlin Press, 1995.

Mészáros, István. *Socialism or Barbarism?* New York: Monthly Review Press, 2001.

Mészáros, István. *The Structural Crisis of Capital*. New York: Monthly Review Press, 2010.

Ministério do Trabalho e Emprego do Brazil, a Previdéncia Social. *Resumo das regras nas medidas pProvisórias* no. 664 e no. 665, n.d. http://www.previdencia.gov.br/wp-content/uploads/2015/03/Cartilha-regras-MP-664.pdf.

Moncada Roa, Patricia. "El fenómeno de la debilidad y el fracaso del Estado: un debate inconcluso y sospechoso." In *Los estados fallidos o fracasados: un debate inconcluso y sospechoso*. Bogota: Siglo del Hombre Editores-Universidad de los Andes-Pontificia Universidad Javeriana-Instituto Pensar, 2007.

Oliveira, Francisco de. *Crítica à razão dualista/O ornitorrinco*. São Paulo: Boitempo, 2003.

Oliver Costilla, Lucio. *El Estado ampliado en Brasil y México*. Mexico: UNAM, 2009.

Pajuelo Teves, Ramón. "Del 'Poscolonialismo' al 'Posoccidentalismo': una lectura desde la historicidad." *Comentario Internacional* 2. Quito: Universidad Andina Simon Bolivar, 2001.

Peña, López, Ana Alicia. *Migración internacional y superexplotación del trabajo*. Editorial Itaca: México, 2012.

Peña, Sergio de la. *El antidesarrollo de América Latina*, 13th ed. Ciudad de Mexico: Siglo XXI, 1999.

Pernett, Erick. *La Geopolítica Tras el 11 de Septiembre: ¿Absolutismo Global o Crisis de Hegemonía Mundial?* Medellín: Lealón, 2005.

Petras, James. *Globaloney. El lenguaje imperial, los intelectuales y la izquierda.* Buenos Aires: Editorial Antídoto, 2000.

Petras, James. "El Neoimperialismo." *Rebelión*, 24 May, 2004. https://www.rebelion.org/hemeroteca/petras/040524petras.htm.

Petras, James. "Brasil: o capitalismo extrativo e o grande salto para tras." Observatório das Nacionalidades, *Tensões Mundiais World Tensions* (Fortaleza) 10, no. 18–19 (2014): 301–324.

Petras, James and Morris Morley. "Los ciclos políticos neoliberales: América Latina 'se ajusta' a la pobreza y a la riqueza en la era de los mercados libres." In *Globalización: Crítica a un paradigma,* edited by John Saxe Fernández, 215–246. Ciudad de Mexico: Plaza y Janés, 1999.

PIA. "China enfría su economía." *Periodismo Internacional Alternativo* (PIA). 6 March 2015. Available at http://www.noticiaspia.org/china-enfria-su-economia/.

Pinto, Aníbal. "Concentración del progreso técnico y de sus frutos en el desarrollo latinoamericano." In Pinto, Aníbal, *Inflación: raíces estructurales.* Ciudad de Mexico: Serie Lecturas del FCE, 1985.

Pinto, Aníbal. "Factores estructurales y modalidades del desarrollo, su incidencia sobre la distribución del ingreso." In Pinto, Aníbal, *Inflación: Raíces Estructurales.* Ciudad de Mexico: Serie Lecturas del FCE, 1985.

Pochman, Marcio. *O mito da grande classe média. Capitalismo e estrutura social.* Boitempo: São Paulo, 2014.

Prado, Eleutério F.S. "O mau humor do 'mercado'." 17 April 2014. https://eleuterioprado.files.wordpress.com/2014/04/o-mau-humor-do-mercado.pdf.

Prebisch, Raul. *The Economic Development of Latin America and its Principal Problems.* New York: United Nations, 1950. http://prebisch.cepal.org/en/works/economic-development-latin-america-and-its-principal-problems.

Prebisch, Raul. *Capitalismo Periferal: Crisis y Transformación.*Ciudad de Mexico: Fondo de Cultura Económica, 1987.

Quijano, Aníbal. "La Nueva Heterogeneidad Estructural de América Latina." In *¿Nuevos Temas, Nuevos Contenidos*? Edited by Heinz R. Sonntag. Caracas: UNESCO/Nueva Sociedad, 1989.

Rawls, John. *El Espejo, el Mosaico y el Crisol. Modelos Políticos para el Multiculturalismo.* Barcelona: Anthropos, 2001.

Reforma. "Quita Pemex beneficio laboral." *Reforma*, 18 March 2015.

Rifkin, Jeremy. *The Age of Access: The New Culture of Hypercapitalism, Where All of Life is a Paid-for Experience.* New York: J.P. Tarcher, 2000.

Rodríguez, Octavio. *La teoría del subdesarrollo de la CEPAL*, 8th ed. Ciudad de Mexico: Siglo XXI, 1993.

Rostow, W.W. "The Five Stages of Growth-A Summary". The Stages of Economic Growth: A Non-Communist Manifesto. Cambridge: Cambridge University Press, 1960.

Salama, Pierre. *El proceso de subdesarrollo Editorial.* ERA: México, 1972.

Salama, Pierre. "Globalización comercial: desindustrialización prematura en América Latina e Industrialización en Asia." *Comercio Exterior* 62, no. 6 (2012).

Salles, Severo. *Ditadura e luta pela democracia no Brasil. O inicio da distensão política* (1974–1979). Salvador: Quarteto Editora, 2003.

Salles, Severo. *Karl Marx y Rosa Luxemburgo. La acumulación de capital en debate.* Buenos Aires: Peña Lillo-Ediciones Continente, 2009.

Salles, Severo. *Lucha de clases en Brasil* (1960–2010). Buenos Aires: Peña Lillo-Ediciones Continente, 2013.

SCA-TUCA. "Informe Final de la Comisión Nacional de la Verdad de Brasil." 10 December 2014. http://www.cnv.gov.br.

Sennes, Ricardo and Ricardo Mendes. "Políticas Públicas E Multinacionais Brasileiras." In A Ascensão Das Multinacionais Brasileiras. O Grande Salto de Pesos-Pesados Regionais a Verdadeiras Multinacionais. Rio de Janeiro: Elsevier, 2009.

Serra, Jose. *El 'milagro' económico brasileño. ¿Realidad o mito?* Buenos Aires: Ediciones Periferia, 1972.

Sicsú, João. "Quem são os novos consumidores dez anos depois." *Carta Capital*, 14 March 2013. http://www.cartacapital.com.br/economia/quem-sao-os-novos-consumidores-dez-anos-depois.

Sonntag, Heinz. *Duda, certeza y crisis. La evolución de las ciencias sociales en América Latina.* Caracas: UNESCO-Editorial Nueva Sociedad, 1989.

Sotelo Valencia, Adrián. "Entrevista con Ruy Mauro Marini: las perspectivas de la teoría de la dependencia en la década de los noventa." *Estudios Latinoamericanos* 9 (1990): 49–58.

Sotelo Valencia, Adrián. *América Latina, de crisis y paradigmas: la teoría de la dependencia en el siglo XXI.* Ciudad de Mexico: Plaza y Valdés – Facultad de Ciencias Políticas y Sociales – Universidad Nacional Autónoma de México, 2005.

Sotelo Valencia, Adrián. *Crisis capitalista y desmedida del valor: un enfoque desde los Grundrisse*. Mexico: Editorial Ítaca, Facultad de Ciencias Políticas y Sociales – Universidad Nacional Autónoma de México, 2010.

Sotelo Valencia, Adrián. *México (re)cargado. Dependencia, neoliberalismo y crisis*. Mexico: Editorial Ítaca, Facultad de Ciencias Políticas y Sociales – Universidad Nacional Autónoma de México, 2014.

Sotelo Valencia, Adrián. *México (des)cargado. Del mexico's moment al mexico's disaster*. Mexico: Editorial Ítaca, Facultad de Ciencias Políticas y Sociales – Universidad Nacional Autónoma de México, 2015.

Sotelo Valencia, Adrián. "Encrucijadas, límites y perspectivas del ciclo progresista en América Latina." http://www.rebelion.org/noticia.php?id=203714, 25 September 2015.

Sotelo Valencia, Adrián. *The Future of Work. Super-exploitation and Social Precariousness in the 21st Century*. Translated by Amanda Latimer. Leiden-Boston: Brill, 2016.

Sotelo Valencia, Adrián. "Apuntes para una comprensión de la coyuntura histórico-política en curso [I], Las nuevas derechas y la contrarrevolución Latinoamericana." *Rebelión*, 23 May 2016. http://www.rebelion.org/noticia.php?id=212538.

Sotelo Valencia, Adrián. "Brasil en la encrucijada." *Rebelión*, June 27 2016. http://www.rebelion.org/noticia.php?id=213860.

Sunkel, Osvaldo and Pedro Paz. *El subdesarrollo latinoamericano y la teoría del desarrollo*. México: Siglo XXI, 9th ed. 1976.

Tavares, Maria da Conceição. *Auge e declínio do processo de substituição de importações no Brasil*. In *Da substituição de importações ao capitalismo financeiro*. Rio de Janeiro: Zahar, 1972.

The White House, Office of the Press Secretary. "Joint Communique by President Barack Obama and President Dilma Rousseff." Accessed 31 August 2016. https://www.whitehouse.gov/the-press-office/2015/06/30/joint-communique-president-barack-obama-and-president-dilma-rousseff.

The White House, Office of the Press Secretary. "Remarks by President Obama and President Rousseff of Brazil in Joint Press Conference." East Room, June 30, 2015. Accessed August 31 2016. https://www.whitehouse.gov/the-press-office/2015/06/30/remarks-president-obama-and-president-rousseff-brazil-joint-press.

Vasconcellos, Gilberto Felisberto. *Gunder Frank. O enguiço das ciências sociais*. Florianópolis: Editora Insular, 2014.

Vergopoulos, Kostas. *Globalização: o Fim de um Ciclo. Ensayo Sobre a Instabilidade Internacional*. Rio de Janeiro: Contraponto, 2005.

Vitale, Luis. *Interpretación marxista de la historia de Chile*. (Three volumes). Santiago de Chile: Editorial LOM Ediciones, 2013.

Vuyk, Cecilia. *Subimperialismo brasileño y dependencia del Paraguay. Los intereses económicos detrás del Golpe de Estado de 2012*. Paraguay: Cultura y Participación para el Cambio Social, 2014.

Wallerstein, Immanuel. *The Modern World-System: Capitalist Agriculture and the Origins of the European World-Economy in the Sixteenth Century* vol. 1. New York: Academic Press, 1974.

Wallerstein, Immanuel. *World-system Analysis: An Introduction*. Duke University Press, Durham and London, 2004.

Weber, Max. *Ensayos sobre metodología sociológica*. Buenos Aires: Amorrortu, 1982.

Williams, Raymond. *Culture and Society 1750–1950*. Harmondsworth, UK: Penguin Books, 1961.

Williamson, John. *Latin American Adjustment, How much has happened*? Washington, D.C.: Institute of International Economics, 1990.

Yoichi, Itagaki. "A Review of the Concept of the 'Dual Economy.'" In *The Developing Economies* 6: 2 (1968), 143–157.

Zibechi, Raúl. *The New Brazil: Regional Imperialism and the New Democracy*. Translated by Ramor Ryan. Edinburgh: AK Press, 2014.

Index

www.ingramcontent.com/pod-product-compliance
Ingram Content Group UK Ltd.
Pitfield, Milton Keynes, MK11 3LW, UK
UKHW022209051026
15624UKWH00001B/78

9 789004 319400